Send Up
The Clowns

Send Up The Clowns

Parliamentary Sketches 2007–2011

SIMON HOGGART

guardianbooks

Published by Guardian Books 2011

2 4 6 8 10 9 7 5 3

First published in Great Britain in 2011 by
Guardian Books
Kings Place, 90 York Way
London N1 9GU

www.guardianbooks.co.uk

A CIP catalogue record for this book is available from the
British Library

ISBN 978-0852-65243-5

Cover illustration by Steve Bell
Text design by seagulls.net
Cover design by Two Associates

Printed and bound by CPI Group (UK) Ltd, Croydon, CR0 4YY

Introduction

I do a fair bit of speaking, mainly at literary festivals, some in villages you have never even heard of. At the end of each talk we usually have questions from the audience, and here are some of the most frequently asked:

How do you find something different to write about every day?

As one of my predecessors said, 'It's easy – I have 649 little helpers who sit underneath me, and they always come up with something.'

He was right. It might be one of the great parliamentary occasions, such as the resignation speeches by Geoffrey Howe and Robin Cook. It might be something ludicrously trivial, like the embarrassing mispronunciation of Jeremy Hunt's name, or David Cameron telling a female shadow minister to 'calm down, dear'.

It might be the weekly jousting match of prime minister's questions, which has little political significance except for improving – or destroying – morale on either side of the house. It is as if a football match were to be decided not by the number of goals scored, but by the votes of the fans. Or it might be some wonderful off-the-cuff remark, as when Gordon Brown announced, on the topic of his handling of the banking crisis,

'We saved the world…' I assumed at the time that this was a slip of the tongue, but on reflection I am not so sure.

As often as not, I find my mind spinning off in unexpected directions. One MP wanted to stop urban drivers from using motorways so as to prevent tailbacks, and I wondered, how on earth would the police decide what is an urban driver, and how would they ban him or her? And what about people who live in the suburbs?

Or the monthly question session on farming and rural affairs, in which hideous euro-jargon is used to set policy for this still, in parts, green and pleasant land. How would Laurie Lee have coped with a pigmeat regime? Or a WEE (waste electronic equipment) directive? Often MPs don't actually listen to what they are saying as it translates effortlessly into politician-speak. I recall one junior minister discussing an experimental plan to introduce better food for children: 'We are rolling out fresh fruit in primary schools.'

What do politicians think about what you write?

Much of the time they don't think about it at all, though some of the more honest ones will admit that they do sneak a look at the sketch before reading more serious articles. (There are five of us sketchwriters, for the *Times, Independent, Telegraph, Mail* and *Guardian*. The *FT* sometimes sends somebody to the house if they think there might be any chuckles in the public sector borrowing requirement.)

The answer is that nearly all of them regard being written about, say once a year, as a small price to pay for seeing their colleagues pilloried every day. I can still recall the joy on the face of the late Alan Clark when he congratulated me on a put-down of another MP who, I later learned, was one of his very best friends. For many politicians, all scrambling up the same greasy pole, *schadenfreude* is the greatest pleasure they have.

Michael Fabricant, the Tory MP for Lichfield, about whom (and whose amazing hair-style head topping) I used to write a lot, hated it at first, but after I had pointed out that he had survived the 1997 massacre of Tories by roughly the readership of the *Guardian* in his constituency – 'they all want me to keep writing about you, Michael!' – he forgave me and we often stop for a friendly chat. Sir Peter Tapsell told me that he used quotes from me in his election addresses. I pointed out that the remarks were usually meant ironically. 'Many of my constituents are strangers to irony,' he told me, while pouring another glass of sancerre. Sir Peter is a very generous host.

But most MPs, wisely, ignore us. I'm always a little surprised if a member I have been rather rude about comes bouncing up for a friendly conversation, as if there is no possible reason for awkwardness. As the former MP Bob Marshall-Andrews pointed out, 'You sketchwriters are really all playground bullies. You just want to hear your victims squeal.' I don't think that's entirely true, but it certainly is a little startling if they not only fail to squeal but come up for a friendly word. But then as Enoch Powell said, for a politician to complain about the press is like a sailor complaining about the sea.

What are Gordon Brown / David Cameron really like?

Brown was actually quite good at being a real human being. On the odd occasion I have chatted to him I found him amiable, thoughtful, with a good sense of self-deprecating humour. But I think the job he had wanted for so very long simply got on top of him. He couldn't quite cope with the intolerable demands of running a country in a TV age in which the news media constantly insist on new sensations, every hour on the hour, and when there was a huge and consuming economic crisis. I always sensed that he felt that if someone as second-rate as Tony Blair could do it, then for him it would be a doddle. When it turned out to be anything but, he didn't know where to turn. And he hadn't got Blair's instinctive political sense of the public mood. Remember that even after Iraq, and the dirty secrets it exposed, Blair won an election with a majority any other Labour leader would have thought a triumph.

I last talked to Brown outside a select committee where he was about to give evidence. For some reason we got onto Raith Rovers, his favourite football team, who had lost 1-0 at home the previous Saturday. Had he been there? 'No, I only go when they win.' But, I asked, how did he know they were going to win before he went? 'Because, when I go, they do win.' I thought that the Labour party might have appreciated some of that magic.

Cameron has quite a share of personal vanity. He was going to have a personal photographer at the public expense until he was laughed out of it. And he hates being drawn by Steve Bell with a condom over his head. Most politicians try to get hold of the most insulting original cartoons and hang them in the loo, just to show that they can chortle merrily at them-selves. I doubt if the lavatory at Number 10 contains any recent Steve Bells.

But he is also – I sometimes think – a cross between William Brown and Tigger, always shooting off with another bright idea. '"I know," said William, "why don't we reorganise the health service, and get the doctors to decide what to do, because they know about stopping you being ill, and stuff…" His voice trailed away. Then he brightened up. "And that Hubert Lane will hate it!"'

He races off after one great idea until someone catches up and tells him it just won't work. So he changes his mind, comes up with an entirely different plan, and declares victory. Or in Tigger's words, 'Worra, worra, worra! Have I won?'

'I know, why don't we serve our guests avocado whelks?'

'Because it would taste horrible, David.'

'All right, so we'll do it anyway – but without the whelks! Or maybe without the avocado! I'll see what Nick thinks.'

It has been an eventful time in British politics, but then most times are. We've had the departure of Tony Blair, Gordon Brown's unsuccessful spell in office, the Iraq inquiry, the expenses scandal, the first forced resignation of a Speaker in 300 years, the general election ending in a hung parliament followed by the first coalition government since the war, the cuts and the return of recreational rioting to our streets. It's all been debated in parliament – sometimes appositely, sometimes ludicrously, sometimes urgently, often self-indulgently, and occasionally conveying the air of an old but loyal Labrador, panting noisily as it tries to keep up with reality.

Simon Hoggart, July 2011

In March 2007, we were all waiting for Tony to go and for Gordon to take over. But there were warning signs. Frank Field, for instance, had compared the PM-in-waiting to the first, mad Mrs Rochester. And he was a Labour MP.

British politics isn't about Tony Blair any more; it's about Gordon Brown. As I scurried into the Chamber yesterday to catch the chancellor's question time, I picked up the leaflet published by Hazel Blears – the diminutive figure known to her colleagues as Mrs Pepperpot – in support of her campaign to become deputy leader of the Labour party.

The pamphlet is just 12 pages long, but it crams in no fewer than 23 pictures of its subject. There is Hazel with John Reid, Hazel at the dispatch box, Hazel with smiling constituents, Hazel as she appeared as a little girl in the film *A Taste of Honey*, and Hazel with Gordon Brown. Both are clearly thrilled to be in each other's company.

But there is no picture of her with Tony Blair. Indeed the Prime Minister, *pro tem*, is not even mentioned, even though his personal popularity must have helped get her elected three times. But then politics is about gratitude in the way that rugby league is about flower arranging – it's not why people go into it.

In the Chamber, Gordon Brown was busy turning the session into a one-hour party political broadcast for himself. As in most such commercials, ordinary members of the public are invited to give their personal testimonies. In this case, the man in the street was played by Dennis Skinner, a jobbing legislator. 'Of all the G7 countries, Britain comes out tops for jobs, stable growth and government debt,' he declared, which I thought was ironic coming from someone who for most of his political life was an adherent of what the late Frank Johnson used to call 'the tree-grown theory of the money supply'.

'If this was a football team,' Mr Skinner continued, 'we would have done the treble nine years in a row!'

'And it will be 10 years in a row,' Gordon smiled through the Tory jeers. He produced some astounding figures, illustrative of his own genius. In per capita income we were behind only the United States, and way beyond the wretched paupers of France, Germany, Japan and Italy. Mr Brown naturally knows that his figures are quite meaningless, being based on the artificially high value of the pound, but this is politics, where truth is regarded like Tabasco sauce, to be used sparingly and never splashed about.

George Osborne, the shadow chancellor, quoted Charles Clarke, the former Labour home secretary, who had said that thanks to Gordon Brown Britain was 'sleepwalking towards disaster'. He added, 'Does Mrs Rochester agree?'

Mr Brown scowled heavily. After all, who would vote for a helpless mad person who sets themselves on fire and burns the whole house down?

How prescient Messrs Field and Clarke turned out to be.

As it happens, Hazel Blears was four years old when Tony Richardson filmed her in his adaptation of Shelagh Delaney's novel. The director wanted her and her brother to appear as ragamuffins – street urchins – but their mother refused to let them appear on camera except in their Sunday best. Indeed the early scenes in the film are full of small children improbably playing in the street wearing white dresses, or jackets and ties. This may be an allegory for political spin.

At the height of the expenses scandal, she waved to the cameras a cheque for £13,300, being repayment for capital gains tax. I reflected at the time that the overwhelming majority of her constituents would think being able to write a cheque for such an amount an improbable dream.

8 March 2007

A joke went round at the time. Tony Blair and Gordon Brown go for a stroll together.

'Look,' says Blair, 'from now on let's be totally honest with each other.'

'All right,' says Brown, 'you go first.'

The rest of the walk passes in silence.

I don't know where Gordon Brown was yesterday, but he wasn't at prime minister's questions. I gather that he likes to watch the session on TV in his office. He can bellow imprecations at the screen, rather like one of my great aunts, who used to shout advice to the characters in thrillers. If they had been able to hear her, none of them would have been killed by the baddies, rather missing the point. As was Gordon Brown.

David Cameron, having noticed that his own poll ratings are higher than the chancellor's, has decided to assault him rather than Tony Blair. The session has become Questions to the Absentee Prime Minister-in-Waiting, and Mr Brown's absence makes it all the more piquant. The Tory leader quoted Sir Stephen Wall, a former policy adviser in Downing Street, who had appeared on television and said that Tony Blair 'couldn't govern without Gordon Brown, but he couldn't govern with him either'.

'Why,' asked Mr Cameron, 'would somebody at the heart of Downing Street say this?'

'Answer!' yelled a few Tories. Answer? I don't think so. Tony Blair does answering the way the rest of us do synchronised swimming, very rarely indeed. Instead he launched into a list of the chancellor's achievements. Mr Cameron pounced.

3

'The prime minister is very good at praising the chancellor, but the chancellor is not so good at praising him.' Mr Blair's love and admiration appear to be unrequited, rather like Violet Elizabeth Bott's feeling for William Brown.

Mr Cameron tried a little stunt. 'Let's ask the cabinet!' he cried. 'Who thinks they will have more say when the chancellor takes over? Come on, hands up!'

No sane person would fall for such an obvious trick by sticking up their arm. So only John Prescott did. The rest sat glowering, contemplating their uncertain futures under Gordon Brown, or else flapped their hands in histrionic contempt. Mr Blair ignored the entire event and started banging on about some bonkers party in the Czech Republic and its views on climate change. He was asked by an SNP member about the apparent sale of peerages.

Did he get an answer? Try to keep up. Instead he got another disquisition on the shortcomings of the SNP. My great-aunt would never have let him get away with it.

9 March 2007

Even before Gordon Brown became leader of the Labour party, other MPs were judging their chances after, they suspected, he turned out to be a disastrous if inevitable choice.

David Miliband claims he has no intention of running for leadership of the Labour party, and indeed he would be mad to do so. He is young (not quite 42) and has time.

Even if he beat Gordon Brown, he might well lose to David Cameron. He would be Labour's William Hague, a man of great ability promoted too soon. And without the consolation of Mr Hague's 17 pints a night.

So there is nothing in it for him. But that doesn't mean that the PGNG (Please God, Not Gordon) people won't have a try, and it is this that makes sleeping Tories sit up in the middle of the night, their wives fearful they have had a heart attack.

Instead of their fresh and youthful leader facing an ageing Scottish grump, their fresh and youthful leader would face another fresh and youthful leader – admittedly one with a face that appears to be skewed to one side (the gap between the left end of Mr Miliband's mouth and his left eyebrow is narrower than the gap on the right side, so it looks as if his face is pointing to its left. Luckily this makes him look not devious and lop-sided but rather engaging).

And he isn't a grump. In fact, he likes to stray off into amusing byways. For example the MP for Burnley, Kitty Ussher (presumably she used to work as a steward at cat shows) wanted Burnley to be a Fair Trade Town. This has something to do with where the council buys its coffee and bananas.

5

Mr Miliband mused affably that he'd heard a rumour Alastair Campbell was to become manager of Burnley football club, 'so maybe that will be their salvation'. (Possibly, though spinning a 5–0 defeat into a triumph would tax even Mr Campbell's powers. On the other hand, football is a game of two halves, and he knows all about the importance of 45 minutes.)

So the Tories are scared. They tried to imply that the cock-up over rural payments made Mr Miliband an evil man, but that didn't work. And the more they abuse him, the more Labour MPs are likely to see him as someone who will fight for their side more fiercely.

The Lib Dems had a go too. They fear their leader, an amiable middle-aged Scot, would do better against an unamiable middle-aged Scot. 'Take off your nappy!' their spokesman, Chris Huhne, shouted at young Miliband.

A disgustingly ageist remark, I thought, but Mr Huhne looked very pleased with himself.

15 March 2007

Nigel Griffiths, who was deputy leader of the house, resigned in March 2007 in protest against the government's decision to replace Trident. His resignation speech was a classic of its kind. Margaret Beckett, then foreign secretary, had once been against all nuclear weapons but had recently said she was in favour of replacing the submarine system.

'I want to be remembered!' cried Nigel Griffiths. Well, don't we all, I thought. Sadly, most politicians are forgotten as soon as they go. I often think, yes, I remember him, wasn't he long dead? The obituary headlines say something like 'doughty fighter on Labour's left wing', or 'loyalist Tory known for his hardline views', but I remember the bloke who never bought his round, or who sprayed you with a little shower of spittle when he talked.

But Mr Griffiths meant more. He wanted to be remembered not generally, but specifically, 'not so much for being the government's representative in the house, but the house's representative in government'.

I realised that this speech was going to require simultaneous translation, and that line meant: 'I am on your side, unlike all those other toadies in government.'

He went on, segueing smoothly to praise for the government from which he had just resigned. The happy children in their new schools! The sick, healed in a brand-new infirmary! 'In my constituency thousands of citizens have been lifted from poverty, and owe this government a great debt!' This is standard boilerplate on such occasions. The implication is that the government is so wonderful, so perfect in every

7

respect, that his bravery in resigning from it is all the more breathtaking.

Having described the new Elysium that is south Edinburgh, he thanked 'this prime minister, and the funding provided by this chancellor!' (Translation: 'I hope to be back one day, promoted by one or the other of you.')

'I have seen colleagues wrestle with their consciences, and lose their beliefs!' he went on. (Tr: 'But since I don't imagine there is the faintest chance of Margaret Beckett getting the top job, I can afford to be rude about her.')

Mr Griffiths concluded with his shiny new catchphrase: 'I leave with a heavy heart, but a clear conscience.' Just once, I would like to hear someone resign and say, 'I leave with a light heart, but a very troubled conscience.'

The imminent departure of Tony Blair, and the coming of Gordon Brown, entirely dominated the political debate. Mr Brown appeared on the Today *programme in March.*

We got Gordon Brown, man of a thousand faces. There was Grim Gordon. 'I made it clear that this was not a fiscal loosening,' he told John Humphrys, grimly.

Suddenly, the quick-change artist slaps on a greasy pork-pie hat and a check suit. He is the bloke in Oxford Street, playing Find the Lady on a folding table. You think you can find the queen? Don't be daft. You probably also thought there was going to be a 2p reduction in income tax!

Things going well? Praise Gordon! Things going badly? It's the fault of someone else. The public debt is way up. 'That was the lower production of North Sea oil – not the fault of the government.' Suddenly his mate spots a copper: Gordon and the table vanish.

Next we had Gordon the Polymath, who had spoken in the past year on security and terrorism, on defence and on public order – every topic a prime minister might handle.

Then just as suddenly we had Gordon the Daddy, with a warm, sympathetic voice and sick stains on his shoulder. 'I've got married, I've had two very young children, and I understand the challenges.'

Next he was a mediaeval king, moving anonymously among his subjects to find out what they really believe. 'I've tried to go about the country very quietly, and it's not really been reported, meeting workers in health, education, Sure Start…'

He was less easy as Gordon the Loveable. Humphrys asked if he thought he was liked. He seemed fazed by the question.

'I hope so, er, ha ha, I hope so. I'm not so arrogant to say I can make up my mind if I'm liked!'

He was suddenly much happier as Gordon, Man of Implacable Principle. 'People don't want someone to come into a room and ask, "What do you want to hear?" and when you hear it, say, "That's what I believe." I think that's the worst form of personality politics.' Who could he have meant?

Were we listening to Batgordon, sworn enemy of The Smiler? 'Tony is a great guy, and I've got an enormous amount of respect for him.' Oh dear, he really does loathe the fellow.

Next we heard Philosopher Gordon. 'If I thought I couldn't make any further contribution, I would go off and do something else. There are plenty of other things I can do.' What? Climb the Eiger, single-handed? Seize power somewhere else?

His most improbable disguise was as Gordon the Saintly Forgiver. People who called him 'Stalin' and 'psychologically flawed' would probably now regret what they had said. 'But I don't hold grudges against people at all.'

What? He is the greatest grudge-bearer in Westminster. I'll bet those people do regret their words, but not for the reason he implied.

Finally we heard from Polyanna Gordon: 'Every day when I get up in the morning, I feel excited and optimistic about the future – and energised!'

In the Chamber, the Tories chanted 'Where has all the money gone?' Sadly he was not present to enjoy this. No doubt he was rummaging through his dressing-up box.

Bob Marshall-Andrews, a man who once rejoiced in being the stroppiest of all Labour backbenchers, was once a great fan of Gordon Brown. But he changed his mind. As he put it, 'He has the decisiveness of Hamlet, the paranoia of Othello, the judgment of King Lear and the loyalty of Brutus. But at least we've got rid of Lady Macbeth!'

28 March 2007

The Rev Ian Paisley, who began his public life as a fire-eating dema-
gogue, finally made it to privy counsellor, which would be a greater
honour if there were fewer of them. In fact there are hundreds, 35
with names starting with 'P' alone. He is now Lord Paisley.

'No!' cried a familiar booming voice. Douglas Hogg had
suggested that the parliamentary oath be changed so that Sinn
Fein MPs would feel able to take their seats in the Commons.

'No!' thundered the voice again. It was an evocative
moment. The Rev Ian Paisley was reprising his greatest and
best-loved hit. For nostalgia fans (I first heard that mighty roar
on the streets of Belfast in 1968) it was like Pavarotti singing
'Nessun Dorma' or John Mortimer telling the story that ends,
'Fax it up, my lord.' Repetition cannot dim its allure.

It was also slightly surprising. On the day that he had
perhaps reached the end of his life's march, from crazed,
bigoted rabble-rouser to crazed, bigoted privy counsellor and
probably the next prime minister of his homeland, he seemed
to be fast asleep. The old turtle was slumped on the bench, his
body immobile, his eyes shut.

Even as the Northern Ireland secretary, Peter Hain, praised
his 'courage and leadership' I thought he might have marked
the hour of his triumph by dying on us. But then there was an
almost imperceptible stirring, as if after 39 years the eggs
might finally be hatching in the sand.

Peter Hain, the Ulster secretary, was explaining why – after
he had promised that if there wasn't a new executive by
Monday the assembly would be dissolved – he had changed
his mind. Some MPs seemed cross about this decision, though

11

every parent knows the feeling; you threaten your child that if they haven't tidied their room by 12 o'clock, they won't go to the cinema. Then at 11.59 they haul themselves up with a sigh and much eye-rolling and start to tidy. So you let them go.

Finally the hero of the hour got the chance to speak. He was not a very cheery turtle. He was anxious to settle a few old scores. His party, the DUP, never got any credit. After the Good Friday agreement, there had been much singing and handshaking, 'and kicking me!' Mo Mowlam had even had him arrested. As for the new era of peace, joy and fraternal feeling, 'I said to the leader of Sinn Fein, "This is not a love-in, it is a work-in!"' There would be difficulties, fights, tough talking and hard riding.

So business as usual, we reflected. Now we wait to see if anyone in Ulster can out-fundamentalise the most turbulent priest since Thomas à Becket.

17 April 2007

In April 2007, 15 Royal Navy sailors were seized by the Iranian authorities for allegedly entering Iran's territorial waters. After they were released there was much outrage that they were allowed to sell their stories to the newspapers. (Not that these were very exciting; one sailor seemed most upset that someone had taken his iPod.) Des Browne, the dry Scottish lawyer who was defence secretary at the time, got the blame and was pressed to express regret.

As *mea culpas* go, it was not exactly gushing. Des Browne, having been nagged, cajoled and hectored, finally admitted to 'a degree of regret that can be equated with an apology'.

Pressed to use the word 'sorry', he said, grudgingly, 'If you want me to say "sorry", then I am happy to say "sorry".' He said it in a very loud voice, which made it seem even less rueful. I don't suppose many parents would regard that as enough. For example, young Des's mother: 'Have you said "sorry" to your sister for throwing her dolls out of the window, young man?'

'I have expressed a degree of regret that can be equated with an apology.'

'You will say "sorry" to her!'

'If you want me to say "sorry", then I am happy to say "sorry".'

'Say it as if you mean it, or you will not be playing football this afternoon!'

'Oh, all right then, sorrr–eeee.'

24 April 2007

The threat of terrorism was forever held up before us. Conspiracy theorists thought it was a plot to keep the population subdued. Cynics like myself assumed that politicians were covering their backs so that if an incident did take place, they could not be blamed. The home secretary, responsible for these matters, was John Reid, a man who had survived the Scottish Labour party – a body in its way quite as ruthless as al-Qaida. People who go to university frequently make friends they cherish for life. People who get their education in the Scottish Labour party make enemies they cherish for life.

I don't know what is scariest about John Reid's disquisitions on terrorism – the 'generation-long' war we are supposed to be fighting against these people, or the preparations he has made to cope. Certainly, as always with New Labour, a massive task force of jargon has been assembled to meet the ongoing, pitiless menace.

Mr Reid spoke to the home affairs committee yesterday. He pointed out that the National Security Board meets weekly, the Committee on Security and Terrorism had met yesterday, and the government is now recruiting someone who will doubtless be known as the Terror Tsar, or Director-General of the Office of Security and Counter-Terrorism to his friends.

It is no wonder that we need so many magnificos with fine titles, since according to the home secretary, 'the level of threat we are facing, and its exponential rate of growth, requires that we re-focus all our efforts'.

And what should these re-focused efforts involve? 'Better oversight, longer strategic planning and thinking, better integrated responses, and central regeneration and capacity to deal with the battle for values and ideas.'

Who should deal with these matters? Why, 'a laterally integrated cross-government centre,' of course. So that's simple enough. But Mr Reid was also in philosophical mood. 'If we had to look at all the changes in the world, and find one defining characteristic, it would be the fact that we are moving from static communities and a static world to a highly mobile world. As the world changes, so we must change our response to the world.'

Here's another one, missus. 'Problems used to come to us. Now we have to go to the problems.' Home secretaries used to bang on about hanging, flogging and prison. Mr Reid sounds more like a hermit on a mountaintop cave, dispensing wisdom to the backpackers and rock stars who have made the stony 8,000 foot climb to consult him.

The threat, the guru said, was so extensive that it could not be handled by only one department. They would all have to have 'a common and overlapping cause: the values that are enshrined in our lifestyle and our liberties, which are common to all of us'.

David Winnick inquired whether we were winning this battle. Any normal, boring, unenlightened politician might have replied, 'yes', 'no', or 'search me'. Not the Swami of Shotts. 'If you will permit me to use one of my favourite quotes to answer your question, I think that the Owl of Minerva will spread its wings only with the coming of dusk.'

I have checked the original quotation from Hegel, and unlike Minerva, am no wiser. But it didn't half impress the committee. They look forward to the terrorists uttering owls of rage.

The prime minister's resignation came ever closer.

Golly, we are going to miss Tony Blair. For one thing, he is the most skilled evader of a question I have ever seen in action. Watching him not answering questions is exhilarating, like seeing Jonah Lomu headed for the try line. Opponents try to grab him, but only come up with fistfuls of air.

I'd love to see him on *Who Wants To Be A Millionaire?* Chris Tarrant asks: 'On which Greek island was the Colossus of Rhodes situated?' Blair: 'Before I answer that, I should say that the British people are not concerned with giant classical Greek statuary. They are much more interested in the reduced NHS waiting times for heart treatment…'.

Or on *The Weakest Link*: 'What was the name of the wife murdered by Dr Crippen?' Blair: 'If, Ms Robinson, you have any evidence that Dr Crippen did murder his wife, then I suggest you forward it to the police. Otherwise, if I were being unkind, I would call that a smear.'

Actually he did use that last sentence yesterday. David Cameron was asking him about the suggestion from a Metropolitan police officer that someone was leaking news of terror raids to the press, even before the raids take place. Mr Cameron was hinting heavily that these leaks came from the government rather than the police. The very idea, that policemen might give information illicitly to journalists, for money! Be still, my beating heart!

It appeared that Mr Cameron wanted an inquiry because he didn't know who to blame for the leaks. Mr Blair did not want an inquiry, because he didn't know who it might emerge had been to blame for the leaks. Puzzling, eh? So the prime minister said that the Tory leader should not just make an accusation and leave it hanging in the air. 'If I were being unkind, I would call that a smear.'

Ming Campbell asked about the Freedom of Information bill, which comes up tomorrow. MPs are trying to exempt themselves from some of its provisions. Ming asked if there should be one law for MPs and another for everyone else. Mr Blair said that this was a private member's bill, and therefore it was not be appropriate for him to make a commitment.

Since the government could swat the bill dead as easily as an obese bluebottle, this was exceedingly evasive. Jeremy Paxman on *University Challenge*: 'Your starter for 10. What is the capital of Vanuatu?'

Blair: 'That is purely a matter for the people of Vanuatu, and it would be entirely wrong for me to answer on their behalf.'

9 May 2007

The Tories held some hi-falutin' press conferences.

The philosophy of the new Conservative party was the theme for the day, and who better to introduce it than the Tories' policy supremo, Oliver Letwin, a man so brilliant that he makes a Cray supercomputer look like an old Amstrad. As with all great intellects, you cannot hear his brain whirring.

We were gathered at a meeting of the Policy Exchange, the right-wing think tank. There were a lot of young men in suits, many wearing shiny neckties, though no hoodies that I could see. Mr Letwin began by saying that the Conservatives had always been a pragmatic rather than a dogmatic party. A political position, he said, might not be theory-driven, but 'may nevertheless disclose deep theoretical dispositions – patterns of thought which, through their internal coherence, lend strength to pragmatic responses'.

Heady stuff, you will agree, and the audience was rapt. Even their neckties seemed to be paying attention. But Mr Letwin had barely started. We had to move, he said, 'from an econo-centric paradigm to a socio-centric paradigm'. We also had to shift from 'a provision-based paradigm to a framework-based paradigm'. There should be no paradigm lost. Then the best bit: the Tories had to 'internalise externalities'.

I wondered how this would go down in the average Conservative club, possibly planning their annual fete using Mr Letwin's precepts – or 'meta-thoughts' as he called them, as in the phrase, 'a penny for your meta-thoughts'.

'Now, Mrs Trubshott, I confess I am somewhat at a loss to know what Mr Letwin meant to tell us with his "framework-based paradigm".'

'Oh, Major, you are such a silly at times! I am sure it is a misprint for "parasol" and of course it must be mounted on a trellis to stop it from falling over. I'm afraid that several of the ladies felt quite faint from the heat last year!'

'Then what on earth d'ye think he means by a "second-order observation"?'

'Well, the entrance ticket includes only one glass of wine or fruit cup. If someone asks for a second one, they will have to pay for it.'

'Splendid! That seems quite clear. But Mr Letwin says we must also "internalise externalities". What does that mean when it's at home?'

'I am sure it's a frightfully clever way of saying that in the event of inclement weather, the event will be held in the village hall.'

The young persons listened respectfully to all this, paying close attention, and continued doing so until Mr Letwin told us it had all been a joke! Yes, he had been demonstrating that you didn't need 'ridiculous, high falutin' language' to express important concepts, unlike Gordon Brown with his 'neo-classical endogenous growth theory'. The audience laughed at this revelation, as politely as they had listened to all that nonsense in the first place.

But in politics, no good idea goes unpunished. As I type these words, I can hear on the Commons TV feed Chris Huhne of the Liberal Democrats reading out Mr Letwin's words in a mocking tone of voice. And we accuse the Americans of not understanding irony!

Tony Blair finally announced that he was leaving. His first farewell – and there were many – came at the scene of his first triumphs.

'I ask you to accept one thing. Hand on heart, I did what I thought was right.' Tony Blair was speaking in the familiar auditorium of Trimdon Labour Club, possibly the last place on earth where everybody loves him. But his message was for the whole planet – for Britain, for America, for Europe, and anybody who might be listening in Basra.

And just in case there was anyone present who didn't want to join in the praise for himself, he had praise for us. We were 'the blessed nation … in our innermost thoughts, we know this is the greatest nation on earth', he told us, almost moist-eyed. Possibly that line was cut from the feed to Washington.

Trimdon, a neat, spruce community in County Durham, had become a media village. Ten satellite trucks were parked on the well-mown green. Hundreds of journalists and party faithful were amassed inside the Labour Club, where in 1983 an agent called John Burton spotted the potential in the young lawyer and employed sleight of rulebook to give him the last Labour seat going in the imminent election. It has been the chosen setting for all the great events of his political life.

And the audience proved much of what he said. I've been going to Trimdon on and off for 10 years and the people have become noticeably more prosperous – better dressed, better fed, the skin glossier. It's only the old men, the former miners, who look pinched and stooped, their faces lined as if they had never quite been able to scrub the last of the coal dust away.

We waited. Vaguely inspirational pop music boomed out. 'Search for the Hero Inside Yourself', 'Higher and Higher'. People appeared with placards, many in suspiciously similar styles: '10 Years, 3 Elections, 1 Great Britain'; 'Britain Says Thanks'; 'Tony Rocks'. Without evident irony they played 'Things Can Only Get Better' at top volume. A woman tried clapping and dancing to this tune – which might be better re-titled 'Still Some Room for Improvement'. Some people joined in, but most didn't, so it looked as if a happy-clappy congregation had been infiltrated by Anglicans.

Then he arrived. He began in folksy style, thanking Maureen, and, er, Maureen's friends. 'She said to me "four more years", and I said, "Maureen, that's not on message for today."' He thanked John Burton. He thanked Cherie and the children, 'who never let me forget my failings'. Surely, there are other people around to do that, millions of them?

Then he was up and away. Most prime ministers are actors, and this was a performance worthy of a Wolfit or a Sinden. He was revealing about why he had clung on for so long. 'Sometimes the only way you can conquer the pull of power is to set it down.' He made it sound like levering yourself out of bed on a cold morning.

We rushed through the politics of the past few years, and soon realised that this was not merely a description of Blairism – it was a description of Blair. No cabinet colleague – indeed nobody else – was mentioned. Even the word 'government' appeared to have been banned. It was him, him, him! He listed his achievements, all of which we have heard many times. We now lived in a country that was 'confident in the 21st century, comfortable in its own skin', which made us sound like a particularly lazy sausage.

Some thought he had been Messianic. Not so. He had suffered doubts, hesitation, reflection and reconsideration.

Changes had been 'hellish hard to do'. Suddenly and briefly we were on to Iraq, and 'the blowback from global terrorism'. Had he been wrong on that one? No. 'It is a test of will and belief, and we can't fail it.' So no apology there. But he did say that in 1997 expectations had been 'perhaps too high … apologies to you for the times I have fallen short'.

But apologies for what? He has always been willing to admit being wrong, but will never tell us exactly what he was wrong about. But, 'good luck,' he said to us all, and was away, flanked by a guard of honour mounted by Trimdon's Labour supporters, to cries of 'Thank you!' from them, and 'Move out the fucking way!' from the photographers. And I did see one woman dabbing her eyes.

Gordon Brown was the only candidate for the Labour leadership.
Nevertheless he felt the need to run as if there were dozens of rivals.

Gordon Brown began his campaign in London yesterday. It will be a lonely business travelling round the country asking people not to vote for anyone else, since there is no one else. But he is a truculent chap, and can easily pick a fight with himself. The launch was at a trendy design centre, all white-painted brickwork and open steel stairways, as if Richard Rogers had created a Victorian prison.

A claque of young persons had been gathered. They were the kind of young people politicians love to have around, but who make other young people look at them strangely, as if they were train spotters, or evangelicals. News came through that Tony Blair had endorsed him on television. The words were warm enough, but the body language was awful. The outgoing prime minister umm'ed and ah'ed. His eyes flickered wildly.

'I am absolutely delighted, um, to give my full support to Gordon. As. The next leader of the Labour party. And – er – prime minister.' It got worse. The teeth were so gritted you could have sprinkled them on a snow-covered motorway. The words sounded as if they had been dragged from the bowels of his being, like a potholer with a broken leg being pulled, inch by inch, to safety.

Finally Mr Brown arrived. The claque clapped him for far too long. It was like a mass Moonie wedding. He looked happier than I've seen him for a long time. He had a new haircut. He worked the crowd, chatting and smiling. He resembled a second husband trying to be chums with his new wife's children. He is the Stepfather of the Nation. ('Awright, I'll have the iPad 2, but I'm not going to call you "Dad".')

His speech was, of course, an attack on Tony Blair. Why break the habit of a lifetime? You had to read between the lines. Like the way he kept talking about 'a new government' with 'new ideas' and 'new leadership for this new time'.

Get the drift? We needed to change. We must embrace change. Communities must embrace change, and 'as the world changes, our priorities must change'.

'We must restore power to parliament,' he said. I wondered who had taken it away in the first place. 'We must uphold civil liberties' – against the tyrant who has been stripping them away, as he meant, but didn't quite say.

But then it was clear that, alarmingly, he was morphing into Blair. He talked about his 'core beliefs' – remember Blair's 'irreducible core'? He spoke with misty eyes, and no evident sense of irony, about 'security with good pensions'. The claque, which had been applauding every line with bright-eyed zealotry, failed to express astonishment at that, coming from the biggest pension-purloiner since Robert Maxwell.

Like Blair, he began to speak in verb-free sentences. 'Faith in people and in their potential! A belief that Britain can lead the world!' He spoke about his parents. Like the parents of every politician who ever lived, they taught him integrity and decency, and provided him with his moral compass. Why does no one ever say, 'They taught me to grab what I can, and look after Number One...'? And the last jab at Blair: 'I have never believed that presentation is a substitute for policy.'

Mind you, if anyone in his team had cared about presentation yesterday he would not have been speaking from behind an autocue that managed to mask half his face. On television it looked weird. But then being there is never any substitute for watching an event on TV.

As well as a new leader, Labour had to elect a new deputy leader to replace John Prescott. This was a real fight, with lots of candidates. First up was the ultimate winner, Harriet Harman.

'Cactus Jack' Garner, Roosevelt's deputy, famously said that the vice-presidency of the US was 'not worth a pitcher of warm spit'. From the excitement at Harriet's launch, you might imagine that the deputy leadership of the Labour party was a bucket of molten gold.

She had backing from 61 MPs, of whom 31 were women. They were, along with a handful of men, marched into a committee room at the Commons like Japanese tourists who have lost the lady with the flag. They knew it was important, but weren't quite clear why they were there.

Harriet walked in to a sound probably unfamiliar to her – loud and enthusiastic cheering. The women clustered round her. It was like the famous picture of the 'Blair babes', though I would hesitate to call them Harriet's Harem. She told us what we had to bear in mind. First, it was time to 'rebuild the Labour party and renew the trust of the people of this country'. That didn't sound too good. A party crumbling like Tintern Abbey, mistrusted by everyone.

But, secondly, we had to remember Labour's great achievements. In other words, 'We are wonderful, but everybody hates us.' It's a problem politicians have faced down the ages.

Then she announced that she had to be interviewed by the BBC, and walked off. She had abandoned her own launch! So we traipsed outside for another one, this time by Hazel Blears, or 'Mrs Pepperpot' as she is known to her fans. She had quite a team, including John Reid and Ruth Kelly. Fashion notes: Sir Gerald Kaufman was wearing a cheese-cutter cap, a two-tone orange and beige anorak, a faux-denim suit with orange stitching, and a striped shirt decorated with little diamonds. As Raymond Chandler once wrote of a gangster: 'He was as inconspicuous as a tarantula on a slice of angel food cake.'

Ms Blears arrived. The weather was awful – soaking rain interrupted by showers. One of her supporters, Stephen Pound, dramatically whipped off his coat and put it over a puddle for her. Unlike Queen Elizabeth, she looked horrified, and steered frantically to one side. Dozens of cameramen and photographers sat morosely under umbrellas, like fishermen having an awful day.

Ms Blears is very short, and James Landale of the BBC is very tall, so he had to crouch to interview her, like one of those cringe-making interviews with children they used to show on the BBC. 'Now, little girl, what's your message for the British people?' (Cheesy smile to camera.)

She could reply – and did – that her message was as resonant in the Labour heartlands as it was in the marginal seats, code for 'I am still a loyal Blairite'. But the fun was not over. Later we learned that John McDonnell hoped to be the leadership candidate of the left. But he was doubtful that he'd get enough support to get himself on to the ballot paper. There was an air of mild desperation. I was reminded of Bob Geldof at Live Aid – 'Give us your fookin' nominations!'

I sometimes wondered if it was coincidence that Tony Blair's late mother was called Hazel Blair. Many people wondered how Ms Blears had come to be so highly promoted; was it a subconscious, atavistic loyalty to his mother's memory?

16 May 2007

Another candidate, who in the end came second in the contest, was Alan Johnson.

He is running as a real human being, always a risky strategy. His launch was held in the Methodist Central Hall, Westminster. Labour famously owes more to Methodism than to Marx, and Mr Johnson has little time for the irascible German savant. He is no more a Marxist than Richard Dawkins is a Jehovah's Witness.

He does have a claque, like every modern politician. They are bright-eyed and eager, and applaud everything their candidate says, for slightly too long. 'Good morning,' he said. 'Yee-haw,' they replied, as if attending a barbecue in Texas.

Mr Johnson's aides had distributed endorsements. One began with the most improbable statement I have seen for some time. 'We are a group of 53 Labour peers from all sections of the party and walks of life.' Lords from all walks of life! How inclusive can you get? The literature contained many pictures of Mr Johnson. In nearly all of them he had his mouth wide open, as if to cram in a cream bun, or flick out a tongue to catch flies.

His message is that Labour must keep the middle classes on board (thus: 'we have signalled our determination to build a coalition of aspirants as well as the disadvantaged') and at the same time, support the unions. This is because the unions, as part of mature and modern democracy, have a third of the votes.

And he is backing Gordon Brown, which is lucky, because he hasn't got much choice. He read out an extract from his diary ('more Pooter than Pepys,' he told us – 'film rights available, Johnny Depp should play me') written in 1992 when he first met Gordon. 'Could he be a future prime minister?' he had asked himself. 'He knows his stuff.'

And this is the difference between the average political lickspittle and a genuine human: he realised that we might think he had made this all up, and added, 'You can carbon date it if you like.' His other message is, that unlike the lawyers and consultants he is running against, he has done a real job. 'I did stack shelves at Tesco – they sacked me at 16.' He has also been a postman.

And he admits when he got it wrong. 'We are on a long flight – we are having a bit of in-flight refuelling, er, we are changing the pilot and the co-pilot, er, so maybe this analogy doesn't work...'

Someone asked if his campaign team were not all men in suits. 'For those who believe that the deputy leader should be a woman, there's not much I can do. The operation is very expensive, and wouldn't be over by June 27.'

John Prescott, darling of the sketchwriters, had to leave with Tony Blair. He had a last deputy prime minister's question time.

I felt we should send Mr Prescott a retirement present, though it might make him angry, and like the Incredible Hulk, he is best avoided when in a mood. In the end there was something poignant about his farewell tour. I was reminded of the late Max Wall during his comeback. It was less a great comic turn, more a reminder of past glories. The timing was slightly off, and a certain weariness tinged what had once been all brio and panache.

Mr Prescott reminded Vince Cable that he had once been a member of the Labour party. 'He has gone through more parties than Paris Hilton!' he said. Almost, but not quite there. Mind you, we did get value. Fifteen minutes with Prescott as deputy prime minister were followed by half an hour of him standing in for Tony Blair. 'One third of the way through!' he said triumphantly, as Big Ben struck 12.

William Hague, standing in for David Cameron, said: 'He has been told that he will be missed on his own side. He will be even more missed on this side.'

Perhaps feeling that this fell short of an encomium, Mr Prescott vigorously praised himself and the government he served. Then he returned to a favourite theme – the fees Mr Hague is paid for public speaking. 'I notice that he wasn't in the first session. Is that his fee to be in the first session was too expensive for this one? Or is the charging for Tory overtime rates at your speaking rates is too much money?'

The brave Hansard reporters could be seen struggling to put all that into English, though it was fairly clear what he meant all along.

He turned on his tormentor, 'I remember him in the general election and getting horribly beaten!' Since it was Prescott who did most of the horrible beating in the 2001 election, this made the Tories fall into tucks of happy laughter. Then he was asked about Dick Cheney who, improbably, is his equivalent in the Bush administration. Mr Prescott strode off down memory lane. 'I recall that we met for the first time via video screen [after 9/11] when he was in a cave somewhere under security control...'

Which, the Tories thought as they cheered and gurgled and chortled and wheezed, is almost exactly where Tony Blair would like to have kept his deputy. Mr Prescott strolled out, grinning because it was all over. For ever. There'll never be another one, missus.

Gordon Brown was on the brink of the ultimate power. He set out his stall in a speech in London.

'I am truly humbled,' said Gordon Brown as he prepares to accept the job of prime minister. Hmmm... Gordon Brown does humility rather in the way he probably does tap dancing: fun to watch, but not entirely convincing. He didn't look especially humble. He looked rather more like a man who has steamrollered all of his colleagues into voting for him.

After 13 years of flopping over to have their tummies tickled by Tony Blair, Labour MPs have clearly decided they want more of the same. They yearn for someone big and strong to tell them what to do.

He was invited several times to say that he regretted not having any opponents. But he didn't. Instead he seemed thrilled. He was especially pleased that there were no left-wing candidates. 'The party has been unwilling to give candidates of the far left any space to put forward their views, because they simply don't have support in the Labour party.'

In other words, if a left-wing candidate had won lots of votes, that would have given the misleading impression that people supported him. It is a very New Labour point of view. But this wasn't just New Labour. It was new New Labour! A 'new' government with 'new' priorities, working with a 'renewed' Labour party.

How new can you get? Think of Chardonnay-flavoured hand soap, or paw-paw Doritos – incredibly, nose-bleedingly new. His speech was in the headquarters of Bloomberg, the huge financial information provider. Bloomberg takes a very dim view of employees who do not demonstrate total loyalty. Anyone who says they intend to leave is marched directly from the building and their records expunged. They become non-persons, rather like Tony Blair. So it was the perfect place for Mr Brown's apotheosis.

The Bloomberg offices are highly futuristic. The landings on the stairs are illuminated, from below. The room we met in was lit in magenta, purple, violet and *eau de nil* shades, so the effect was of being inside the shirt of a gigantic estate agent. The claque that accompanies him everywhere was in place. The Queen is said to believe that everywhere in Britain smells of new paint. Gordon Brown must believe that every British person is under the age of 30 and wears a suit.

His speech was the usual coded attack on Tony Blair. He finished by clasping his hands together and declaring: 'This is who I am!' At this remark which, so far as I can see, is entirely devoid of meaning, the claque rose to give him the kind of standing ovation which might have been earned by, say, a 19-year-old who at the last minute had triumphantly under-studied the role of Mimi at La Scala.

13 June 2007

Tony Blair marked his imminent departure with a blast at the media.

The outgoing prime minister seemed very much at home at Canary Wharf. It's a place that gleams and glows with money, like sunshine on the bronzed skin of a trophy bride. There are cafes selling caviar and champagne, and presently an open-air show of expensive cars. I found my way by turning left at the Lexuses, and straight ahead past the Cadillacs.

Blair loves modern buildings (unlike the Houses of Parliament, which were designed to look ancient 150 years ago, and which he spent much of his premiership avoiding). Much of Docklands resembles a rather old-fashioned notion of what the future would be like. There are even those driverless transport pods that used to appear in visions of the next millennium, back in the 1950s. They are part of the Docklands Light Railway.

Inside the Reuters building, where he spoke, there are computerised security checks, televison monitors, and endless rows of mineral water, the new sentinels of sobriety. He had come to complain about the media, but the in-house media were all showing *Blair: The Movie*. There was Blair smiling, Blair the statesman, Blair doing his Henry V act in Iraq, playing cricket inside Number 10, Blair with celebrities: Bush, Mandela, Sarkozy, Bono, Geldof. It was Jonathan Livingstone Blair – the hero who dares to fly alone! And to think we are about to lose him.

As he said yesterday, in one of his celebrated profound yet meaningless remarks: 'The public does understand that the future is constantly changing.'

33

How can it? It hasn't happened yet. It's like saying that the result of next year's Cup Final is constantly changing. Even Einstein would have had trouble with that.

His speech assailing the media reads more harshly than it sounded. It was filled with caveats and get-out clauses, like raisins in muesli. Yet few people could disagree with much of what he said – the media do love impact, they are obsessively in competition with each other, 24-hour news does force politicians to make decisions too fast, comment may be free, but most facts, unadorned, are simply boring.

But Blair hates confrontation. He spoke as if afraid that the assembled media might rise up and pelt him with water bottles. 'There is no point in blaming the media – they are not the master of this change, but the victims.'

The problem is that New Labour began by identifying the gruesome faults of the modern media, then using them for their own purposes. They knew all about the demented competition, the need for exclusives and speed, the terror of being left behind, the relentless pressure for the new. Like drug dealers hanging round the school gates, they were delighted to satisfy these cravings.

As the almost premier emeritus admitted yesterday, several times, he and his team had given 'inordinate attention to courting, assuaging and persuading the media'. For several years it worked. Then it stopped working. I do have some sympathy, but it's limited. Blair is rather like a black belt in judo who loves showing off, but when he lands flat on his back, he's moaning that it's not fair.

14 June 2007

This was one of Tony Blair's last jousts with David Cameron.

We witnessed a magnificent moment yesterday. As a piece of pomposity it made a coronation look like karaoke night in an Essex pub. But was it a joke? Or an example of superb, hand-stitched irony? I still do not know.

Let me set the scene. David Cameron was twitting Tony Blair about his speech on the press this week. He pointed out that the government had promised 'Sarah's Law', a statute that would make it easier for vigilantes armed with petrol bombs to find the homes of cowering nonces. The law had been dropped. What's more, the home secretary's promise of 'chemical castration' turned out to mean giving a few paedophiles Prozac. And the Bichard report on co-operation with the police had disappeared. 'Is the prime minister at all surprised that the press are cynical about this government?'

Mr Blair declined to answer these questions. He is a maestro when it comes to not answering questions. He is the Lewis Hamilton of the Formula One not-answering-questions circuit. With his sublime self-confidence and flame-proof suit, nobody can get near him.

Then, in his majesty, up rose Sir Gerald Kaufman, whom I think of as the Sir Peter Tapsell of the Labour benches, in that both men are elder statesmen possessed of an iron certainty about every word they speak. When they are called by the Speaker, the editor of Hansard himself enters the gallery to take charge of the record. He is an equally superb figure with mutton-chop whiskers and pince-nez, and he logs every spoken word with a goose quill.*

'Why,' Sir Gerald demanded, 'did the prime minister pull his punches when speaking about the press yesterday? Is he not aware, that over these years, a huge proportion of the press coverage of politics has consisted of fiction, propaganda and gossip?'

At this, delighted Tories pointed scornful fingers at the Labour front bench – in their view the greatest of all purveyors of fiction, propaganda, and gossip.

But then Sir Gerald brought them close to ecstasy. 'A serious deterioration has occurred since I worked as a political journalist!' The Tories collapsed with chortling, knee-hugging glee. Sir Gerald, one of the best-known writers for *That Was the Week That Was*, the TV show that did more than anything to destroy deference towards political leaders! And the man who worked at Number 10, alongside Harold Wilson, on whose shoulders fiction and propaganda perched like witch's familiars! So it must have been a joke, surely, delivered with the straight face only a comedy genius can manage. Or was it? Could he, just conceivably, have meant it? I honestly do not know.

* *I was gently chastised for this passage by the real editor of Hansard, a charming woman called Lorraine Sutherland. She has never had mutton-chop whiskers.*

15 June 2007

Gordon Brown appeared in front of a select committee, a short while before he became prime minister. He spoke almost entirely in jargon. I imagined how the actual replies he gave – these are verbatim – would go down if he were interviewed on, say, Radio 2.

Jeremy Vine: Mrs Figgis of Daventry, it's your call to the prime minister.

Mrs Figgis: I don't know, Mr Brown, everything is so expensive these days. I bought these school shoes for my daughter, and they were £37, and that was in the sale!

Gordon Brown: Well, Mrs Figgis, our long-term policy objectives include the symmetrical inflation target. Inflation expectations have remained firmly anchored to the government's target, and that has enabled us to maintain international best practice.

JV: Does that answer your question, Mrs Figgis?

Mrs Figgis: Yes, it does, it's all perfectly clear to me now.

JV: Jim Bedstead of Surrey, you're talking to the prime minister.

Mr Bedstead: Our local market, it's been there all my life. But the health and safety, they're threatening to close it down, because they say rotten fruit falling off the stalls might make people slip. It's political correctness gone mad.

GB: I have to tell you, we are doing the right thing for the British economy, in a market-sensitive environment.

JV: Now, let's hear from a pensioner. Mr Pettifer of Truro, what's your question for Gordon Brown?

Mr Pettifer: I had a pension scheme, and it's worth nothing now, absolutely nothing. After 43 years in the same job! To live, I have to eat dog food, and old copies of the *Sun*, mashed up in warm water.

JV: Sounds dreadful. What's your reply, prime minister?

GB: Well, Mr Pettifer, you should know that we have conducted an examination of monetary aggregates in an open economy, which is far more global in its capital markets. The notion that you had a fixed relation between the money supply and inflation was found to be unreliable … and you are ignoring the second-round effect of oil prices on utility prices.

Mr Pettifer: Can't argue with any of that.

JV: Now let's hear from Kerry Skillet, she's a student in East Anglia.

Kerry Skillet: I just wanted to ask…

GB: If I may just say, when we moved from an RPI to a CPI we moved from an RPI of 2 per cent to a CPI of 2.2 per cent.

Kerry Skillet: That is exactly what I was going to ask about. Thank you.

No wonder the Tories are rubbing their hands in glee.

Shortly before Blair gave up the premiership, he was visited by the governor of California.

It was the Terminator meeting the terminated. Arnold Schwarzenegger paid a visit to Downing Street, where he held talks on the environment with Tony Blair. The two men held a joint press conference.

Tony is almost the same height as Arnie, but Arnie has the bigger face. When he dies they can embalm him and stick him straight onto Mount Rushmore. Then there's the accent. You can't listen to him talk about climate change without seeing him waving a howitzer-size gun at various villains. He had, he growled, just gained five pounds from eating a 'delizious Briddish breqqfast'.

Someone must have been sprinkling the sausages with fairy dust, because he seemed to imagine that Tony Blair had, almost single-handedly, saved the planet. 'He came to California ad a criddical stage – [you can talk Arnie by substituting the letter D for T and using the hard G in place of the hard C, in the middle of words] – and whad was grade aboud id, was he invided Demograds and Rebublicans and thad way you can agomplish anything. He showed grade leadership, and the Briddish model has inspired everyone in California.'

Really? Relaxing in Santa Barbara, cruising the freeways of LA, pruning vines in the wine country, do they really discuss Tony Blair and the Briddish model?

'You are falling back emissions to the 1990 level, in Grade Briddain you're 9 per cent or 10 per cent behind the 1990 level…' Who told him this stuff?

Then it clicked. We were at the Oscars. Anything less than gushing, glowing, demented praise for everyone within earshot is virtually an insult. They say that politics is show-business for ugly people, though in Mr Schwarzenegger's case it may be the other way round.

We turned our gaze to Tony Blair, who was busily not denying that he would soon be going to the Middle East. He said he had been told by his minders not, under any circumstances, to say 'I'll be back!' But in his new job he could have used a less well-known Schwarzenegger quote: 'If it bleeds, we kill it.'

28 June 2007

Next day, after what felt like the longest farewell since Frank Sinatra, Tony Blair finally left.

'We won't miss you at all!' cried Cherie Blair, graceful as ever, as she waved goodbye to the press gathered outside Number 10. They were leaving the place for the last time. As so often, she shouted aloud what her husband thought it more prudent merely to think. Tony Blair played the media with brilliance, so it was a bit like Alfred Brendel's wife complaining about piano tuners.

He arrived at prime minister's questions and began, as ever, with a tribute to fallen soldiers. His voice was on the edge of cracking as he said that there were those who thought that they faced the dangers in vain. 'I do not, and I never will.' Was he hovering on the edge of bad taste, using the dead to back his case for war? He raced on through his list of appointments, adding: 'I will have no further meetings today. Or any other day.' The house, quivering with sentimental anticipation, chortled merrily.

The next 27 minutes were a bizarre mixture of the traditional and the frenetic. We had all the usual lists of higher spending, of shorter NHS waiting lists, of once-failing schools whose alumni could walk into Harvard if they chose.

David Cameron produced an encomium. 'No one can doubt the huge efforts he has made in the public service … considerable achievements that will endure.'

The Tory leader is trying to establish a myth of the golden Blair years, a sort of Camelot, which he can contrast with the dark, dour, dire Age of Brown that we are entering. But this did seem genuine.

Blair thanked him for his courtesy. Clearly 'courtesy' was the word of the moment. Ming Campbell praised his courtesy. Blair in turn thanked him, for his courtesy. And he thanked Ian Paisley. The entire House was leaving some for Mr Manners.

Richard Younger-Ross, a Lib Dem bag person, brain as haywire as his hair, attempted a complicated question about disestablishment. The prime minister emeritus – almost – wearily threw away: 'I am not really bothered about that one.' You can get away with that when you're leaving.

Then it was time to go. He admitted he had never been a great House of Commons man – yup – but he did pay the tribute of 'fearing' it. 'The tingling apprehension I had at three minutes to 12 today I felt as much as 10 years ago.'

'I don't like you, you're scary' seems a curious farewell, especially as they almost never laid a glove on him. MPs have, with a few rare exceptions, been the poodle's poodles.

Then some of his trademark clunky phrases: politics had included 'harsh contentions' but it was a profession where 'people stand tall'. And if there was 'low skulduggery' it was more often a place for 'the pursuit of noble causes'. Again, his voice was on the brink of breaking up.

As he left, by prior arrangement, all Labour MPs stood up to applaud him. Against the rules, or at least against custom and practice, but who was going to stop them? Cameron waved the Tories to their feet, and though only a few clapped, all of them stood. As he left Gordon Brown slapped him on the back, and then again, as if to say, 'There's the exit, that way.'

Over in Downing Street we learned that Mr Brown cannot wave. He raised a hand to hip height, as if patting a passing dog. 'Wave!' shouted the snappers. He tried again, but failed. Finally he managed to raise an unwilling arm, and disappeared inside – to start, he said, 'the work of change'. By which he presumably meant, 'undoing all the harm done by the last occupant'.

5 July 2007

In early July a series of bombs were planted, in London and Glasgow. Luckily nobody was killed, but the event was a harsh reminder of the presence of terrorism. Almost immediately Gordon Brown faced his first question time as prime minister.

I felt sorry for David Cameron. For months he has been waiting for his chance to demolish the Jabberwock, training himself to peak fitness to face the jaws that bite, the claws that catch. He had his vorpal sword sharp, all ready to go snicker-snack.

And the slithy toves were lined up behind him, all hoping for some action. But then came the bombs, and the whole country was combined in wanting unity. Gordon Brown had caught the national mood, and there was little the Tory leader could do.

It must have been galling, especially as the new prime minister appeared to be very nervous – surprisingly, when you consider how often he has stood at this same dispatch box. At one point, sounding like a CD that's been left on a hot radiator for too long, he said: 'Then, then, then, then we will not be able to agree on the way, the way, the way, the way, the way forward.'

'Miss, miss, miss, miss,' he uttered, like a schoolchild desperate for the toilet. 'Miss, mister Speaker.' I have never heard him stutter like that. Clearly there was some real anxiety banked up inside that mighty frame. There were other weird remarks. At one point, he said, 'The leader of the opposition forgets that I have only been in the job for five days...' It was meant to say, 'Look, we're realists, I'll get round to it when I have time,' but it sounded like Pooh Bear reminding us that he was a bear of very little brain.

For the first time Ming Campbell won the session. He asked a series of harsh questions, about Iraq, corruption and extradition to the United States. The prime minister climbed back into his national unity suit. 'My door is always open to you,' he said graciously.

The courtesy was not reciprocated. 'The prime minister's door seems more like a trapdoor to me,' said Ming. That may not sound like a particularly damaging wisecrack, but in parliamentary terms it is as if Oscar Wilde had risen from the grave, and strolled into the Chamber, green carnation aloft. MPs were, quite literally, rolling around the benches.

It was left to John Reid, one of Brown's greatest enemies, the man who pre-resigned so as not to serve under him, the original frumious Bandersnatch, to come to the rescue, which he did by implying that old hands like him understood and that Gordon would pick it up in time.

Oh well, to coin a phrase, things can only get better.

10 July 2007

The new home secretary was Jacqui Smith, a former chief whip of whom few people had heard. She began her term of office by making a statement about the bombings, during which she wore a very low-cut dress showing off an impressive décolletage. While my colleagues from the less politically correct newspapers made much of this, I, as a Guardian *writer, forbore even to mention it. This time, while her costume fell short of being a full burqa, it was certainly much less revealing when she answered Home Office questions.*

The main talking point came from Mr Henry Bellingham, the Tory MP for NW Norfolk, who wanted to know when Ms Smith would meet the local police to discuss illegal raves in East Anglia.

The minister, Vernon Coaker, replied that the police were busy gathering intelligence and car registration numbers. (Haven't they got more urgent work these days?) Then Mr Bellingham inquired, 'Are you aware that there was a time when raves were generally low-key, good-humoured events?'

At this the entire place collapsed in laughter. What was he talking about? Was there a golden age of raves, perhaps between the wars? Young men in boaters would arrive, carrying jugs of lemonade and a wind-up gramophone with a wooden horn. They would have some records by 'Hutch' which they would play while 'flappers' danced to music so loud that it could sometimes be heard in the next field.

These events were so low-key and good-humoured that the local clergy were often invited, hence the phrase: 'More "E", vicar?'

45

In his second PMQs, Gordon Brown effectively ended the notion of a super-casino in Blackpool. Instead, he suggested, the town should go ahead with a new museum of the theatre. He seemed to imagine that people would cancel their trips to Las Vegas in order to cross the Fylde for a look at John Gielgud's smoking jacket, and a programme for the first night of Separate Tables.

You can get some idea of how a new administration works by looking at the language it uses. The most important word these days is 'issues'. This appears to mean no more than 'problems', though it sounds more impressive. So Ed Miliband, the new cabinet office minister and brother of David Miliband, the foreign secretary, and presumably of Gummo Miliband too, banged on about 'social inclusion issues' and 'special needs issues'.

Ruth Kelly, the transport secretary, told us that there were 'passenger issues at Birmingham New Street'. Did she mean that passengers were facing difficulties, or that the very existence of passengers was interfering with the smooth running of the station?

Either way, the word is out of control. Suppose you published a magazine like *Parents*, devoted to the care and upbringing of one's offspring, and your edition about children's problems ran into snags, would you then face issue issues issue issues?

A feast of jargon followed. Mr Miliband announced 'a national programme for third sector commissioning', whatever that might be. Even the Tories joined in. 'Have you consulted the new Volunteering Tsar, Baroness Neuberger?'

asked Greg Clark. Only under Gordon Brown could we have such a personage, though of course it should be the Volunteering Tsarina, or possibly a Volunteering Rasputin.

Then John Healey made a statement about giving more power to local councils. The centrepiece was the abolition of John Prescott's regional assemblies, which are, so far as I can see, to be replaced by other equally unelected, unknown and inefficient bodies. Or, as Mr Healey put it, 'We will combine new regional economic strategy into a single integrated strategy.'

So impenetrable was this oratory that another Tory, Tony Baldry, was driven beyond endurance. He quoted the minister's words back to him. 'What does the phrase, "develop proposals for multi-area agreements encouraging local authorities to agree collective targets for economic development priorities and work with interested city and sub-regions on the scope for statutory and sub-regional arrangements which could allow greater devolution of national and economic functions" mean in plain English?' he inquired.

Astonishingly, Mr Healey was able to translate into the demotic. So why use such gibberish in the first place?

Question time for all prime ministers comes round once a week.

Gordon Brown seems incapable of taking a decision. Time and again he ponders things, promises to give them a bit of thought, to chew them over. Yesterday he was asked if he thought that cannabis should be legalised for medical purposes. 'There will be a consultation document to review our strategy.'

What about serious criminals who are being released from prison early? 'The new justice secretary will investigate.' Will these early releases become a permanent fixture in the justice system? 'We will continue to review it.' Darfur: what is the aid minister, Douglas Alexander, doing there? Like Fagin, 'he is reviewing the situation'.

What about the very large number of missing children in this country? He looked forward to meeting children's charities 'to talk about this very grave problem'.

The death of four cyclists from Rhyl cropped up. 'I will look into this with ministerial colleagues.' Had the Royal Navy got enough ships? 'We look forward to making an announcement.'

But he's had 10 years to sort this stuff out. What on earth was he doing all the time, except sticking pins into a wax model of Tony Blair?

24 July 2007

The agonising failure to commit himself to anything continued. In late July 2007, Britain suffered severe flooding. Mr Brown came back from the scene of the deluge, and told a press conference that his 'first thoughts' were with the victims, though he didn't tell us what those thoughts were. Alastair Campbell would have found, on behalf of Tony Blair, a fireman who rescued a kitten from a roof or some other convenient hero, but Brown spoke entirely in stiff, formalised jargon.

He batted aside criticisms of failures by the emergency services by saying, 'In each of these instances where people have raised questions, the answers have been given.' This was the Ted Heath school of debate: 'There are those who disagree with me. They are wrong.'

There would be a review. In Gordon Brown's Britain there is always a review. If he had been stopped by Dick Turpin demanding 'Your money or your life,' he would have announced a review to consider the options. Passing a child drowning in a duck pond, he would leap into action and set up a committee to look at the matter of aquatic safety for the under-fives.

His first press conference was a fairly dour event. He was asked what he enjoyed most about being prime minister, and he gave a long, rambling reply about facing terrorism, and regaining trust, and building eco-villages. Unexpected questions hit him like swirling flood water, and you could see his brain desperately scrambling for dry land, which he invariably reached with a triumphant 'meeting the aspirations of the British people', which apparently is what he wakes up every morning determined to do.

What had been the biggest surprise of his new job? 'I think, er, er, it's a new challenge every day, and you're not able to watch sporting events such as Wimbledon and the Tour de France...'

What on earth did he expect? Did he imagine that civil servants would murmur in his ear, 'Pretty quiet day today, prime minister. You just sit down with a nice cup of tea and watch a bunch of drug-soaked junkies pedal up and down a mountain!'

20 September 2007

Every year, the three main parties hold their conferences, one after the other, starting with the Liberal Democrats.

Liberal Democrats are proud of being ahead of the pack, of spotting in advance problems that soon become mainstream concerns. Years ago I invented a Lib Dem campaign against the menace of cocktail sticks, which lurk in otherwise innocent buffets and can cause horrible damage to people's mouths. Recently, I went to a reception where there was a little label marked: 'Warning! Contains cocktail sticks.'

So even the Lib Dems' fantasy campaigns work in the end. No other party can make that claim. Yesterday, for example, they had a debate on excess packaging. They devoted quite some time to toothpaste cartons. One man said he had invented a form of tube that did not require packaging, yet he had seen that very tube, on sale, in a carton! He was outraged.

But why stop there? Do we even need tubes? Can't we buy toothpaste loose? And instead of using fresh paste every time we brush, can't we recycle it and help save the planet that way?

There were other fine, Lib Dem moments. One delegate, Crispin Allard, touched a rueful chord when he said, 'These are good, intelligent arguments. They work with Liberal Democrats, but are likely to fail with the people we are trying to reach.' Ah, yes, the party's fundamental problem.

Then they moved on to a longish discussion about whether the next – indeed the first – Lib Dem government should draw up a constitution before writing the constitution and holding a referendum on the written version. It was like watching the Flat Earth Society debate the existence of New Zealand.

28 September 2007

At the end of the Labour conference they handed out cards with the words of 'The Red Flag'. Time was when you'd no more have needed to remind delegates of that lyric than you would have needed surtitles for 'Happy Birthday to You' at a children's party. There was a brief period, during the Blair years, when it was banned altogether, but once it had been safely defused it returned, sung yesterday by a willowy blonde, so it sounded less like a call to the barricades than Proms in the Park. In the recent past, the leader and his wife would have appeared on the platform with the deputy leader and his wife, all four twirling round the stage and waving their armpits in our direction. Rock music would have pumped out at nose-bleeding volume, and there would have been a video describing Labour's many achievements, some less exciting than others: 'More pine nuts in pasta salad ... better teeth for *Big Brother* contestants ... a little plaid jacket on every dog.'

But yesterday Sarah Brown appeared with her husband and simply waved us goodbye.

The home secretary, Jacqui Smith, adopted the demotic approach. She quoted the Sex Pistols, something earlier, stuffy, whiskery home secretaries would never have done. She was planning to cut down on alcohol-induced crime by 'taking the licences away from dodgy premises'. I didn't know that 'dodgy' was a legal term.

'What is the charge, officer?'

'Being dodgy in a public place, and you'll come quietly if you know what's good for you.'

Drug users would be helped to 'get their heads together'. The authorities would seize criminals' 'bling'. At one point, she even said 'sumfink'. This may be due to spending too long in police canteens.

The wind-up speech came from Harriet Harman. Just as John Prescott once seemed to be taking credit for the absence of a hosepipe ban, she praised the government for the disasters over which it has presided. 'If the money market wobbles and you are worried about your savings, if torrential rain threatens your home, if foot and mouth threatens your farm, you want people who can sort it out ... you need Gordon Brown and his cabinet!'

This is the ripest, vintage, special reserve *chutzpah*, thickly cut and served with mango relish on a seeded bun.

The Tories always hold the last party conference.

There was a fine symbolic moment at the conference yesterday – the handover of the great blond Mop of State. First we had Michael Heseltine, once the man who could drive the conference into a frenzy of mingled rage and pleasure. Julian Critchley famously remarked that Heseltine always knew where to find the clitoris of the Conservative party.

But he is older, and would need bifocals now. Oh, there were distant echoes of the glorious days past. The hair is as thick, strong and perfectly sculpted as it ever was, propped up like a Suffolk cliff that would otherwise plunge into the sea. The voice would occasionally peak with anger. But the very thought of socialism, which twenty years ago would have driven him into a spittle-flecked spume of fury, now evokes regret rather than rage. He even stuck to the topic in hand, something he never did before.

At the end he lingered, perhaps waiting for the standing ovation that would once have been his due. A handful did rise, but no one followed them. Perhaps they recalled his part in the fall of Margaret Thatcher. Perhaps some younger delegates weren't even sure who he was. He walked off slowly with – was it my fantasy? – his head slightly bowed.

Half an hour later we heard from another blond. By contrast, Boris Johnson got a standing ovation simply for walking on stage. They cheered and they whooped and they yelled. They love him. The Great White Corona, with its power over men's minds, is now his! What we actually got was his stump speech for Mayor of London – no more high-rise buildings, no more 'jack-knifing, self-combusting, cyclist-crushing bendy buses'. And we returned to his great obsession – the theft of his own bicycles. Seven since Ken Livingstone had come to power! Had 'the great newt-fancier' been personally stealing Boris's bikes? We were not told. 'Once they stole my saddle, to whatever voodoo end!'

As slogans go, 'Vote Conservative and stop my bicycle saddle from being nicked' lacks both pith and resonance. But it didn't matter. The conference rose as one, as if bidden by the Mighty Mop. Even David Cameron appeared on the stage, as if to annexe some of that love, fervour and sheer blond magnetism.

In October, Gordon Brown suddenly announced that he would not call the election which had been long expected, and for which he and the Labour party had made careful preparations. This is known in the trade as 'bottling it'. He was anxious about the success of the Tory conference, and feared that opinion could quickly turn against him. It is thought that this one decision did more damage to his reputation than any other.

The prime minister wanted to tell his press conference that he hadn't called off the election merely because the polls were against him. It must be ghastly to have to stand up and say things to roughly 100 people, all of whom have decided you are fibbing.

Seriously fibbing. Lies, whoppers and porkies! Pants ablaze, nose growing so long you could peg your washing out on it.

There is a psychological condition known as Munchausen's Syndrome by Proxy. But this was Munchausen Unplugged. It was Billy Bunter saying, 'I didn't steal your cake, and in any case it tasted horrid.' It would have been embarrassing if it wasn't so funny, and it would have been funnier if it hadn't been so painful for the poor man.

Mind you, he may have believed what he was saying. Politicians have a gift for convincing themselves of what they say. You can fool some of the people some of the time, but you can fool yourself whenever you want.

This was his case. Yes, he had contemplated an election. But his 'instinct' had been against it. What he really wanted to do was to put his 'vision of the future' to the people of Britain. He used the word 'vision' over and over again, though I stopped counting at 30.

As for the notion that the Tory lead in the polls had anything to do with his decision, well, heavens to Murgatroyd! (I paraphrase.) How could it possibly have been a factor, when Labour was certain to win whenever the election was held? Why, candidates in marginal seats had been begging him to go to the country now.

Foot and mouth, terrorism, floods and the collapse of Northern Rock had all prevented him from setting out his 'vision'. Now at last he could! The debate was 'stepping up to a new level'. There were commissions, citizens' juries, deliberative assemblies. But you could tell he was rattled by the waves of cynicism billowing towards him by the way he repeated himself. He 'relished the chance' to debate Tory tax cuts, and would 'relish' telling the electorate why they wouldn't work. 'I would relish the chance for a forensic examination!'

Someone asked, incredulously, 'Are you saying that your decision had absolutely nothing to do with the state of the opinion polls?'

'Yeah,' he said curtly. 'I saw the opinion polls, and how many seats we would have won … but I returned to my first instinct … to give time for our vision to be realised, to implement our vision.' He would 'relish' the debate.

Was he a ditherer? He went off on a ramble about how 'I did the right thing [in 1994] when I said I wanted Tony Blair to be leader of the Labour party, and that was the right decision!'

If he had been hooked up to a polygraph, at that point it would have exploded in a shower of sparks.

Not long after the conferences ended, Ming Campbell, the Liberal Democrat leader, was summarily dispatched. He was replaced by someone guaranteed to be far more popular: Nick Clegg.

At Mafia funerals, we're told, it's always the *capo* that ordered the hit who makes the most fulsome speech over the coffin – about the departed's wonderful qualities, his integrity, loyalty and love of family.

So it was yesterday when Simon Hughes and Vincent Cable emerged from Lib Dem headquarters to announce the 'resignation' of Ming Campbell. We gathered there in the gloaming, as brisk young women marched out to tell us that there would be short statements from two of the conspirators (no, of course, they didn't use that word) and that they would answer no questions.

Where was Ming? 'He is not available,' one of the brisk young women said.

'But where is he?'

'He is not available,' they repeated, and for a gangster that would be a euphemism for 'dead'. For a politician, 'unavailable' is a real place, like London, or Patagonia.

Norman Baker, the Lib Dem MP who believes that Dr David Kelly was murdered, arrived muttering that Ming should have been given more time. He may well believe that his leader was the victim of a massive conspiracy, and for once he might be right.

The two hit men emerged. They looked very solemn, though there is always something faintly ludicrous about Lib Dem leadership crises, like watching a struggle for power in a Buddhist ashram.

What a paragon their late leader had been! The huge purpose and stability he had brought to the party! He had taken every decision for the benefit of party and nation, never for himself. What a massive debt we all owed him! That was just Mr Hughes. The deputy leader, Vince Cable, came next. It was he who had said that there was a 'debate' about Ming's future. This is the political equivalent of the knife between the shoulder blades, or the horse's head in the bed. There must have been a bubble of rage in Mr Campbell's throat when he heard that. 'Et tu, Vince,' however, lacks a certain gravitas.

Like the Walrus and the Carpenter as they surveyed the beach full of empty oyster shells, Mr Cable seemed to be close to tears. He spoke of the gratitude, respect and admiration felt by all Liberal Democrats for this great man. In his speech to the party conference (a mere four weeks before) he had set out a superb vision of a 'fairer, greener country'. Throughout, the Cable eyebrows were leaping up and down, as if trying to convey a quite contrary message in semaphore.

'Did you wield the dagger?' someone asked. 'Where is he, what have you done with him?' someone else shouted. A voice demanded, 'Is he dead?' and I realised it was mine. At such a time you wonder why, if he was such a cynosure, he should have been dispatched so ruthlessly.

There was a great fuss over the new European treaty. Gordon Brown had promised a referendum on a new constitution, but decided not to hold one, on the grounds that he might lose it. As old political hands will tell you, never hold a vote unless you know the result beforehand.

The prime minister had gone to sign the new treaty, but waited till all the other European leaders had gone before he showed up. Quite what this was intended to prove we never learned.

Gordon Brown returned from Lisbon to face his first big test over the non-existent referendum. He is agin one. I took a copy of the new treaty into the Chamber so that I could refer instantly to every topic that was raised. It includes 294 'articles', plus 63 pages of protocols, and it makes for a gripping read.

On page 26, for example, we find article 37 (b): 'In the first sub-paragraph, the words "without prejudice to paragraph 1 and Article 14 (3)" shall be replaced by "in accordance with Article 11 (3)" and "as well as the High Representative" shall be inserted, "keep the latter".'

And in the view of many Tories, you can certainly keep him, or her.

There are fascinating sections that tempt the reader onward, such as: 'The words "AND SPACE" shall be added to the heading of Title XVIII', which hints at the longest-ever series of sci-fi movies. Or new article 32 which reads in its entirety: 'The Union shall have legal personality.' Like Rumpole of the Bailey, perhaps.

I mention this only because if we do have a referendum some of us will have to read much of such stuff. Gordon

Brown has latched on to the fact that nobody, apart from a few lawyers and Euro-fanatics, has the slightest interest in it, so he has decided to bore us into submission. If yesterday's debate is any indication, he is well on the way to success.

David Cameron accused him of reneging on his promise to hold a referendum. Brown saw his opportunity. He leapt in with a stunning new piece of euro-jargon, the 'passerelle'. Apparently it was Lady Thatcher who, unknown to the entire population, first legislated for passerelles.

I logged on to the EU website, hoping that a passerelle would be a delicious Belgian pastry, filled with cream and pralines. Instead it means, 'a footbridge, referring to the possibility of either moving a policy area from the intergovernmental third pillar to the supra-national pillar, or changing the voting rules in the council, or the extension of the article's scope of application.' No wonder we are not getting a referendum.

Every year the Queen opens parliament, and every year her speech becomes grimmer.

They call it the 'gracious' speech, but it sounds more like the verbal equivalent of clinker scraped from an old coke oven. And every year the Queen reads it without a flub, implying that she has rehearsed it – and so has had to read it twice! It must be horrible. You can imagine her hurling it aside, crying: 'Where are the tumbrels when we need them? Who is building the guillotine to bring me merciful release?'

The session is the same every year, yet subtly different. It used to look like the inside of Grayson Perry's dressing-up box, but with the departure of the hereditary peers, the Chamber has a much lower tiara count. One peer's wife, in blue silk and a mink stole, wore diamond earrings, necklace and brooch with a tiara that could have been worn in a Las Vegas casino. It takes a lot to be over-dressed at a state opening.

Then the Commons came over. Jack Straw (he is not the first member of the Commons to be Lord Chancellor, since St Thomas More got their first. On the other hand, sainthood is one title you can't buy in Downing Street) handed the speech over to Her Maj and restored the ancient tradition of walking backwards down the steps. If he had ever dreamed, as a student activist, that he would one day be dressed as a bit-part player in *A Man for All Seasons* paying full-bottomed obeisance to the Queen, he might have woken up screaming.

Then came the speech. I will spare you all but a sample of its horrors. The 'meeting the people's aspirations', 'realising full potential', 'promoting regeneration', 'financial inclusion', 'binding frameworks', and 'meeting millennium development goals' – all the breeze-block prose that New Labour has been deploying for 10 years. They are words that have been drained of meaning. Like Blair's verb-free sentences they express a vague aspiration, in language so distant from the way people think and talk that they convey only an unformed, inchoate desire.

At last it was over, and I hope the Queen got a very large gin and tonic.

9 November 2007

A new star appeared in the Conservative galaxy.

The scene is Tory HQ. In a basement room, a team of people wearing security passes has been locked in. A middle-aged man in a lab coat steps onto the dais. 'Ladies and gentlemen,' he says, 'your requirements were specific. You wished my team to create a Tory MP who would refute the public's suspicion that your party consists entirely of wealthy, privileged people, who have no knowledge of, or connection with, the north of England.

'I am pleased to report that we have succeeded. In fact, we have done more. We have brought you today's version of Alderman Foodbotham, the 25-stone, awesome-jowelled, iron-watch-chained, crag-visaged chairman of the Bradford City Tramways and Fine Arts committee, created by the columnist Peter Simple!'

As an excited buzz runs round the room, his voice drops. 'And I can inform you that this is the first time anyone, anywhere, has managed to clone a fictional character. In all modesty, I believe it is the greatest scientific achievement of the century!'

A curtain is pulled back. There stands a gigantic figure, with a great moon face, a rubicund complexion and an iron watch chain. The room erupts in a hubbub. Cries of 'The next election is won!' and 'Wozziz name?' ring out. The scientist looks slightly embarrassed. 'We gave him a joke name for our amusement, but of course you'll need something more serious. We called him "Eric Pickles".'

'But that's wonderful! I love it!' says the party leader. 'Eric Pickles he is, and Eric Pickles he shall be!' Yesterday we were privileged to watch the new creation in action. Mr Pickles, who like Alderman Foodbotham was leader of Bradford council, faced Hazel Blears, the tiny communities secretary whose poppy was level with the dispatch box. As always, she looked terrifically pleased with herself. If she had done a little jig, just to celebrate the sheer joy of being her, we would not have been surprised.

Mr Pickles rose, and the floor of the Chamber shook. He spoke with the air of one who would have been handing down the Ten Commandments if he hadn't mislaid his chisel. He told us that his great-grandfather had been chairman of Keighley Co-op. How utterly authentic! How sad that the Speaker does not allow MPs to wear flat caps in the Chamber, or keep ferrets down their trousers. He quoted from Ms Blears's blog. (The original Alderman Foodbotham would have imagined that a blog was a cheap substitute for cod for poorer people, to be served battered with chips.) 'Snap election,' he said, 'reet on!' (Only fictional northerners say 'reet' any more.)

He speeded up, but as he did the microchip in his brain broadened and lengthened his words. 'Agency' became 'age-gunn-say'. The government had 'roared ruffshud' over local councils. 'I gre-e-ew up in a terruuss house. I kno-o-ow what it's like to be poo-wuh.' A fantastic tribute to British technology.

13 November 2007

Like an anthropologist on a visit to the reclusive Amazon tribe he has spent decades studying, I went to inspect the annual Conservative women's conference, held in central London. Comparison with my last field trip showed many changes. In the past few years the session has attracted a sparse crowd. Yesterday there were 700 of them. And the average age has plummeted faster than a drunken bungee jumper; around a quarter were under 60. And several looked like men. On closer inspection, many were men.

It was a puzzle. So were the topics. In earlier times, debates would have had titles such as 'The Undeserving Poor – Tax Them Till They Squeal', or 'Hanging Drawing and Quartering – What's Wrong With That, I'd Like To Know?'

Yesterday they spoke about Africa. They heard Zainab Salbi, who does good works in war zones. Another was Shirin Tahir-Kheli, an advisor to Condoleezza Rice on women's empowerment, and who focuses on 'multi-faceted outreach to women in the Muslim world'.

Women's empowerment? What sort of talk was that, Tory ladies of 25 years ago would have asked. Since all men, including their husbands – especially their husbands – quailed at their every word, they already had more empowerment than they could handle. And 'multi-faceted' could only refer to a sherry decanter.

They heard from Sir Christopher Meyer, the former British ambassador to Washington. In the past their greatest hatred would have been directed at some figure in the Labour party. Now they have a different target.

'Heather Mills!' Meyer mused, and you could hear the sharp intake of breath. 'You could say she brought it on herself!' There were cries of 'yes!'

'She liked the publicity when she liked the publicity, but she didn't like it when she didn't like it!'

This remark, somewhat runic, brought loud applause. Later, asked about George W. Bush, he offered the view that he was cleverer than most people thought. 'But you don't have to be stupid to be stupid,' he added, giving us all something to chew on.

He also gave us a learned exegesis on the advice he had been given to him by Number 10. 'Get up the arse of the White House and stay there!' The meaning is complicated, but many of the women must have been recovering from hearing the word 'arse' at a Tory ladies' conference.

Finally the delegates heard from David Cameron, who gave a harrowing speech about violence against women. In the past, they'd have sung 'Land of Hope and Glory'. Nowadays they get a dose of grim reality.

The constant figure in all governments is the cabinet secretary, famously played by Nigel Hawthorne in Yes, Prime Minister.

Watching a top Whitehall mandarin in action is like sitting in a Bentley as it whispers up the drive towards a stately home. Only the parkland gliding past and the almost imperceptible purr of the engine tell you that you're moving.

Yesterday we heard from the most majestic mandarin of them all, Sir Gus O'Donnell, the cabinet secretary and head of the civil service. His parents may have had some inkling of his destiny, for they enabled him to sign his initials 'GOD'. There was something a little wrong. Usually cabinet secretaries speak in a language called British, similar to English, but subtly different. They do not 'think' things, but are 'minded to take the view'. They never admit that they don't know something; instead they say, 'You are probing the depths of my ignorance.' 'The situation was well short of a counter-allegation' is their way of saying 'true'. But Gus is a south London lad who went to a provincial university. He has a flattish London accent and tends to use words like 'yes' and 'no', which rarely crop up in British. Instead of saying 'I find myself locked in a position of some perplexity,' he says, 'I'm puzzled.' But he is still a mandarin. I suspect there is something of an internal struggle between 'Gus' the football fan, and 'Sir Augustine', to give him his real name.

Sir Augustine was questioned about the police inquiry into the alleged sale of peerages. He clearly felt very strongly. But he could hardly shriek in rage, or denounce the Metropolitan police. So here is what he said in reply to MPs on the public administration committee yesterday. 'It was a very intense process,' he began, referring to the police investigation. This meant, 'The idiot flatfoots took up all of our time.'

'Some of my staff were doing other work, and had to spend time, sometimes a long time, on other matters, and to take work home at the weekends.' This meant, 'They had us climbing the walls 24/7.'

'It was extremely disrupting. So many things that were going on, some accurate, some wildly inaccurate, appeared in the media.' This meant, 'On top of demanding every spare minute we had – as if we weren't trying to run the country – they were leaking lies about us to the media.'

He didn't need to spell out what he meant. Short of using the F-word, the C-word, and the entire contents of the Profanisaurus, he had conveyed precisely what he meant. It was his way of leaning out of the back seat of the Bentley and shouting, 'Rot in hell, you bastards!'

One of the worst things that can happen to a politician is for someone to make a joke at his or her expense – a joke that sticks. It happened to Gordon Brown a few months after he became prime minister.

It was ghastly – the most horrible, tooth-rattling, goose-pimpling, stomach-heaving prime minister's questions since John Prescott stood in for Tony Blair. I was reminded of the only bullfight I ever saw: the great beast, tormented by the picadors, charging around the ring, lowering his head and bellowing with futile rage and pain.

Sheer pity made me want the bull to have a chance – not to kill the matador, but at least to toss him once, perhaps briefly to wipe the thin, satisfied smile from his face. I felt the same for Gordon Brown. It started when he got up to answer the first question, and Tories jeered at the near silence from Labour. David Cameron had darts to plunge into his hide, and he planted them with cruel care. The prime minister had promised to be open, trustworthy and competent. Could he stand there and make that claim again?

He asked about the cash for peerages inquiry. 'Does he expect us to believe that someone even Labour members believe is a control freak was preparing for an election, sorting out the finances with everyone involved in this scandal, yet did not have the first idea of what was going on?'

Mr Brown lowered his head and charged blindly. Wretchedly, he even raised Black Wednesday, which happened fifteen years ago. The Tory leader delivered the *estocada*, the final sword-thrust: 'We have had 155 days of this government, with disaster after disaster. The prime minister's excuses go from incompetence to complacency and there are questions about his integrity. Are people not rightly asking, "Is this man simply not cut out for the job?"'

The attack was more lethal than it might have been. Mr Cameron could have gone over the top and raved about the worst government since George III. Saying, like Attlee, 'not up to the job', was far worse.

But far, far worse was yet to come. The agony was heightened. Vince Cable, the acting leader of the Liberal Democrats, said in his voice like a sheep with a tummy ache, 'The house has noticed the prime minister's remarkable transformation in the past few weeks – from Stalin to Mr Bean.'

A great howl of laughter seemed to fall from the ceiling. Even Labour MPs tried desperately to hide their laughter from the whips. Apparently many stab victims feel no pain at first, but are aware how much it will hurt later. This one will go on hurting.

The only relief came when Sir Patrick Cormack bizarrely asked Mr Brown what he would like for Christmas. Perhaps he expected a reply on the lines of 'an iPhone, or perhaps a giant bar of Toblerone'. Instead the prime minister said, from deep inside his pit of misery, 'I might have one day off.'

Mr Cable later revealed that he had thought the gag up in his bath. His wife had advised against using it, but he went ahead all the same.

The sight of Boris Johnson in a rage, hair flapping apparently independently from his scalp, was always terrifying. The sight of him flapping with fake fury – and in his new, shortie haircut – was bound to be sensational.

Yesterday he sat on the fringe of prime minister's questions. A Labour MP asked what appeared to be a planted question. (Like Bill and Ben, Labour's flowerpot men sit in the pots, waiting to be sprinkled with Baby Bio by prime ministerial helpers.) It concerned Boris's plan, when he becomes mayor of London – which once appeared as likely as the job going to a Teletubby but now seems increasingly possible – to reduce funding for the Metropolitan police.

Since the question had been, I assume, scripted by the prime minister's aides, Gordon Brown was in a good position to reply. 'He [Boris] wishes to cut spending on the Metropolitan police. That would be disastrous for the police and disastrous for London.'

In a distant corner, we could see Boris harrumph. It was a mighty harrumph, worthy of a well-lubricated walrus who's just realised that the fish he has swallowed was rotten. You would not have wanted to be downwind of that harrumph.

Ten minutes later the session was over and Mr Brown had scuttled away. Boris rose to a mighty roar of acclamation, sincere from the Tory side, ironic from Labour – or possibly a mixture of both on both sides.

'I am sure that the prime minister INADVERTENTLY misled the house…' (The capital letters were meant to indicate that Mr Brown was lying through his teeth, while keeping Boris within the rules of order.) Amid the swelling roar, he continued, 'That is the EXACT opposite of the case. I want to get MORE policemen ... will you, Mr Speaker, ask him to come here as soon as possible and rectify that mistake?'

Well, the Speaker is not in the business of dragging prime ministers back to apologise to backbenchers, however famous, so the walrus was told, in effect, to shut up and slide off the ice.

Earlier in the session, we had heard from Nick Clegg, the Lib Dem leader who has, to put it mildly, kept a low profile since his election last month. But he asked a ferocious pair of questions about services for the armed forces. Did the prime minister not care about them? Could he even be bothered to provide proper medical care for those who risk their lives for our country?

Mr Brown looked like someone who has been attacked by the neighbour's rabbit. He repeated, as he usually does, a string of statistics which may well be true but don't appear to be relevant.

One topic nobody mentioned was sleaze. This is because both main parties are terrified about what might emerge about them. It is like the fear of Mutual Assured Destruction. Or like wrestling on cable TV. It's quite fun, but you really want both sides to lose.

Every now and again New Labour coins a spanking cliché: a phrase that sounds bold and resolute, but actually implies nothing of the sort. 'Challenges' has been used for years to indicate 'a pressing problem which we have no idea how to tackle'. So yesterday during transport questions a minister, Tom Harris, spoke about the 1,300 railways carriages that are to be acquired by 2015, by which time many of us will have died, after having to stand up for hours a week, pressed against pregnant women to whom nobody will give up a seat, young persons with their iPods turned up to 'melt soft brain tissue' volume and people with bulging rucksacks on their backs, apparently filled with granite boulders.

'We will not eradicate all the capacity challenges that we face,' intoned Mr Harris. You can say that again, especially as it turns out that under current plans only three of those carriages will be used, for example, on the East Midlands line, an increase of, say, 20 seats per year.

Ruth Kelly is probably the only transport secretary to be a member of Opus Dei, the Roman Catholic organisation which encourages self-flagellation (not perhaps the perfect niche for most politicians). Older readers may recall a column by Michael Frayn, a satire on the Catholic debate about contraception. He imagined fundamentalists wanting to ban rear-view mirrors, on the grounds that the story of Lot's wife told us it was sinful to look backwards.

I doubt that Kelly would go that far. But she was deeply evasive when asked about reducing the number of short car journeys. These have been increasing, and the rapid closing of post offices has made the problem worse.

Her reply was that the government 'intended to encourage local leadership … to think through how people get around'. I took the phrase 'encourage local leadership' to mean precisely nothing beyond, 'not our baby', or 'search me'. But it would be the perfect cop-out for almost any government problem. What will ministers do about unemployment? 'We shall encourage local leadership in the creation of jobs.' The crime rate? 'Encouraging local leadership in assisting with police work.' You could slap it like a poultice on any problem – sorry, any challenge.

6 March 2008

Under the leadership of Nick Clegg, the Liberal Democrats became somewhat silly. They walked out of the Chamber en bloc in protest at a ruling by the Speaker. Then a week later most abstained in an important vote on Europe.

The government won the big vote last night. The greatest losers were the Liberal Democrats, most of whom abstained.

All other MPs were milling about and enjoying the occasion (we had the wondrous sight of the majestically bellied Nick Soames, a Tory, chatting to the majestically bellied Ken Purchase, left-wing Labour. How could they get close enough even to hear each other?)

Last week the Lib Dems stormed out of the Chamber in protest against a Speaker's ruling. Last night they sat on their hands. If there is one thing sillier than a petulant walk-out, it's a pretentious sit-in.

The Commons is at its most ferocious when all sides know they are wrong. Labour knows that it should have held a referendum on the Lisbon treaty, but it wouldn't because it would have lost. The Tories know that a referendum would be catastrophic and would set us back in Europe for years.

And the Lib Dems want a referendum on whether we should stay in at all – which they all believe we should – because they can't think of anything else. It is like the war in *Gulliver's Travels* between people who open their egg at the big end and those who passionately believe in cracking the little end – with the Lib Dems saying we should have a vote on whether to eat the egg at all.

It was a bad day for them. Since their angry mince-out a week ago, almost all other MPs have decided that the Lib Dems are a pitiful joke. Their poor leader, Nick Clegg, could barely be heard above the sarcastic jeers. Yesterday he just managed to say, 'He talks about leadership...' before dozens of MPs erupted in a great, camp, 'Whoooo!' noise. That was before William Hague got to work. He quoted Mr Clegg as saying that pro-Europeans lacked the '*cojones*' to take their argument to the people. 'This might explain why their interventions have become ever more shrill. They have become separated from their *cojones*. These unfortunate objects are now to be found, impaled on a distant fence.' There were screeches of laughter, and even some grim smiles from the Lib Dems. It's the way he tells 'em, and worth a grand of any Chamber of Commerce's money.

Poor Ed Davey, the Lib Dems' spokesman on Europe, had invented the 'mouse argument', which is supposed to demonstrate the difference between the treaty and a new constitution. Apparently 90 per cent of our DNA is shared with mice, but it's the 10 per cent that matters. 'The difference between a man and a mouse is an intriguing question,' mused Mr Hague, ironically, and from that moment on, whenever Mr Davey rose, there were cries of 'Squeak, squeak!'

Does it matter? Not really, except that deep down, all politicians yearn to be taken very seriously.

The new chancellor gave his first budget.

Is Alistair Darling the most boring chancellor ever? Put it this way: he sent Geoffrey Howe to sleep. This is an epoch-making achievement, like beating Roger Federer at tennis – a sign that the torch has been passed to a new generation.

The former chancellor, now Lord Howe, was the proud holder of that ancient title, the ultimate mega-snooze, Denis Healey's 'dead sheep', a man whose first throat-clearing could empty a packed room.

Yesterday he took his place in the gallery across from the whipper-snapper bidding to depose him. Mr Darling had barely started talking in his soft Scottish monotone about 'stability', 'challenges of the future', 'flexibility and resilience' when Lord Howe's head slumped dramatically forward. For almost the entire speech, he slept in peace. Very occasionally he would wake with a start, look across the Chamber, and observe that Mr Darling was still speaking. Instantly his head dropped down again, and there it stayed.

It was a fine, touching tribute from the crasher's crasher, and Mr Darling must be very proud this morning. Indeed, so dull was his speech that for much of the time he heard the sound that other, lesser, public speakers dread – the audience talking among themselves.

Normally during a budget speech they'd be discussing new rules for mortgages; yesterday I suspect they were asking if their neighbour had caught Delia on TV, or how the kids were doing at school – anything to drown out the drone. But we know that Mr Darling regards being boring as a wise political strategy, so deep down he must have been delighted.

If you actually listened, your eyes propped up by matchsticks, a ballpoint pen lodged under your chin, it was eerily familiar. As Nick Clegg said later, 'I watched the prime minister very carefully and his lips scarcely moved while the chancellor was speaking.'

For example, Gordon Brown's budgets – at least the last 10 – all described an Elysium, a happy land of smiling children, of warm, well-fed pensioners, with wealth-creating entrepreneurs thronging every street corner. He would contrast their earthly paradise with other, wretched countries such as the United States, Japan and the miserable peoples of Europe condemned to live in hunger and squalor. We got the plasma screen TV and they got the box – to live in or to eat, according to necessity. I exaggerate, but only slightly.

Amazingly, Mr Darling did exactly the same as his boss always had. Faced with the worst economic crisis for decades, he told us again how much better off we were than all those snivelling nations, how vastly better prepared we were for the tempests ahead, which in sooth would hardly affect us at all.

Tories listened in disbelief. Whenever he made a faint concession to reality, they went 'Aahh,' like a field of cynical sheep.

When he said, blandly – no, 'blandly' makes it seem too exciting – that 'given the fundamental strength of our public finances' some of them woke up long enough to emit a bellowing shout of mockery. Somewhat shrieked 'What?!?!' in a falsetto, like Frankie Valli in that musical about the Four Seasons.

Like all the great bores, Mr Darling was unfazed. His fiscal rules were all in place, he said. His forecasts had proved accurate. Debt would be lower than – of course – that of the US, Japan and the euro area. (David Cameron said that our debt was actually as bad as Hungary, Pakistan and Egypt, proof once again that you can make statistics say anything you want.)

The speech trundled on, like the heavy roller on a cricket pitch, crushing everything in its path. Now and again, Tories would catch on to the fact that he was saying something quite nonsensical: the business minister, he told us, was going to consult on ways to reduce bureaucracy and regulation – a review, after 11 years in office!

He promised no change in the charges on non-doms 'in this parliament or the next', he said, a piece of brass neck (does he really believe they have a chance of winning, or was it a wind-up?) that roused a few scoffing Tories.

Finally it was over. Lord Howe, still asleep, was woken by the mass stampede of fellow peers pushing past him to seek gallon jugs of black coffee.

19 March 2008

In London, there was an election for mayor. The candidates were the sitting mayor, Ken Livingstone, and his Tory rival Boris Johnson.

'This election is not *Celebrity Big Brother*,' said Ken Livingstone. Yesterday was the formal beginning of the campaign for mayor of London. I apologise to non-metropolitan readers, except that with Ken and Boris running, *Celebrity Big Brother* is exactly what it resembles. I wouldn't be surprised if instead of going to the polling station we are all obliged to vote off the contestants by phone – 50p a minute, calls substantially more from mobiles. And in the meantime, they'll all have to jump around performing silly tricks.

Ken was introduced by Doreen Lawrence, the mother of the murdered black teenager Stephen Lawrence. She said, 'Ken has always been there for London, time and time again.' I should hope so too. We don't pay for him to be there for Glasgow, or Kalamazoo, Michigan.

His large claque clapped almost everything he said. They clapped when he claimed to have performed miracles for the city. And we didn't have to take that on trust. He told us so himself. Miracles in transport, better than ever. Miracles on crime, lower than in living memory. Miracles on the environment, the cleanest yet. 'If we get it right in the big cities,' he said, 'humanity has a future!'

Yes, Ken's proposed £25 daily charge on Chelsea tractors will not just raise money – it will save the planet! Vote for Boris, and the few survivors of the great cataclysm will be scrabbling through dust and cinders, fighting over the last scraps of food.

The polls currently show Boris in the lead, possibly because the voters don't realise that this is actually a hit TV show (*Dancing on Thin Ice*) and want to give Labour an old-fashioned, ballot-box thumping. So Ken has started to talk less about his own genius, and more about Boris's shortcomings. For example, he said, in Ken's eight years in office, Boris had asked just three parliamentary questions about crime, while Ken had put 1,000 extra police on the streets. 'What do Londoners want? A thousand extra police or three questions?'

This is more than slightly unfair, since as MP for Henley, Boris is not in a position to do much about policing in London. Still, as I may have remarked when Ken was called by some other politician 'the greatest threat to London since the V2 rocket', with Ken you know that the time to duck is when the whining noise begins.

Ken finished off by misquoting Dr Johnson: 'When a man is tired of London, he slopes off to Henley.'

We walked the five minutes to Boris's launch. Unlike Ken he didn't have a claque or even a mini-claquette. But he did have a bold proposition: people should vote for him because he is a journalist. Journalists have the skills a mayor would need – asking questions, getting answers, championing great causes.

This is a very high-risk strategy, like saying: 'Vote for me, I'm an estate agent!' Or, 'You should choose me, because I know how to run a paedophile website.'

The unspoken secret is that you could hardly slot a bus ticket between the two candidates' platforms – both want better transport, cleaner air, safer streets, good community relations and a bag of gold for every voter, or its equivalent. All we have to do is choose between the old-fashioned machine politician and the even more old-fashioned toff. But that is the genius of *Big Brother*, forcing entirely disparate people to co-exist for what may seem like an endless period.

The president of France came to visit.

He loves us. He adores us. He reveres us! Listening to Nicolas Sarkozy address parliament yesterday was like being underneath a torrent of crème Chantilly sprayed from a high-pressure hose.

He actually said 'thank you' for the liberation. Previous French presidents have implied that events in Normandy were mere skirmishes while the French got on with the real work of throwing off the German yoke.

But Mr Sarkozy could not thank us enough. Grateful? It was surprising that he didn't grab the Speaker round the legs to thank him personally for everything his forebears had done. France would never forget – never! She would never forget the English blood, the Scottish blood, the Welsh blood, not to mention the Irish blood. France would never forget the welcome given to General de Gaulle in London (an event that seemed to slip the general's mind quite quickly). 'France will never forget because it has no right to forget!'

(Compare and contrast with de Gaulle's decision to throw all American troops out of France. One diplomat asked then, 'Does that include the ones under the ground?')

The setting for this geyser of gratitude was the royal gallery in the House of Lords. The president is partial to a spot of bling, and this is bling on a mega scale. The gold, the scarlet leather, the stained glass and gilt statuary – it is a mad Victorian's idea of what a mediaeval castle ought to look like, and it makes parts of Versailles look like something knocked up by Mies van der Rohe. And we had the vast battle pictures on either side of the room – Waterloo and Trafalgar. 'We got them lit especially brightly,' said one of the attendants. Denis MacShane had come over from the Commons, bubbling brightly as he always does when anything European is in the air. 'Did you hear him on the *Today* programme?' he asked. 'He was completely over the top about Britain. He probably only talks to Carla like that!'

Ah, Carla. She entered, cool, poised, as if the nude pictures in the tabloids had never appeared. (Why do I suspect that Sarko doesn't care; in fact may be rather pleased?) She sat at the back of the stage and the audience was transfixed. Crusty old codgers who spend their lives buried in policy documents smiled for the first time in years.

For her husband, the remarks about our help during the war were the merest throat-clearing. He also loves our parliament. Over the years, our nation had become 'aux yeux de beaucoup d'hommes, un idéal humaine et un idéal politique'. So it wasn't just him; the whole world thought we were brilliant!

His listeners were entranced. Even the translator could be seen to chop the air and wave in excitement, as if she were delivering the speech herself.

'My dear British friends,' he continued. He needed us. The Franco-German axis was all very well, but it was the Anglo-French axis that mattered now.

'I was so often inspired in my youthful days by the greatness of Britain,' he reflected. And now he would never forget the hospitality he had just been shown. 'Vive le Royaume-Uni! Vive la France!'

Somehow we slithered through all that cream and gave him the ovation he so obviously, so desperately, craved.

Disasters continued to arrive on the government's doorstep.

Alistair Darling announced a £50 billion bailout for the banks. But he did it all in that maddeningly calm way he has. If my house was on fire, I hope the brigade wouldn't send him to tackle the blaze. 'This is a serious situation. I intend soon to make available a wide range of fire extinguishers. Asbestos blankets will also be an important part of the rescue package…' A shower of sparks goes up from the roof with a great swooshing noise. 'This house is better placed to withstand the effects of fire than most others in the street,' he intones, with the same infuriating placidity.

'But can't you hose it with water?' you ask desperately.

'We are conducting an urgent review of the use of water as a fire retardant and I have tasked the committee to present its conclusions within six months…'

In transport questions we might have heard about the Terminal 5 fiasco, which left hundreds of passengers without baggage, or indeed flights, and which has once again made Britain's reputation for incompetence a by-word round the world. Or we could have heard about the crawling queues along motorway roadworks in which no roads are being worked.

But that got only the odd glancing mention. What MPs wanted to talk about was Mrs Gwyneth Dunwoody, the Labour chairwoman of the transport select committee, who has just died. She kept her position in spite of tireless efforts by the government, who regarded her as a terrific nuisance.

I have to say that there was an ever so slightly sinister air to yesterday's tributes, as if people could not quite believe she was dead, and might one day return with her rasping tongue and harsh, angry laugh. Ruth Kelly, transport secretary in the government that did so much to get rid of her, called her 'a truly outstanding parliamentarian and a great servant of the people', but at least had the grace to add that she made 'pertinent, if sometimes mischievous contributions to debates'. This is obituary code for 'I personally found her as agreeable as a septic goitre'.

It was the Tories who went over the top, possibly because they could never hope to rival, and would love to copy, Mrs Dunwoody's ferocious disdain for the Labour government. Anne McIntosh even evoked Rupert Brooke: 'There will always be a corner of this Chamber that is forever Gwyneth,' she said.

It sounded like an MR James ghost story. A new member, arriving perhaps in 2010, insouciantly sits down in her old place and immediately feels a cold shiver down his spine. Later he is found in his office, dead, a look of indescribable terror on his face. 'It looks as if he's been sat on, by a very large person, sir,' says the copper who finds the body. The Inspector shudders. He guesses what has happened. A black cat appears from nowhere and emits a terrible screech.

'It seems very strange to be here without her watchful eye,' said the Tories' Louise Ellman.

Without her watchful eye? I wouldn't be so sure. Did I detect in the distance a mirthless cackle of contempt? Or was it just an old rafter creaking?

3 May 2008

We finally got the result of the mayoral election in London.

It was the greatest triumph for Eton College since Harold Macmillan won the 1959 election. After half a century, the toff is back on top. Boris Johnson's victory may owe as much to the voters' desire to rub Gordon Brown's nose in the mud as to any of his policies or personality, but the fact remains that once again one of Britain's most successful politicians wore a tailcoat and wing collar to school, and spoke in slang they probably don't understand down the Queen Vic.

Boris's victory had been predicted for 24 hours, though when the moment came his margin was lower than most people had expected. He responded with a victory speech that might have been written with the sole intention of having the word 'gracious' slapped on it. He praised Ken Livingstone – 'a distinguished public servant', the man who had truly spoken for London after the 7/7 bomb attacks. 'You have the thanks and admiration of millions of Londoners, even if they have a funny way of showing it... To the vast multitude of people who voted against me, I shall work to earn your trust,' he added. Etonians do tend to be alarmingly polite, even to their enemies.

Ken must have felt bitter. In 2000 he was first elected in spite of the Labour machine opposing him. Then he was grudgingly taken back into the party. This week the same Labour party dragged him down to defeat. In the American west, they teach a dog not to kill poultry by strapping the rotten carcass of a chicken round its neck. Ken had Gordon Brown trussed round his neck and the voters hated the smell.

Boris said, 'Let's get cracking tomorrow, and let's have a drink tonight!' He had given up booze for the course of the campaign. Ken then thanked 'everyone' – politician-speak for 'me' – for 'setting this city on the path of being the greatest city in the world of the 21st century'.

It had been a long night. Admittedly there had been a record number of votes. But computers had been brought in to delay the process, taking hour upon hour to compute the votes that a few human beings with moistened fingers could have managed in a morning.

It would be nice to think that Boris will now perform all his duties in a silk hat, and insist on having fags to toast his crumpets in the mayoral office. But that would be triumphalism. Instead he will have to cope with bendy buses and signal failures in the Stratford area.

Gordon Brown launched yet another fightback yesterday with a preview of the Queen's speech at Prime Minister's Questions. The solemnity of the occasion was only slightly reduced by the presence of Bruce Forsyth, who sat on a visitor's bench at the back of the Chamber, along with his wife, Wilnelia Merced, a former Miss World. She added a touch of glamour missing since, oh, since the death of Gwyneth Dunwoody.

It was a good day for Brucie, as we learned there is talk of Mr Brown becoming a judge on a reality show for aspiring politicians, called *Junior PM*. This gave David Cameron the peg for a scripted gag: he claimed the show would be a cross between *The Apprentice* meets *Maria* meets *Strictly Come Dancing*. Brucie looked very pleased at that.

'But I've got a better idea,' said the Tory leader. 'Why not a reality show involving the whole country, called *General Election*? Then everyone could stand up in front of the prime minister and say, "You're fired!"'

Mr Brown, who probably knows as much about popular culture as Wayne Rooney does about Armenian palimpsests, merely glared at Mr Cameron, and grunted that he was 'a salesman without a substance', a remark greeted by much Tory mockery.

The trouble with Brucie is that just as some pop songs can lodge in your head for days, his catchphrases rattle round your brain while you're trying to focus on something else. Labour MPs had been asking the usual 'questions' about Gordon's greatness. ('Nice to see you, to see you nice!') Nick Clegg asked about the million or so people who won't be compensated for the temporary removal of the 10p tax rate.

'Why should they pay for the prime minister's incompetence?' It was a good point, well made. ('What do points mean? Points mean prizes!')

Mr Brown could only reply with a flurry of statistics, which he ended by saying that poverty had 'trebled' under the Conservatives – an entirely meaningless statistic unless you define what you mean by poverty. You might as well say there had been three times as much weather under Labour.

At least the Lib Dems looked pleased to see their leader being taken seriously, rather than being regarded as the school swot, booed by the oiks in the rugby team. ('Didn't he do well?')

Then the prime minister outlined his programme for the next year. ('I'm in charge!') It was welcomed by Mr Cameron, on the grounds that nearly all the ideas had been pinched from the Conservatives. 'As well as elected officials, why not an elected prime minister?'

Mr Brown managed a wintry smile. 'The grin is back!' chortled the Tory leader, and indeed it was the first time we had seen the prime minister smile in public for many a month. Maybe he feels he is on his way back. Perhaps next week he'll give us a twirl.

Even before Gordon Brown had been in office for a year, Number 10 began to resemble the House of Usher. Labour had just lost the by-election at Crewe, even though their candidate was the daughter of the popular late member, Gwyneth Dunwoody.

It was the first prime minister's questions since the by-election. It was no better for him than beforehand, but no worse either. Tories kept jabbing at the wounded bear. Bill Wiggin referred to his practice of ringing random members of the public to elicit their views.

'What advice does he have for people who receive nuisance calls?' Mr Wiggin asked, as if Mr Brown had been saying, 'Have you always dreamed of a wonderful new kitchen? Our representatives will be in your area and will be happy to provide you with a free estimate, without obligation...'

This is the equivalent of boys ringing a doorbell and then running away. Mr Brown, the eccentric old geezer who lives in the big spooky house, had no reply except that the Tories could ask any question, but chose to concentrate on trivia. He said it again when he was asked if we might have not one, but two, unelected prime ministers in this parliament.

You'd imagine that someone in Downing Street would have a word with him in the morning. 'Look, Gordon, they're going to ask about the phone calls. We need to provide you with a real zinger to reply...' But clearly no one does. In the House of Usher there is no room for levity. Lace curtains flap, rats scuttle in the wainscot, moss grows through the floor, but in between all we can hear is the rustle of paper as the occupant leafs frantically through another 800-page Treasury document.

Tony Blair made his first return visit to the Commons, to talk about his work in the Middle East.

The last prime minister strolled confidently into the Thatcher room in the Commons – how apt that her portrait should be looking down on him, her most successful pupil! He looked, and I choose this word with care, radiant. His skin glowed with the warmth of the sun we so seldom see at home. His teeth gleamed so brilliantly you could have used each one as a tiny shaving mirror, for a vole. He looked more relaxed than I've ever seen him since his 1997 election victory.

He flashed us a smile that I would call cheesy, except that it was much, much more. It was Brie, Camembert, Stilton – a whole board full of the finest, most luxurious cheeses (*supplement menu, 6 euros*). The teeth even greeted the press, as if he was pleased to see us.

'How you guys doing?' he asked the international development committee. Somebody said it was good to see him back.

'Good! Better not take a vote on that!' The grin returned, looking like a very clean cemetery. He had left Westminster as just another pol. Now he was returning as a global superstar.

The committee's remit was to ask about the occupied territories. Fascinating though that is, one felt they would rather ask him about himself and his life. For example, 'When you're on your own, in a quiet moment, don't you just gloat about the terrible trouble Gordon is in? Or do you shout it out gleefully, to everyone you meet?'

Or: 'All that stuff in Cherie's book about not taking the "contraceptive equipment" up to Balmoral. Did you read it beforehand? Wasn't it hideously embarrassing? Or, worse, did you like it because it made you sound like Mr Mucho Macho Man?'

And finally: 'Haven't you got enough money by now? How many houses does any one family actually need?'

As it was, he had dodged all those questions, or at least versions of them, on the GMTV sofa earlier in the day. So they were stuck with Palestine.

17 June 2008

George W. Bush paid his final visit to the UK.

Two of the least popular politicians in the world appeared together in London, propping each other up like drunks in need of a lamppost. People age in plateaux, looking much the same for much of the time, then suddenly appearing old. Bush looks thinner than before, more lined, more worn. It was as though he was physically disappearing. Brown, by contrast, looks like a poster boy for two hours' sleep a night.

The pair were speaking in the totally over-the-top Locarno room in the Foreign Office. It's like being inside a wedding cake. The prime minister spoke at length. The president favoured him with his 'I know I've seen this guy somewhere before, but I can't remember when' look.

Mr Brown's talk may have been long, but at least it was coherent. Bush sounded as if he were floating down his own stream of consciousness. 'Some are speculating that this is my last trip, well, let 'em speculate, who knows?' he said.

The language remains strange, random. He had no quarrel – pronounced 'kwarl' – with the Iranian people. He wanted free elections for the 'good folk' of Zimbabwe, which made them sound like the congregation at a Texan church supper.

Even after eight years of Bush, we still need to untangle much of what he says. 'Freezer eye-tie', for example, is 'free society'. Later he said that it wasn't 'only, you know, white gang Methodists who are capable of self-government'. Or it might have been 'white guy' or 'white goons' – hard to tell. We pondered for a moment on all those Episcopalians and Catholics who are, apparently, incapable of self-government.

18 June 2008

David Davis, a Tory frontbencher and runner-up to Cameron as party leader, resigned his post and his seat. He stood again, in order to demonstrate his opposition to the anti-terrorism policy of both government and opposition. Labour decided not to stand against him.

Gordon Brown walked through Westminster on his way to make a speech, possibly with the title 'David Davis is bonkers, but I am not. Dear me, no. You would have to go a long way to find anyone as sane as me.'

A BBC reporter was waiting. The moment Mr Brown appeared, he shouted, 'Why isn't Labour standing against David Davis? Are you afraid of the debate on terror?'

The role of Corporation Shouter is a long and honourable one, though probably not dating back to the days of Lord Reith, who discouraged shouting at our rulers, even by reporters in evening dress. The modern Shouter resembles the musician who does the gunfire at the end of the 1812 Symphony. It's a brief moment, but a vital one. A trained Shouter will wait for hours until his quarry appears. It's a task that requires great patience, constant alertness and a strong bladder. Sometimes the shout will last barely one second: 'Will you resign?'

No politician is ever going to come over to the Shouter and say, 'Do you know, we are afraid. You see if a Labour candidate stood against David Davis he would be soundly beaten, and it would look like a referendum on our anti-terror strategy.' Likewise he would never say: 'Resign? Do you think I should? It hadn't really occurred to me, but now that you mention it...' Mr Brown, as tradition demands, ignored the Shouter and marched sternly onwards with his protection officers.

8 July 2008

There was a strange, ongoing row over whether badgers should be culled in order to prevent the spread of bovine tuberculosis.

Hilary Benn, the environment secretary, said there was too little hard scientific evidence to justify a cull of badgers. As always, in the Brown government, no matter how urgent the question, there is always time to set up a quango. This will be the Bovine TB Partnership Group, which sounds like an organisation for lonely cows to meet new friends.

The Commons divided largely along party lines, with Labour MPs wanting to save the badger and Tories eager to slaughter the lot and turn them into shaving brushes. Labour's Nick Palmer, for example, said that the Conservative response to every problem was the same: when in doubt, kill something.

My own theory is that Tory antipathy to badgers goes back to their pre-prep schooldays when their parents (or nannies) read them *The Wind in the Willows*. If you remember, Badger is a kindly figure who welcomes the lost Mole and Ratty in from the cold into his sett, where he serves them a huge meal in front of a roaring log fire. Badger's main role in the story is to stop Toad making a fool of himself by driving too fast and escaping from prison. In short, he is one of literature's great spoilsports. He would have strongly disapproved of the Bullingdon Club.

So the Tories associate Badger with pursed lips and Puritanism. They are, however, misreading him. Kenneth Grahame was writing in 1908, when the whiff of revolution was in the air. He is against Toad not because he is the wealthy owner of Toad Hall, but because he, Badger, knows that with great riches and position come great responsibility. Badger knows that if Toad spends his life in dissipation, he will give the stoats and weasels the perfect excuse to steal his property, so destroying the class system.

Which is why Badger leads the assault to recapture Toad Hall. He was, in short, on the side of the toffs. It would be very different today, and would have to be written by, say, Elmore Leonard.

'Why, come in my dear friends, you must be perished,' said Badger.

'Sorry, we're from the Bovine TB Group, and you're going to get what's coming, you furry freak!' Blam!

23 September 2008

The Labour party conference this year was marked by a demented optimism, tempered by misery. As so often, it was Alistair Darling who was the guru of gloom.

The Chancellor unleashed the power of positive pessimism. Things were terrible, he told us. The only good news was that they are better now than they will be soon. It was all perfectly dreadful. We faced tough challenges, unprecedented problems, extraordinary and turbulent times. Financial institutions were on their knees. Crises ... shocks to the system ... nothing would ever be the same again. People were in agony wondering if they were going to stay in work, and how they could ever find the money to pay their bills. Families were reduced to eating their own children in order to avoid having to buy school uniforms. (Of course I made the last one up, but it does convey the general mood.)

He reminded us how morose he himself had always been. Britain led the world in misery. 'I've made headlines by saying how tough times are. I draw little comfort from the fact that many people now understand what I meant.' It was like being at Eeyore's birthday party, during a rainstorm.

However, he did offer us some reassurance. In fact he did twice. 'I want to explain and reassure,' he said. I fear that politicians saying 'I want to reassure you' is up there with other famously misleading phrases, such as 'The cheque is in the post,' and 'Of course I'll call you in the morning.' People want to hear it, but they don't quite believe it.

The conference didn't quite know how to cope with this. They were used to Gordon Brown telling them that everything was wonderful, that Britain was far better off than all those wretched nations, such as Japan, Germany and the United States, who live in comparative squalor. Being warned that the government's new housing programme might involve empty Toshiba boxes is not what they expected to hear.

As a result they only clapped when he attacked the Tories. Quite why they are to blame for the current crisis he didn't explain. He did finish with some spray-on optimism. 'We should have confidence in ourselves. And confidence in the future.' Even here he said it in a way that implied that the best way out of problems was to commit mass suicide. It's being so cheerful that keeps him going.

29 September 2008

All this time there were rumblings about Gordon Brown's leadership. Many people thought that David Miliband would make a good replacement, but he made a lacklustre speech at the conference, and, fatally, was photographed holding a banana.

Why this should have harmed his chances of winning the leadership I have no idea. Perhaps it was the jaunty angle at which he held it. Would it have mattered so much if he was holding, say, an apple?

Gordon Brown pulled off something of a masterstroke when he got his wife Sarah to introduce him to the conference. Poised, relaxed and good-looking, she was everything he isn't. No wonder they gave her a standing ovation just for turning up.

As is the tradition with political wives, she gave us a description of the old man at home, though he didn't sound too much like the rest of us. Apparently he is 'motivated to work for the best interests of people all round the country', she said, as opposed to those of us who are motivated to drink beer in front of the television.

There was no mention of flung telephones, or prime ministers who accidentally staple their own hands to documents.

Then they showed a video of Labour achievements over the past 11 years. Curiously Tony Blair figured only once, for about a second. It was the modern equivalent of the airbrushed Soviet leaders lined up at the Kremlin. (Blair did get one mention in the speech; but apart from that he has become an unperson.)

They played Jackie Wilson singing '[Your Love Keeps Lifting Me] Higher and Higher', a piece of music as dislocated from the image of Gordon Brown as it is possible to conceive.

One always feels that the prime minister should be greeted by a lone piper playing a tragic dirge, possibly lamenting the death of a pet otter.

The great man appeared. He produced an all-new, different version of the alarming grin – the smile of a man who has taken your sandwich but wants you to know that all is not as it seems.

He kicked off by saying that he wanted to talk about who he was and what he believed in. It turns out he believes in fairness. You know that when politicians rip off the facade and promise to reveal their true identities, they are never, ever going to say, 'I am greedy for power for its own sake. I am paranoid and vengeful, and obsessed by unimportant details.'

He did confess mistakes, but again it turned out that the errors made him even more loveable. 'What happened with the 10p [tax rate] stung me, because it really hurt that suddenly people felt that I wasn't on the side of people on middle and modest incomes.' In other words, he knew how wonderful he was, and it startled him that others didn't agree. He did admit to being unpopular, but in a sideways sort of way: 'Understand that all the attacks, all the polls, all the headlines, all the criticism – it's all worth it if in doing this job I make life better for one child, one family, one community.' It seems a modest enough ambition, given that there are 60 million people in this country.

Then he got in a twofer. The Tories, he said, couldn't be trusted to run the economy. They were too inexperienced. 'I'm all in favour of apprenticeships, but let me tell you, this is no time for a novice, David Miliband.'

Naturally he didn't utter the last two words, but that's what he meant.

The Tories were clearly worried about the theme of experience. They were afraid that the electorate might follow Hilaire Belloc's line: 'Always keep a hold of nurse, for fear of finding something worse.' David Cameron responded in his own conference speech.

'I get the modern world!' declared David Cameron, and that was the message of his speech. It's not a claim that, say, Sir Alec Douglas-Home would ever have made, but then I don't recall him groping Lady Home after a conference speech either. Samantha Cameron was not so lucky. She was pulled on the stage looking nervous. Perhaps this was why she got several smackers on the lips, a definite snoggerama, plus innumerable strokes of the tummy, which presently, so far as we know, does not contain another little Cameron.

There was definitely something erotic in the air. The cry, 'Get a room!' hovered unspoken over the stage. 'I understand entrepreneurs,' he said, 'I go to bed with one every night.' Presumably he meant Mrs Cameron, rather than, for example, Sir Alan Sugar. Samantha sells, among other things, upmarket notebooks. I was reminded of the old Donald McGill postcard that shows a man in the shop asking a pert young woman if she keeps stationery. 'Well, sometimes I wiggle about a bit,' she replies.

For the big speech, the conference had moved to the Birmingham Symphony Hall. Some people had been standing in line for three hours to make sure they got their place. They were seething with excitement. I thought some of them might pop. But at first he didn't give them many applause lines.

When he wanted a clap, he paused and scrunched his eyes up. The scrunch, visible on the big screen, was their cue.

Then they warmed up. They loved his line about experience. Experience was the excuse always used by failed incumbents through the ages. Jim Callaghan had had plenty of experience. 'But thank God we changed him for Margaret Thatcher! … If we listened to this argument about experience, we would have Gordon Brown as prime minister forever!'

There were tricky bits, such as the suggestion that prison doesn't always work. 'Come with me to Wandsworth prison and meet the inmates!' he said, and we had a vision of the entire Tory conference turning up at the famous gates and demanding admission.

Nor were they particularly happy about his 'aspiration for the poor and the disadvantaged'. Whoever joined the Tory party to fret about them?

Then another phrase that never dropped from the lips of Margaret Thatcher: 'We won't bottle it when things get tough!' But, being well brought up, he pronounced both t's.

Then it was all over and he scuttled off with Samantha, possibly to the room they had already arranged.

One of Guardian readers' favourite MPs is Michael Fabricant, about whom I have been writing since the John Major era. A former disc jockey, Mickey is best known for his amazing hairpiece that resembles the tail of a My Little Pony toy, being glossy and shiny. He once offered to jump out of a plane with a parachute but without a helmet so as to prove to his local paper that the confection wasn't a wig. The paper refused on the grounds that they couldn't afford the insurance. For a while he hated my writing about him, but after the Labour landslide of 1997 I was able to point out that his majority – 238 – was almost exactly the number of Guardian readers in Lichfield, and so could claim that I had saved him his seat. From that moment on we have been good friends, or at least warm acquaintances.

MPs called on the power of God to solve our financial crisis yesterday. But first they had to welcome back Michael Fabricant from his Latin American hell. Chris Bryant, a new minister who is now Harriet Harman's deputy leader of the house, said how delighted we all were that the Colombian police had finally released him so that he could be with us yesterday.

I was abroad myself when the terrible events unfolded, but it appears that he had been paying a visit to the anarchic nation. Not trusting the local milk, he took with him a jar of Coffee-mate, a white powder that turns black coffee into a brown sludge. Frankly, I'd rather drink milk from a diseased nanny goat, but it takes all sorts.

At some point a policeman spotted the jar and decided that it must be full of cocaine. Officers surrounded him and his friend, pointing their guns aggressively. 'Cocaine, cocaine!' they shouted. 'No, coffee, coffee!' he shouted back.

There was only one way out. He had to eat a large quantity of the powder to prove that it was harmless. The effect was to make him very ill, but not dead, which he would have been if it had been cocaine.

I found the whole story evocative, worthy perhaps of Graham Greene. The broiling South American sun gleaming on the gun barrels of the police and glinting off the hair-style substance on top of Mickey's head! The officers with their swarthy, moustachioed faces! The wretched member for Lichfield, once a successful disc jockey, trying to force down another spoonful as it sprays around his face! Surely a canvas worthy of Goya.

New Labour was always exceedingly partial to jargon, and sprayed it on all its policies, like artificial cream squirted from a can. The education secretary Ed Balls had to deliver it. Peter Mandelson, meanwhile, had been reconciled with his old enemy Gordon Brown, and had been made a peer.

Ed Balls yesterday made a statement that was, to the layman, almost entirely impenetrable, and stuffed it as full of jargon as Paxo in a Christmas turkey. Yet it was, astonishingly, praised by MPs as 'for its clarity of principle and intellectual rigour'. Heaven knows what they would have said if it had been marked by intellectual sloth and obscurantism. Lines such as 'Making Good Progress pilots' (Mr Balls likes to talk in capital letters) whizzed past our ears. 'We are currently piloting "stage not age" single level tests,' he told us. We heard about 'random sampling of particular cohorts'.

At one point, Mr Balls said that to get the reforms right, he would be working 'closely with our social partners, to take them forward without unnecessarily adding to teacher workload'.

I wondered who these social partners might be. Drinking companions? Freemasons? The Castleford Ladies' Magic Circle? I felt for innumerable teachers who for years have assumed that adding unnecessarily to their workload was an important part of government policy.

Mr Balls must be a sad man these days. Once he was Gordon Brown's dearest social partner. Now it appears that he has been supplanted by Peter Mandelson, and we know that there is no greater friendship than an enmity that has been reversed. Poor Mr Balls is now fretting about school tests, while the once-reviled Mandelson parades in scarlet and ermine.

Mr Balls announced that there would be 'school report cards' so that parents would know how their children's schools were performing. Perhaps some schools will try to hide their reports from the parents – 'the dog ate it,' perhaps.

Mr Gove tried to wrong-foot Mr Balls by speaking only in English. He was all in favour of abolishing tests for teenagers. He quoted one of the questions in a science paper: 'What part of a rider's body does a rider's hat protect?'

Peter Mandelson made his maiden speech in the House of Lords..
Nominally he was moving the order that will allow Lords to take
over HBOS. In reality, he was bailing out his own reputation.

It was a tricky moment. Normally peers are somewhat resent-
ful of people injected into their House for political reasons,
even though that's how most of them arrived in the first place,
and if not them, their ancestors. So Mandelson found himself
in the position of a used car dealer who has unaccountably
been elected to White's Club and has to explain that he won't
use his mobile phone on the premises and won't comb his hair
in public.

He succeeded triumphantly. The Lords, always insecure in
their constitutional role, love to be told what splendid folk
they are, and he laid it on, not with a trowel but a steamroller.
He lathered them with a thick creamy lather made from the
richest, thickest whale sputum. It was a great honour to speak
there. What a wonderfully warm welcome he had received,
and – here was the cunning part – 'also from the staff who
work here and who add so much to the character of the house.
It means a lot to me!' They adore people being nice about the
staff – so much more rewarding than a tip!

The warm sticky foam was sprayed around. 'One of the
great privileges of being a member of your lordships' House
is the richness of the political experience gained from the
decades, and available for our debates today.'

By this time, I thought that some older peers must be
gasping for air through all the gunk. But he wasn't finished.
He stuffed their mouths with molten marshmallows. 'There is

not only a breadth but a depth in this House, which might be more generally acknowledged…' The message was, 'Nobody appreciates you. But I do.'

The Tory Lord Hunt was equally glutinous. 'A very accomplished maiden speech!' he gushed. 'He led us on a fascinating and absorbing journey … his impressive career to date … his tributes to colleagues and, in particular the staff, were much appreciated and reciprocated by us all. He has indeed joined the aristocracy!'

Just when I thought I might gag – how awful to die, choking on someone else's vomit! – Lord Hunt quoted the Bible and specifically the bit about lilies of the field: 'They toil not, neither do they spin.'

'While he toils, I am sure he will reflect deeply on the second part of that quotation,' he said, with a refreshing gust of sarcasm, and I found my own breath returning.

One of the joys of covering the Commons is the occasional reminder of just how batty some MPs can be.

Sir Nicholas Winterton called for 'harsher' penalties against young hoodlums. Nothing unusual there, you might think. Sir Nicholas's mindset is, in Alexander McCall Smith's phrase, 'traditionally built'. He harks back to a time when Tory back-benchers used to call for the return of the birch and capital punishment, or possibly both. Miscreants could be thrashed to within an inch of their lives, and then hanged. Or, in less serious cases, the other way around.

But this is 2008, and Sir Nicholas seems to have softened over the years. What was his recipe for dealing with tearaways and scofflaws? 'They should be set to removing graffiti, removing chewing gum, and picking up litter!' he said.

You could almost hear the knights of the shires rolling in their mausoleums. What did their wraiths imagine that Sir Nicholas had in mind? 'Get those vandals out of bed before noon, and set 'em to scrubbing those walls!' Or, 'They don't like the taste of cold Brillo pads.'

Or, 'I don't think they'll be terrorising old ladies once they've tried lifting chewing gum with a garden scraper! A couple of hours of that and we might see a change of attitude! No, they won't be so keen to rip up train seats once they've picked up a few Coke cans and old burger boxes – and had to throw them in a black plastic bag! It's the only language these young thugs understand.'

So that was weird enough. Then things got stranger. Norman Baker, a Lib Dem, took up the cause of protesters at the Kingsnorth climate change camp in August. They had been the subject of over-zealous police action, he said. He had been told of officers confiscating items such as 'toilet rolls, board games and clown costumes'. He wanted an inquiry.

David Drew, a Labour MP, said that one of his constituents had been arrested at the camp for 'aggressively picking up litter'. I was reminded of the old *Not the Nine O'Clock News* sketch about Constable Savage, carpeted by his superior for arresting a man for 'loitering with intent to use a pedestrian crossing', 'smelling of foreign food', and 'wearing a loud shirt in the hours of darkness'.

One wonders how the police were debriefed after the ructions at Kingsnorth. 'Constable Savage, I see you have seized several dozen rolls of toilet paper. Might I inquire why?'

'Yuss, sir, I apprehended the toilet paper before it could be thrown, creating a potential hazard for my colleagues.'

'Did it not occur to you, Savage, that they might have needed the toilet paper to wipe their bottoms?'

'No sir, I assumed that with them being tree-hugging types, they would have utilised grass and leaves for that purpose, sir!'

'And why did you impound the board games?'

'Because they were in possession of metal irons, boots, a cannon and a warship, sir.'

'You blithering idiot, Savage. They were playing Monopoly. The only way anyone could have been injured was if they had stuck the pieces up their own noses! And what, in the name of all that's holy, is the penalty for "offensively picking up litter"?'

'Obviously, sir, picking up litter, like Sir Nicholas says.'

7 November 2008

With the accession of Gordon Brown to the premiership, John Prescott ceased to be deputy prime minister. We missed him, but help was at hand.

Secondary Prescott, the affliction that makes members of parliament sound like our recent deputy prime minister, continues to be a problem. Otherwise normal people begin to gabble, swallow their words, repeat themselves, confuse definite and indefinite articles, ramble unchecked, and altogether sound like an ill-tempered bull in a Meissen factory outlet.

Yesterday we discovered a new sufferer. He is Huw Irranca-Davies (presumably the preacher had a coughing fit at his baptism, but since his parents may have belonged to a fundamentalist sect, they could have believed it would be in defiance of God if they changed the name back to the one they had planned). Mr Irranca-Davies is a new under-secretary at the environment department, and yesterday was his first trip to the dispatch box.

He was replying to a question from my old chum Michael Fabricant, who had asked about the extension of broadband services to rural areas. Here was Mr Irranca-Davies's reply, as transcribed from my digital recorder. I have inserted very little punctuation because he himself included almost none.

'Well, the honourable gentleman makes among other things a very good point and he and I served together in debates on the communications bill quite some time ago when these issues were raised with the original roll-out of broadband among other things and what I can assure him that issues of "not-spots" which are at issue in Wales and England are being tackled not least by CLA and Defra, research which we are taking forward also coming up what I always call the "ciao" review but the Ciao review looking at this issue of how we extend it market-driven but also how we fill in those market failures so what government can do as well but also what regional development authorities can do but also what local authorities can do!'

The whole thing seems to boil down to, 'We're seeing what we can do about the problem.'

I had expected him to get a round of applause for this performance, especially as there was no sign that he had drawn breath once, though MPs on all sides seemed to regard it as perfectly normal. I would like to pay tribute to the lads and lasses at Hansard, who within three hours of Mr Irranca-Davies speaking had translated it into English and posted it on their website. It is much shorter than what he actually said, but makes an awful lot more sense.

Gordon Brown gave a press conference yesterday to explain his plan for rescuing the economy. This involves spending much more money while at the same time cutting taxes.

An intelligent layman asks: 'What does this mean?'

Brilliant economist: 'We call this the Looney Tunes strategy. It's like this. A cartoon animal, such as the Road Runner, dashes off a cliff top into mid-air, looks down at the canyon below, goes "Yikes!" then runs back on to the cliff top.'

Layman: 'Does it work?'

Economist: 'It does in the cartoons.'

The prime minister was speaking at a press conference, just after David Cameron had given his own press conference. The Tories had offered us bacon sandwiches. Mr Brown did not. Offering breakfast snacks is not what serious politicians do. Serious politicians offer nothing extraneous – no ifs, no butties.

Mr Cameron had also offered tax cuts, only bigger, shinier ones than the government was offering. It was getting a little like those competitive ads you see on American television: 'Hi, I'm Cray-zee Dave, and you are not gonna believe the deals I'm offering on tax cuts! I gotta be outa my mind! If you can find a better tax-cutting deal in the metro area, I'm not only gonna slash taxes to match 'em, but I'll set fire to myself!'

Two minutes later, same channel: 'Are these tax cuts completely insane? They gotta be, because I'm "Gaga" Gordo, and these cuts are completely dee-mented! If you find a better deal you can come over, cut off my head, and eat it!'

The nub of the matter seemed to be that both sides took entirely contrary views of the state of our nation's financial health. The prime minister maintained that we have a very low level of public debt, better than – and here he gave us a long list – France, Germany, Italy, Spain, Ireland, the US, the Planet Tharg, etc.

By contrast, according to Mr Cameron, we were worse off than every country in the world except for Pakistan and Hungary. Nevertheless the Tories are offering their own tax cuts.

Knowing the way that the government at first claims to despise everything the Conservatives stand for before taking up their ideas with exaggerated enthusiasm, we can expect at the next presser a groaning sideboard, including bacon, eggs, sausage, fried potatoes, black pudding, kedgeree, breakfast chops and bio-active yoghurt.

Now Mr Brown is off to America to use his amazing powers – you may recall that last month he saved the world banking system from complete collapse with the ease of Superman stopping a runaway train. He is going to 'stimulate' the economy. He spoke so much about stimulation that he began to sound like one of those kindly sex advisors who help chaps when things go wrong in bed.

'Dear Gordon, I love my economy very much, but I find it hard to stimulate it. I am at my wits' end.'

'Dear Frustrated, kindness and gentleness are the key. And tax cuts.'

The gist of his message appears to be that all the countries that have saved money for a rainy day should not splurge it in order to help countries that have been on credit binges. Like us.

Now and again, people from the real world come to parliament to speak to MPs. Or in the case of Peter Stringfellow, the not-so-real world.

Mr Stringfellow, the entrepreneur, appeared at the Commons culture committee yesterday. He was helping MPs with their inquiries into lap-dancing clubs. He had flown over specially from Majorca, and was wearing, so he told us, his only suit. He was also wearing what appeared to be a badly raddled sheep on his head. Or possibly it was his normal hair, only backwards.

He followed two women from Object, an organisation that tries to make it easier for local authorities to close lap-dancing clubs on the grounds that they objectify women. One was a former lap dancer, Ms Nadine Stravonia de Montagnac, of whom Mr Stringfellow said, 'She was a dancer, and with all due respect, it must have been a long time ago.'

This less than gallant remark brought a shout from Ms Stravonia de Montagnac, who had to be called to order by the chair. The chairman, that is, not the piece of furniture on which she used to perform.

Mr Stringfellow appeared with members of the Lap Dancing Association. He made sure we did not confuse them with him. 'I do not like the term lap dancing,' he said. 'My term is "adult entertainment", or in my case, "Gentleman's Entertainment".' He somehow managed to pronounce the capital letters.

He also appeared to have succumbed to a case of secondary Prescott, the affliction that affects so many people in the Palace of Westminster. This caused him to speak at great speed and at great length on a series of apparently random topics. Here is a selection from some of his answers: 'All they have to do now is to say "no nudity" and they have to explain why no nudity, and they bring up police and everyone else, and we have to go up and explain all objections regarding alcohol, dancing, I'm not going into history lessons, we've gone into these very correctly because I don't want to be quoted by the press and be made a fool of later on, we say I want to open one, they say you can't, and off we go...'

But this was the plainest common sense compared to the contribution made by Mr Simon Warr, chairman of the Lap Dancing Association. Mr Warr wanted to insist that his members' establishments were not a turn-on. 'People go for the alcohol and the entertainment – so, the entertainment is nude. But it is not sexually stimulating.'

MPs were incredulous. 'If you asked a customer,' said Philip Davies, 'whether it was sexually stimulating, would the answer be a big fat "no"?'

'That is not part of our business plan,' said Mr Warr.

'So you must have a lot of dissatisfied customers,' said Mr Davies.

You would imagine that was like a football club chairman insisting that all his customers went for the Bovril rather than the match. But help for Mr Warr came from Mr Stringfellow. Lots of things were sexually stimulating, he said, 'such as discos, or David Beckham in his Calvin Kleins'. We were rapidly reaching information overload. 'It's the personalities,' he said, adding, 'the ambience of the club and the male environment.'

So men go to strip clubs chiefly to be with other men. MPs and public digested this thought in silence.

The Speaker, Michael Martin, did not have much longer in office. The decline of his reputation was accelerated by his actions in the case of Damien Green, a Tory frontbencher, who was arrested by the Metropolitan Police on suspicion of having received leaked intelligence from the Home Office. MPs were appalled at this and especially appalled at the fact that the Speaker seemed to have co-operated with the rozzers. The affair moved towards its climax on the day of the Queen's speech at the opening of parliament.

After the flummery, the flannelling. The Queen, as she read out each leaden line through what sounded like a very tickly cold, gave the impression, even more than in previous years, that she had lost the will to live. The Speaker managed to stay alive another day – just.

The gist of his explanation to the house was that his dog had eaten the arrest warrant. To clear the whole thing up, he would set up an inquiry by seven senior MPs, all selected by him. In other words, the Speaker's behaviour will be investigated by a top team – chosen by the Speaker! That is the way we do things here.

Mr Martin read out his statement, printed out on plastic-backed paper like those books children read in the bath. 'The precincts of the house should not be above the law,' he said, to at least one Tory cry of 'Shame!'

The police had explained the situation to the serjeant at arms, Jill Pay, possibly due to become Jill 'suspended on full' Pay if the inquiry goes badly for her.

But the police had not explained that, since they lacked a search warrant, she had a perfect right to stop them coming in. 'That's an outrage!' bellowed another Tory, giving a half-decent imitation of someone being outraged.

'I regret that consent was signed for by the serjeant at arms without her consulting the clerk of the house,' Mr Martin went on, neatly dropping an employee into the mire, or in his famous catchphrase, 'Ordure, ordure!'

Over in the upper house, Her Majesty had to wait for the Commons to attend upon her. Gordon Brown was at the front of the procession, and we could see him haranguing David Cameron all the way. Damien Green was close behind, which was slightly surprising, like seeing Captain Dreyfus feted on Bastille Day.

'The strength of the financial sector is vital for the future vibrancy of the economy,' the poor Queen had to intone. 'Proposals to create gateway savings accounts...' she continued. At this point, a peer emitted a loud 'Urghhhh!' – probably a cough being suppressed, or perhaps someone actually dying of boredom.

My theory was that neither Gordon Brown nor Tony Blair were invited to the Royal Wedding in April 2011 as revenge for the terrible drivel both men had forced Her Maj to read out.

11 December 2008

Shortly before Christmas, Gordon Brown came out with a quote to stay with him until the end of his days.

It was a slip, but was it a Freudian slip? There is no way Gordon Brown would have announced during prime minister's questions yesterday that he had saved the world, if he'd been in full command of his brain.

But did it express some profound, half-secret feeling buried deep in his id, or ego, or wherever these things lurk? Did he really mean it, or did he just sort of mean it?

Other countries have congratulated him on the way he prevented British banks going bust. Some have followed his example. Possibly there is a small cluster of synapses that believes he really did save the world from sudden and total disaster. Perhaps the thought just popped out like champagne from a badly corked bottle. Or he could, like so many politicians, be in thrall to his own publicity. Here's what happened.

David Cameron was launching into his assault for the day. Putting money into the banks was all very well, but it hadn't worked. When was Gordon going to change his strategy?

He replied: 'The first point of recapitalisation was to save banks that would otherwise have collapsed.' So far, so predictable. He went on: 'We not only saved the world...'

There was a pause, in which MPs looked at each other and wondered whether they had heard what they had heard. In that moment, the prime minister had a chance to correct himself – 'saved the banks and led the way,' he said – but it was too late. He was buried under a sudden, overwhelming, mountainous avalanche of laughter – laughter, hooting, derision, chortling, spluttering, screeching and general mayhem filled the Chamber like oil in a lava lamp, bubbling and swirling.

The Tories, of course, were the most affected. Genuine hilarity mixed with the joy of seeing the hated Brown discomfited. They slapped thighs, anybody's thighs, waved their order papers, rolled around, and allowed their faces to turn a deep red colour like a Christmas glass of port.

I was more fascinated by the Labour benches. Some MPs laughed openly, mainly those who thought the whips couldn't see or who didn't care what they thought. Some could be seen twitching horribly, trying to hold back their merriment. Others, such as the chief whip, Nick Brown, glowered ahead, as if the Tory laughter was as grossly inappropriate as it would be at a funeral.

The laughter had gone on for 21 seconds (an age in parliament) when the Speaker first said 'Order!' When it showed no sign of dying down, he again said, 'Order!'

The prime minister tried to plough his way through. But he is hopeless at snappy comebacks; so, having repeated what he really meant to say, he decided to claim that the Conservative hilarity was in some way an affront. 'The opposition may not like the fact that we led the world in saving the banking system, but we did!'

But nothing would help. The laughter just kept bubbling up. When you thought it had finally died down, it erupted again.

Thus MPs were in the mood for more fun when Nick Clegg – often a figure of jest, I fear – rose to ask a sensible question about people who couldn't give back overpaid tax credits.

But all MPs remember his claim in an interview that, in his time, he had made love to 30 women. 'Recently,' he began, 'a single mother with two young children came to see me…' and he too was buried under a cloudburst of laughter, while one Labour MP shouted '31!'

The government continued its bold attempts to solve the financial crisis. At Prime Minister's Questions, Gordon Brown tried repetition as his key weapon. He answered what we took to be a planted question about small businesses.

He said that his plan offered 'real help for business now. It is targeted and focused and ... it is real help for small businesses. It is real help for businesses looking for working capital over the next year. It is real help for technology firms, real help, and real help with credit insurance. This is real help, real help funded by the government!' He used the phrase eight times. It was a Hogmanay eightsome reel.

There followed one of those entirely mad scenarios that we sometimes get. David Cameron wanted to assail the government over the recent cut in VAT, which has achieved almost nothing except make a lot of retailers rather angry. Gordon Brown pointed out that the cut saved the average family £5 a week. 'That £5 a week might not matter a lot to members of the opposition front bench,' he said, in a desperate attempt to make a failed policy look like a mighty blow for equality against wealthy snobs.

But they didn't want to talk about the same thing at all. It was like watching a heated argument between two men who have no interest at all in the topic raised by the other.

Cameron: I don't know how you can suggest that Liverpool could win the Premiership! Steven Gerrard might not even be playing for them soon.

Brown: You are wrong. It is nonsense to suggest that bacon and eggs make for a healthy breakfast. Porridge, by contrast, is full of fibre, and provides all the energy needed for an active morning's work.

Cameron: The whole House will know that is absolute rubbish. Why, only this week Ronaldo was named Footballer of the Year.

Brown: I don't know why the Opposition cannot simply listen to what I am saying. Yoghurt and fruit work splendidly in reducing cholesterol levels…

21 January 2009

Many committee meetings are held in Portcullis House, the vast new building opposite the Palace of Westminster that houses MPs' offices. I think it is quite hideous, resembling a gigantic municipal cremato-rium. And the cost – more than £300 million – would be enough to buy every MP who uses it a large house in the country, with a few acres and a horse paddock. But the building has to be used and so we dutifully troop in there most weeks for one reason or another.

Across the Atlantic they were swearing in the new US presi-dent. Here it was the usual shambles. The home secretary was due to speak to the home affairs committee about the arrest of the Tory MP, Damien Green.

At the instant Jacqui Smith was supposed to walk in, a crisp, she-who-must-be-obeyed voice informed us over the PA system, 'A *fyah* has been confirmed in your area. *Livv* the building immediately and *geoh* to your *essembly* area. Do not use the lifts!'

The voice repeated this several times. Some of us decided that it might, just possibly, be a genuine alarm, so we sham-bled out of the room in a British sort of way, asking 'Where is our *essembly* area?' It must have been like that moment on the *Titanic* when they finally decided that perhaps it had been an iceberg after all. The home secretary peered in, looked startled, and cleared off to whichever essembly area home secretaries go to.

Outside the building a large crowd had gathered, creating that strange democracy of the fire alarm, in which the great and famous mix with the totally unknown. There were MPs such as Michael Howard and Geoffrey Robinson, people you've seen on TV such as Jonathan Dimbleby (why no ceremonial Dimbleby in Washington?) plus witnesses, journalists, researchers, visitors, lobbyists, cooks, waiters, cleaners and schoolchildren getting a scary lesson in how politics really works.

I fell in with a Labour backbencher. 'The cut-glass voice that told us to get out,' he said, 'belongs to Judy Scott-Thompson. We were all terrified of her when she was the accommodation clerk. But she is still with us, whenever there is a fire. Or a *fyah*.'

Or rather, when there isn't a fire, which there usually isn't. It was a false alarm. Apparently this is usually caused by a piece of bread getting stuck in the toaster.

As my MP chum pointed out, 'This building is supposed to be terrorist-proof, but it can't even cope with a piece of burnt bread. Of course, when there is a real fire, we'll all ignore the alarm and be incinerated.'

And if that isn't a perfect metaphor for the present economic crisis, I don't know what is.

3 February 2009

The Chinese premier visited Britain on a snowy day.

Back in China, it was the annual spring festival. Here in Britain, the capital had seized up. There were no buses. The Palace of Westminster was covered in snow, and as Wordsworth pointed out, the earth has not anything to show more fair. Cars, lorries, taxis and tourist coaches were bowling across the bridge as if it were a fine summer day.

But London buses are delicate, like elderly ladies in danger of toppling over if they venture on to white stuff, and they were all obliged to stay tucked up and warm in their garages. What the premier, Wen Jiabao, made of it we cannot know. If his expression is not necessarily inscrutable, it certainly isn't as scrutable as, say, Graham Norton's. Lord Mandelson, however, is as scrutable as they come. He arrived looking furious for some reason we could not discern.

The two premiers finally turned up. They had assembled a mass of clichés between them. Co-operation was important, we learned. There would be no retreat into protectionism. Monumental decisions would be made. We could expect to face global challenges. The challenges were, Gordon Brown repeated, global. ('Challenges' is New Labour-speak for 'difficult problems we can do nothing about'.)

I turned to the Mandarin translation of his words on my headphones. Lines such as '*Lei minh sharo kao yao tung*' meant nothing to me of course, but I was struck by the speed and confidence of the interpreter. Clearly Mr Brown was saying nothing unusual or unexpected.

126

Wen had his chance. He called us 'my dear friends in the press' – a line you would have had to drag out of Gordon Brown with a boat hook. He said that the discussions had been 'a new starting point' and we no longer had to cope with 'the baggage of history'. I took this to be a reference to the Opium Wars, which to the Chinese are as recent and immediate as the weekend's football results are to us.

He turned out to have as majestic a grasp of resonant platitudes as any of our own politicians. 'Global challenges ... working together for stable and harmonious development,' he intoned. But things would soon get better. 'The world will feel the warmth of summer in this harsh winter,' he told us, proving that some Chinese politicians really do rely on fortune cookies for their inspiration.

We were allowed a total of four questions, which he answered at enormous length. This is clearly not a man used to being interrupted, even by his dear friends in the press. The travelling Chinese dear friends turned out not to have been trained in the Jeremy Paxman school of interrogation. One asked Wen for 'your comments on your visit'. That set him off on another spiel about friendship, confidence and co-operation.

'Time's up,' said a young foreign office official, too wet behind the ears to be a mandarin.

'I am flying home today,' said Wen, and I thought, 'Not from Heathrow, you aren't, my old china...'

Can Gordon Brown ever admit that he has got something wrong? It seems unlikely. He hasn't yet confessed making a mistake when he said that he had abolished boom and bust in the British economy. As for his line at the last party conference, 'British jobs for British workers' – you can't say that he stands by it, but he certainly won't renounce it. It's as if the line were an ex-girlfriend who had turned up at the same party. He can't really ignore her, but he doesn't want to associate with her. He just wishes she would leave.

This is perhaps how he would respond to other challenges to his accuracy. 'Will the prime minister admit that when he said that the Battle of Waterloo took place in 1945, he was completely and utterly wrong?'

'I will tell the right honourable gentleman what is wrong. It is completely and utterly wrong to disparage the tremendous achievements of the brave British soldiers who fought against Napoleon and in many cases laid down their lives in the cause of our freedom!'

Or this: 'Will the prime minister tell the house that he was in error when he said last week that there was no prospect of snow in the immediate future?'

'May I say that it is a bit rich for the right honourable member to talk about snow? When will he admit to the role white powder played in his youth? I for one will take no lessons…'

Public resentment against the bankers who got us into this mess remained high. The Commons Treasury committee hauled several of them in for questioning.

The disgraced former bankers appeared at the Commons yesterday. They were sorry. God, they were sorry. They didn't care who knew how sorry they were.

On the other hand, they weren't to blame. Not personally to blame, you understand. Nobody – nobody at all – had seen it coming. Everybody had got it wrong. So they apologised, but wanted to make it clear that it Wasn't Their Fault.

And they had lost money themselves. Oodles of money! Andy Hornby, the former chief executive of HBOS, had taken his bonuses in the bank's shares, so he'd been cleaned out. Sir Fred Goodwin, who was CEO of RBS, said he had personally lost £5 million. Somehow, MPs avoided breaking down in wet, salty tears at this news. In fact, they got even angrier.

'You're in bloody denial,' cried George Mudie after hearing yet another explanation of how nobody had seen it coming, and suffering bursts of jargon such as 'increasing the longevity of wholesale funding', presumably lobbed out in the hope that nobody would know what it meant.

Viscount Thurso said that 99 per cent of his constituents felt that if a great big black hole opened and every banker fell into it, the world would be a better place. The four bankers in front of him grimaced, as if they felt it had already happened. Or wished that it would.

They had marched into the room so confidently – or at least as confidently as they could through the crowd that had gathered hoping for the modern equivalent of a public hanging. They sat down looking quite, but not very, nervous.

Sir Fred, sometimes described as 'the worst banker in the world', seemed almost relaxed and certainly measured, adopting the tone of a manager explaining to a customer why he is being charged 17.5 per cent on his overdraft, even though the bank rate is 1 per cent. The chairman, John McFall, asked them all if 'sorry' wasn't the hardest word.

It turned out to be the easiest word. They had indeed been sorry. Profoundly, unreservedly sorry, 'about the turn of events', one of them added, making it clear they meant 'sorry' in the sense of regret about something they could do nothing about ('sorry it rained at your picnic') rather than 'sorry' in the sense of 'I apologise.'

They didn't seem to feel any sorrow for the taxpayer. Sir Tom McKillop, past chairman of RBS, decided to come a bit cleaner. Why had they bought the Dutch bank ABN Ambro for €72 billion? Wasn't that much more than it was worth?

'Everything we paid for it was more than it was worth,' he said grimly. But look on the bright side – 94.5 per cent of their shareholders had supported the purchase.

Once again, their judgment was in error. But only because everyone else's was too. They blamed Alan Greenspan of the US Federal Reserve, who appeared to think that the good times would be rolling on forever. They were like people who believe that, since the average daytime temperature has dropped 20 degrees since July, we'll all need igloos next May.

Labour's John Mann asked whether they knew how much the JSA was currently. The jobseeker's allowance is actually £60.50 per week, but they didn't even know what JSA stood for.

After the session we learned that RBS was firing some 2,300 people, all of them paid far, far less than Sir Tom and his friends.

It was round about this time I bumped into Mervyn King, governor of the Bank of England, who had been an undergraduate at my college, though a year behind me. 'You know you're getting old,' I said, 'when the governor of the Bank of England looks young.'

He groaned softly, and replied, 'I looked an awful lot younger six months ago.'

Meanwhile, in the Commons, MPs found that getting an apology out of Gordon Brown was like extracting a grizzly's tonsils – a lot of bother, and probably not worth the effort.

'Sorry' is the word of the week, and yesterday David Cameron tried to get Gordon Brown to say it. Fat chance. Politicians find it easy to apologise for things they had nothing to do with, such as the slave trade and the Irish potato famine, but not for something they themselves got wrong. Gordon Brown simply can't do it. If he let the swing door slam in your face, he'd say, 'I am well aware of the very real issues involving swing doors. I will say, however, that keeping doors open on a permanent basis is not an option at this time.'

Actually I don't suppose he would have apologised if he had been running things at the time of the potato famine. 'I have commissioned an independent inquiry into the challenges presented by the shortage of edible tubers in Ireland, and this will report in due course. In the meantime, I have appointed a special advisor, Dean Jonathan Swift, who has produced a paper recommending that, in the meantime, Irish people should consider eating their own children. The whole House will have an opportunity to debate this modest proposal...'

No, the day Gordon Brown does a proper apology is the day that Boris Johnson combs his hair, Amy Winehouse runs the London marathon, and Harriet Harman does the can-can down the aisle. Tories know this, and so every time he spoke they bellowed 'Sorry, sorry, sorry!' so the place sounded like the inside of a very crowded tube train during the rush hour.

It should have been a terrible day for the prime minister. Unemployment had gone over two million, and the governor of the Bank, normally a Pollyanna figure compared to some economists, had warned gloomily of a 'deep recession'. Ed Balls, Brown's closest advisor, had said that we faced the worst recession in more than one hundred years. A hundred years! What a triumph for the government! How long before all those converted wine bars and chic executive apartments are re-opened again as workhouses?

Cameron and Brown spent what seemed eternity slagging each other off on these and other related topics. Cameron: 'Incompetence plus arrogance equals two million unemployed!' Brown: 'Wrong, wrong, wrong!' Labour MPs: 'More, more, more!'

The apology? Perhaps I just missed it.

When the prime minister is away, his deputy takes over at prime minister's questions. The papers had been full of stories to the effect that Harriet Harman, the deputy leader of the Labour party, had hopes of becoming leader.

Miserable, gloomy, sad, depressed, sorrowful, pain-racked, down-in the-mouth: these are just some of the words and phrases under the heading 'unhappy' in *Roget's Thesaurus*. And they all applied yesterday when Harriet Harman took over prime minister's questions.

You could almost see what was going on in their brains. 'My God, if she takes over the party, it will be like this every week!' Meanwhile, the Tories opposite were happy, smiling, cheerful, exhilarated and gleeful, looking collectively like a party that has in the space of 30 minutes lost a quid and won the lottery.

She wasn't dreadful – just not good enough. She was dogged and determined. And it wasn't her fault that she was up against William Hague, who may be the most nimble combatant in the house. He nagged her over the government's working capital scheme, which was supposed to provide immediate help for businesses that are short of money, but which six weeks later isn't even in operation.

She rose and said primly, 'The provisions under that scheme are being finalised.' That was the magic moment for the Tories. They realised that she had not come prepared. They began cheering. Like school bullies, they can sniff victimhood right across the playground.

'But the prime minister promised real help for businesses now!' said Hague. 'And they only applied to Brussels for permission last week!' He had combined two fat Tory targets: government incompetence and EU bureaucracy. The Tories were happier than ever.

Then he got personal. 'When Chamberlain lost his party's confidence, Churchill stepped in. When Eden retired, Supermac came forward. This could be her moment!' he said to Tory cheers, loud and thumping as a sarcastic pile driver. They would love Hattie to become Labour leader.

She must have known for weeks that the subject of her leadership ambitions would come up. She had all that time to produce a zinger in reply. Perhaps something really cutting such as, 'When Hague failed, they sent for – Iain Duncan Smith!' But she didn't have a riposte ready. Instead she said, 'He focuses on political gossip. We focus on fighting for Britain,' in the tones of a bossy big sister reprimanding her brother for saying 'poo'.

She did score once when she pointed out that Hague had received £30,000 for two after-dinner speeches for the hated, and now nationalised, RBS. He went a deep red colour that suffused his head and scalp, making him look like a beetroot lollipop, perhaps invented by Heston Blumenthal. But then she spoiled it all by wrongly claiming that Sir Fred Goodwin had got his knighthood for charitable work, rather than for banking. She left the Chamber to morose muttering from her own side, with the only cries of 'More!' coming from the joyful, delighted, rapturous, blissed-out Tories.

Mervyn King kept being called back to answer MPs' questions about the crisis. He realised that the only help lay in confusing them with jargon, of the type that they were obliged to pretend they understood.

It was a bright, sunny day, and the governor was in a perky mood. He quantitatively eased himself into a comfy chair in the Thatcher Room (isn't there some way we can blame her for this crisis?) and faced the Treasury committee yet again. There was some minor confusion when the chairman seemed to call two MPs at once. 'It's like Aston Villa's passing,' said Mr King, cheerfully. 'You're not quite sure where it's going to!' It may be a green shoot of recovery when the governor of the Bank starts making football jokes again.

But that was the last part of the session that a normal human being could follow. Take Mr King's response to Peter Mandelson's complaint that the government wasn't making money available for the car industry. 'We opened last autumn for asset-backed security paper,' the governor told us. Members of the committee nodded sagely. It was comforting to know that in these difficult times, we have MPs who are capable of pretending they know what on earth he is talking about.

The rest of us, however, were openly confused. 'We have been engaged in asset purchases in those corporate credit markets,' he vouchsafed, before going on to mention 'the quality of leverage such purchases might have on credit spreads in the markets'.

Clearly this required more explanation. 'The spreads on commercial paper have come down by 30-50 basis points,' he said.

At this, I realised that under the surface there was some tough, competitive jargon-wrestling going on. A Tory, Peter Viggers, mentioned 'the purchase of high-quality, temporarily illiquid assets'.

That was a gauntlet that had to be picked up. 'Yes,' said the governor, 'that's what I call conventional, unconventional purchases.'

Oof! It was Viggers's turn to look baffled. The governor rammed home his advantage with mentions of 'distorting private sector yields', 'the final impact on broad money supply and final demand', finishing off with a bravura 'quarterly forecast horizon'.

At this point I thought the committee might simply admit defeat and clear off. But they didn't. Instead they implied that the government actually wanted inflation to rise, since it would make paying back its enormous debt somewhat less painful.

'A clear inflation target is the anchor to which everyone should cling,' said the governor, which made it sound a pretty quick way of drowning. But economic jargon always produces weird images in the head. 'Many of those vehicles went off-balance sheet,' the governor mused, making me think of Jeremy Clarkson testing a four-wheel drive car. 'Okay, gang, let's go off-balance sheet!'

Michael Fallon wanted to know his exit strategy. 'Having put £75 billion into the system, how do you get it out?' he asked. Mr King said he did indeed have an exit strategy, and I had a vision of him leading billions of little pound coins down the tunnel from Colditz and to freedom.

'What will keep our feet to the fire is our inflation strategy,' he said. So we must cling to the anchor while keeping our feet to the fire. Sounds simple enough.

No wonder he seemed to be in such good fettle yesterday.

1 April 2009

*In April, world leaders arrived in London for a summit on saving
the planet from the economic crisis. There were several events
attached to the meeting, including one at St Paul's.*

Gordon Brown is trying to talk his way out of recession. At St
Paul's yesterday he was the morning's star preacher – sorry,
teacher. The cathedral was packed with around 2,000 people.
They were there for a debate. Several world religious leaders
were also there, including the Patriarch of Jerusalem and the
Grand Mufti of Egypt.

(What do muftis wear when they are off duty?) He looked
rather exotic, and the crowd strained forward to get a shufti
at the mufti.

Gordon spoke for a long time. It was actually his stump
speech about the need to restore values and confidence. He
talked about 'the fierce urgency of now' and warned us that
we could be 'literally too late for history'.

I don't know exactly what this meant, though it may be like
school where some of us were too late for geography and
French as well.

He also gave us his well-worn non-apology. 'I take full
responsibility for all my action. But I also know that this crisis
is global in source and global in scope.' This translates, as
always, as 'I am responsible but not to blame.'

Suddenly he was on a tour of world religions. Apparently,
on the general topic of being a good egg towards the next chap,
they all agree. 'We are all our brother's keeper,' he intoned,
'when those with riches help those without, it enriches us

all…' This was the stuff the troops wanted, and he gave it to us hot, strong and very long.

His key word turned out to be 'themba'. Not a new Disney character, or a brand of grass-powered car, but the acronym for 'There must be an alternative'. Also, by co-incidence, it is the Zulu word for 'hope'. Maybe it will be a hit with the 'kidz' – 'Hey, man, themba!'

He finally sat down after 26 minutes. Kevin Rudd, the Australian prime minister, said much the same but managed to say it in only 14 minutes. Next we had the debate. One man was determined to keep speaking. Total times: Gordon Brown: 9 minutes. Rudd: one minute. Bishop of London: one minute. Kev and the Rev looked as if they might resemble cream horns crushed under a lawn roller. But the Aussie battler fought back and grabbed some more minutes for himself. 'Young people are enormous vessels of hope,' he said. Or freighters full of themba.

But nobody could best the champ. As I left I could hear him thanking young persons for giving him faith in the future. Glad somebody has.

3 April 2009

The freshly inaugurated US president came for the summit. Politicians jostled to be near him and get some of that fairy stardust sprinkled over them. He gave a press conference with Gordon Brown. Rather like Sarkozy, Obama loved Britain – just adored being among us. I will spare you the feast of platitudes. Next day we had to go to Docklands in London to be briefed on the summit itself.

The summit took place on the dark side of the moon. We left normal humanity behind us on the Tube – idealistic young folk with piercings to protect the planet – then were ushered into a series of buses, swept past driverless trains, deserted roundabouts, abandoned building sites and empty docks, with not a single human being in sight except for groups of police officers, holding back nobody.

You had to go through security in order to be admitted to security. At one point we had our ID checked at the entrance to a huge shed. It was completely empty. But at the other end we had our ID checked again. The buses swirled around in figures of eight, like the route taken by the Mafia to make sure blindfolded victims can't work out where they are.

Inside the hall, the size of the hangar in Seattle where they put together Boeing 747s, there were around 2,000 journalists. It is amazing these days how, thanks to the miracle of modern communications, information of no use or value to anyone can be flashed instantly around the world. Hacks interviewed each other. Cameras filmed camera crews. The British had laid on free food – great dunes of sandwiches and salads for the most part. It must have cost enough to rescue a small Midlands auto parts maker. The soup was watercress – green shoots of recovery flavour, perhaps.

Now and again a world leader, or at least a world under-study, would appear and be fallen upon like a wounded gnu being spotted by a pride of lions. Peter Mandelson glided from table to table, briefing stealthily between the snacks. This is a man who can skulk in broad daylight.

A reporter from an American company was told to find out how the various world leaders felt about being 'at the fulcrum of history'. Lord Mandelson pondered the question for a moment, then said that the soup was nice.

There were two prayer rooms, for men and for women. The little image of a praying person was the same on both doors, which would have led to confusion if either of them had had any customers.

Then, finally, the talking was over and Gordon was among us. The summit had been a huge success. The global economy would be back on track faster than anyone could have imag-ined. He unreeled unreal figures, like a trader in an Arab souk unrolling an overpriced carpet. There would be $5 trillion to rescue the global economy. 'A new world order is emerging, and a new era of co-operation!' He was full of the fulcrum.

Two British TV reporters asked, in effect, the same question: what's in all this for your voters? What they wanted was a soundbite for the news, something like, 'safer homes, safer jobs, and a quicker end to the crisis,' perhaps.

But Gordon Brown does not do soundbites. Instead he does bread and butter puddings, great bowls full of stodge, lumpy with facts, judgments and declarations. You could almost sense the despair back at TV centre as his reply went on.

Around the centre, national leaders were all recounting how it was their personal efforts that had made the summit such a success. Only a curtain separated the leaders from each other, so we could hear Gordo and Sarko explaining, in stereo, how it was all to their own personal credit.

It was in this summer that the great expenses scandal broke out. MPs were caught out in all manner of dodgy practices, such as charging for maintenance that including moat-cleaning, for floating duck-houses, for their husband's porn films, and for interest on mortgages that had long been paid off. Some went to jail. Oddly enough it was often the smaller amounts that enraged the public most. The home secretary charged 18p for a bath plug. Jeremy Browne MP spent half an hour on Radio 5 Live being quizzed aggressively about a Kit Kat he had claimed from the public purse.

Oddly enough little of this was debated in the Chamber, not least because all sides knew there were enough skeletons in each party's closet to keep a Bart's anatomy class going for a year. Instead we heard the sound of the stable door being clanged shut time and again. Take Gordon Brown's appearance on the internet, shortly after the scandal broke.

The prime minister announced the swingeing cuts in MPs' allowances yesterday – on video. In the old days, premiers spoke to the Commons. But that has one huge disadvantage – MPs can answer back. Viewers of YouTube can't. (But they can show their interest in other ways: for instance, 'Gordon Brown picking his nose' has had 376,000 hits and counting.)

Anyhow, there is his latest policy pronouncement on number10.gov.uk. What was most amazing was not the content of his statement, but the brand new smile. This smile has clearly been worked on for a long time, possibly by a professional smile consultant. ('Now, Gordon, darling, lift the corners of your mouth. Let's see those incisors! No dribbling, mind.')

It cannot have been tried on a focus group, since it is quite terrifying. Think of the Joker in the *Batman* films. Imagine Munch's *The Scream* only upside-down. Then again it is the kind of smile you might deploy on a first date with someone you'd found on an internet site. ('Hmm, it says "good sense of humour essential". Maybe if I smile a lot, she'll think I have one.') It's the smile a 50-year-old man might deploy on the parents of the 23-year-old girl he is dating in a doomed attempt to reassure them. It's a doctor saying, 'Now this is going to hurt just a teeny bit, but if you're a brave little soldier, the nurse might give you a biscuit.'

It is certainly meant to be friendly, even though it is scarier than anything Hannibal Lecter might have come up with. I thought of a supply teacher with the worst class in the school, desperately hoping to win them over by sheer niceness. It's a smile a terrified kidnap victim might use on his captors: 'I must say, I think you chaps have got an awfully good case.'

But what makes it truly scary is that the smile is deployed entirely at random. 'Going round the country, I have been struck by the comments of young people.' Big cheesy smile. 'A detailed written statement setting out our plans will be made by Harriet Harman.' Again, the manic grin. Does the very thought of Harriet Harman cause him to smile uncontrollably?

'Those ministers who live in official residences would not be entitled to this allowance.' Again, the smile leaps from the screen for no discernible reason. I began to wonder if he was wired up to something, possibly operated by a nine-year-old boy who is having a lot of fun.

'While the committee on standards in public life looks at the issue...' Smile! Now he is almost at the end, and able to visit his plastic surgeon for a face-drop, or whatever is the opposite of a nip and tuck – a slice and stuff, perhaps.

There comes a point in many governments when everything seems to go wrong. It happened to Jim Callaghan in the late 1970s and to John Major in the mid-1990s. When disasters begin to arrive on a daily basis, there is no comeback and no hope.

Gordon Brown has been travelling the world like a mediaeval penitent, seeking a shriving that he never receives. Instead he is being pelted with rotten fruit and vegetables. Yesterday he was in Poland, being hectored by the Polish prime minister, Donald Tusk, who said that he would never follow the British policy of fiscal stimulus. This, from a country that has already had to ask for help from the IMF! Last month he suffered a similar harangue in Chile. Thank heavens he doesn't have to go to Zimbabwe for a lecture on inflation.

This was all a bonus for George Osborne, the shadow chancellor, appearing at Treasury questions. 'We are used to Poles telling us to fix the roof while the sun is shining,' he said, 'not Polish prime ministers!' Richard Ottaway cruelly added, 'The Polish prime minister made ours look like a bit of a novice.'

But nothing fazes Alistair Darling, not even the sight of Sir Peter Tapsell hurtling towards him, like that gigantic boulder that threatens Indiana Jones in the first of those films. As always, when Sir Peter arises (other MPs rise, he arises), the Hansard reporters throw away their ballpoint pens and take up sheets of vellum on which they can record, with ample use of illuminated lettering, his words for posterity.

He unrolled himself, like priceless, hand-blocked wallpaper. 'Does the chancellor agwee [Sir Peter has a slight speech impediment] that the objective of the unannounced pwogwam of quantitative easing is to incwease and facilitate the lending by banks to businesses? So why, the Bank of England having warned against another fiscal stimulus, is it pwoceeding with QE in such a half-hearted manner as to actually waise the yields on gilts … would Montagu Norman not be pwoud of him?'

This last barb brought sustained laughter from the more economically literate Tories, who recalled that Montagu Norman was the governor of the Bank whose inaction in the late 1920s and early '30s is thought to have prolonged the great depression. So, if you decoded it, it was quite an offensive remark, like comparing a military leader to Custer, or the Grand Old Duke of York. Most Labour MPs, of course, believe that history began in 1997, and so have never heard of Montagu Norman.

Darling said that was a matter for another day. I can't help wondering what he would say if someone walked up to the dispatch box and emptied a bucket of manure all over his head. 'I cannot necessarily agree with the honourable gentleman's approach to this problem,' perhaps.

Peter Kilfoyle of Liverpool made a harsh and bitter intervention about the '17 millionaires' on the Tory front bench. The Labour left resemble those Japanese soldiers who got lost in the forests and didn't realise – in the left's case – that the class war was over. Now they have returned to civilisation and discovered that it's still going on! They are very happy.

MPs' expenses were the huge issue, Gordon Brown was accused of throwing office equipment at aides whose work had failed to come up to scratch ... the government's travails just kept increasing. Joanna Lumley took up the cause of Gurkhas who, having served in the British army, had no right of residence here. The actress proved far more competent at getting her way than most politicians.

We gathered near the Commons for what has become Joanna Lumley's daily matinee. It was utterly, majestically, chaotic. She had just heard that five Gurkhas, including two who had been injured in the Falklands, had been refused right of entry. It was, said one of her sidekicks, 'beyond betrayal'.

The press conference was beyond farce. The Atrium restaurant near the house was heaving with snappers, TV cameramen, journalists, soundmen, politicians and even some baffled diners who hadn't finished their lunch.

There was no sign of Ms Lumley. Then word came down that she had 'bumped into' the immigration minister, Phil Woolas, on the stairs. There had been a heated exchange of views, which in Downing Street would mean flying tea trolleys, though in this case probably meant no more than strong words.

The Lib Dem Chris Huhne muttered, 'What a way to run a government! "Bumped into on the stairs"!' The *on dit* among the politicians was that the Home Office would willingly let the Gurkhas in, but the MoD was hanging tough, because of the money.

Upstairs, it turned out, Ms Lumley and the minister, plus innumerable aides, had piled into an executive's office, closely followed by a TV crew. Ms Lumley has no more problems with a TV crew than a top batsman with a cricket ball.

'What do we have to do,' she said – or rather, breathed – 'to end this cartwheel of emotion?' Crash! Over the sightscreen and out of the ground!

Downstairs, excitement was boiling over. There was to be a joint press conference, Woolas and Lumley, Phil and Patsy, the Beast and Beauty. On the stairs down into the restaurant came a bizarre pile of people as the cameramen, locked together like a stroppy chain gang, walked perilously backwards down the curved flight while filming the scene above them.

At the bottom of the stairs was a single man in a white jacket who appeared to be holding up the whole tottering mass. If his arms had given way, there would have been a terrible disaster, with appalling injuries and thousands of pounds' worth of equipment smashed.

She made it to the microphones unharmed. 'The enormous shock we felt!' she said, her words hovering in the air as if they had bounced off a waterbed. Hopes had been so high since she had met Gordon Brown last week. But it turned out that the prime minister hadn't even been informed about the latest exclusions. Did some civil servant think it so unimportant that he hadn't thought it worth informing Number 10? Behind me, opposition MPs sighed with pleasure.

Mr Woolas tried to put his case. The Gurkhas had indeed been rejected under the rules, but they could try again with the new guidelines. 'And we are going to help with the formation of the new guidelines!' respired Ms Lumley, and Mr Woolas could only nod in mute, if sorrowful, agreement.

Ms Lumley's co-campaigners were behind him, and had arranged it so there were pictures of injured Gurkhas behind each of his ears. What a terrible fate for any politician, to be doughnutted by hideous lacerations! If Alastair Campbell were dead, he would be turning in his grave.

The principal victim of the expenses brouhaha – apart from the MPs who later went to jail – was the Speaker, Michael Martin, whose handling of the whole affair made matters horribly worse.

The Speaker stood up to make his statement about the scandal. The house was far from full; no doubt many members were saving money by hitch-hiking to London.

Michael Martin began: 'We face a catastrophic loss of public confidence in the entire democratic process. The public are enraged. At a time when millions are facing financial hardship, they see us sucking up their money like thirsty camels at an oasis. As the man who presided complacently over this mounting chaos, while claiming extremely generous expenses myself, it is clear that my continued presence can only delay the crucial task of cleaning out the stables. I hereby tender my resignation.'

Did he say that? Of course he didn't! Instead he gave a performance that, to use today's fashionable word, was truly lamentable. Oh, he did say that things would have to change and that MPs should stick to the spirit as well as the letter of the rules. But then he got on to what really bothered them: their (or rather, our) money. The police had been called in. The person who had leaked the details of the expenses to the *Daily Telegraph* was clearly capable of selling MPs' account numbers, signatures and passwords. The Commons commission would look into the whole subject, that very night. In other words, the crime was the leak, not the pilfering.

Great. The whole statement lasted about three minutes. But as soon as he left his script things started to go the shape of an over-ripe pear. Kate Hoey, for one, wanted to know why the Met had been called in when they had a huge job to do in London. As it happened, the *Telegraph* had been very discreet with members' bank details.

You would have thought from his rage that she had questioned the Speaker's parentage. 'Might not this be seen as a way of hiding…' she started to say, but he shut her up. 'I listen to the honourable lady often, when I turn on the TV at midnight, I hear her public utterances and pearls of wisdom on Sky News … it's easy to say to the press, this shouldn't happen, it's a wee bit more difficult when you don't have to give quotes to the *Express* – to the press, not the *Express* – and do nothing else. Some of us in this House have other responsibilities, not just talking to the press!'

This sort of semi-coherent abuse is not what Speakers are supposed to do. Norman Baker, a Lib Dem, was next in the line of fire. He wanted the expenses claims to be published more quickly. 'Another member keen to say to the press what the press wants to hear!' barked Mr Martin. He was losing it. You knew his head was somewhere distant when he referred to Ann Widdecombe as 'the right honourable gentleman'.

At the time it seemed that Michael Martin might even survive this appalling display. Gordon Brown, a fellow Scot, seemed ready to defend him, and Tories were not keen to have a new Speaker chosen before they had a majority. But it turned out that Mr Martin's petulance – he had admitted being 'in a bit of a bad mood' – was the beginning of the end for him.

You cannot overestimate the mood of paranoia, hilarity and madness that pervades Westminster. Normal-looking MPs seem to have messages branded on their heads, reading 'tennis court repairs', 'wife's tampons', or 'moat cleaning', like Hawthorne's scarlet letter.

In the Chamber, members were still doing the bowing and scraping bit – 'with your permission, Mr Speaker – as if he were someone who still mattered. I haven't met an MP yet who doesn't think Michael Martin should go, even if they doubt that he will.

News broke that Andrew MacKay had been obliged to resign as an aide to David Cameron, who has been trying to win the 'holier than thou' vote all week. MacKay and his wife, Julie Kirkbride, had been 'double dipping', each one claiming the second-home allowance on one of their two houses, while the other claimed the moolah for the other house, if you follow me. Since 2001 they cleared £282,731. (In a magnificent irony, Ms Kirkbride last claimed expenses when she was a political correspondent for the *Daily Telegraph* – the paper that has brought us all this information.)

MacKay made his way down the latter-day Via Doloroso that leads to the Millbank studios of the 24-hour news services.

With his weird complexion and bulging eyes, MacKay looks like a kipper that has been smoked before it's dead.

'I was advised to do it [by the fees office],' he said plaintively. The fees office seems to have been run on the lines of a dodgy car dealership. 'If you got cash, I can knock the VAT off, mate ... don't worry about those bloodstains on the back seat, I can clean that off for you...'

MacKay's interviewer seemed puzzled. 'You said that you had a friendly conversation with David Cameron,' he said. 'But he has told the media that he is angry.'

MacKay: 'Well, it was friendly within limits.' Friendly within limits! What a wonderful euphemism for sheer, gibbering rage!

Things swiftly got worse for the Speaker.

It was gruesome, pathetic and miserable. You had to watch it through your fingers, with teeth clenched and stomach knotted. It wasn't even tragic, if tragedy means a great man brought down by his own weakness. Michael Martin is a weak man brought down by his own weakness. He resembled a boxer totally outfought, tottering numbly around the ring, barely aware of what was happening, staggering into his opponents' fists, somehow staying upright amid the swaying. In any more humane arena the referee would have stopped the fight ages ago. But he is the referee, and he's not stopping anything!

One felt one should feel sorry for him. But it is hard to feel pity for someone who has blundered into a situation and shows no awareness that he needs to blunder right out again. He not only failed to announce that he would resign, he didn't even mention the possibility. Instead, he intends to hold a 'top level meeting'. Faced with the Great Fire of London, he would have told the fire brigade to stay where they were and announce a commission, to report in the autumn. He just doesn't get it.

One MP after another rose to tell him to resign. To his credit, he did call the ones most likely to attack him, though of course if he hadn't, the subsequent furore would have blown him away like a dandelion seed in a hurricane.

He did give a sort of apology. 'To the extent that I have contributed to the situation, I am profoundly sorry.' It was, everyone kept saying, a historic day for parliament. Or at least a hysteric day.

Two MPs, Gordon Prentice and Douglas Carswell, who had signed a motion calling on him to resign stood up and duly told him to resign. They wanted a vote on their motion. The Speaker took refuge in procedure. 'It is not a substantive motion,' he said. 'Oh yes, it is!' said Prentice. Carswell, who it must be said exudes a sort of prune-faced Puritanism, said that the house should be allowed to 'choose a Speaker with the moral authority to clean up Westminster'. This breathtakingly rude remark drew a gasp of outrage from some Labour members, though as gasps of outrage go, it was pretty lacklustre.

David Winnick, an aged Labour sage, pleaded with Mr Martin to give some indication of when he intended to retire. But the Speaker was no more going to do that than drop his trousers and dance on the table of the house. 'You know that is not a subject for today!' he said. Wrong. It was the only subject of the day.

Even Sir Patrick Cormack, second grandest – after Peter Tapsell – of the grandees, had a pop. 'The condition of the house is very like the condition of the country during the Norway debate,' he said. This reminder of the vote that ended Neville Chamberlain's premiership could not have been missed by anyone. It was also breathtakingly rude. 'In the name of God, go!' hung unspoken in the rafters.

The only good news for the Speaker was bad news. He was supported by Bob Spink, a former Tory MP turned UKIP member, and so largely despised by all sides. It was like being praised for your banking skills by Fred Goodwin. The end must be very near.

20 May 2009

And so it was.

The first Speaker to be forced out in 300 years was gone in 30 seconds. I popped down at 2.30pm to see the ritual of the Speaker's procession and joined the daily gaggle of tourists who cluster round to see the sight of a middle-aged man walking, preceded by a badge messenger wearing a badge and the serjeant at arms bearing a mace, and followed by his train bearer. It may be the only job on the planet that involves a man being paid to lift up the back of your jacket. Even the Queen usually makes do without a train bearer. The chaplain and various other functionaries follow on. Everyone is wearing black, so that the whole resembles a condemned man's walk to the scaffold.

Aptly enough, as it happens. The Speaker even managed a small, sheepish smile, and I thought that perhaps he looked like someone who has just shrugged a great weight from his shoulders.

Then into the Chamber for prayers, which members of the public and press are not allowed to attend, but we were once admitted by accident, and I can report that they all turn round and face the walls, so that the whole Chamber looks like the Gents at half-time in a football match. The Speaker said that the house was always at its best when it was united. This is a myth to which MPs cling, though it is the exact opposite of the truth, since they generally pass the worst legislation when they are all agreed, as they see no need to debate it properly.

He was resigning, he said, to maintain that unity. He would go in five weeks, he said, and that was that. It was wise to be so laconic. In the past his lengthy ramblings have made the situation far worse.

With that we were on to foreign office questions, with David Miliband saying that we would save the tributes for later. And they will – thick, sticky, glutinous tributes – as nauseous as the attacks this week were acrid and bitter.

A queue of members lined up to shake his hand. A watching colleague said it was like seeing pilgrims at the Vatican kiss the Pope's ring. I was reminded more of a tea lady retiring. There have been a few tea trolley disasters of late, and she has finally realised it is time to go. Relieved colleagues cluster to wish her a long and happy retirement.

With the government coming to bits like candy floss in a wind tunnel, many people at Westminster were astonished to learn that Gordon Brown had made anxious inquiries about the health of Susan Boyle, the chanteuse who only just lost in the final of *Britain's Got Talent*.

But I wasn't puzzled. They have a lot in common. (1) Both come from small Scottish towns. (2) Neither are the loveliest creatures on the catwalk. (3) Both come from a religious background. (4) Susan Boyle, we are told, has imaginary friends who aren't real. Gordon Brown has imaginary friends who exist, but who aren't really friends. (5) Both might have won if the poll had been held earlier.

Meanwhile, we all trooped in to hear Hazel Blears, the communities secretary, answer questions. There is something a little poignant about seeing a minister perform for what is almost certainly the last time. She stood at the dispatch box, trying to reach up. She resembled one of those jokey seaside postcards that show little kittens pretending to drive.

Blears is in huge trouble for having failed to pay capital gains tax on her 'second' home. But we also heard from Phil Hollobone (gas, water and electricity bills) on the subject of the business rate. They discussed 'regional spatial strategies', whatever those might be. The minister answering that was Margaret Beckett (hanging baskets, failed claim).

My old pal Michael Fabricant (numerous claims for £240, just £10 less than the maximum claim allowed without receipts) wanted to know about greenfield sites. Caroline Spelman (nanny) demanded a change of government. Several

Lib Dems took part, including Julia Goldsworthy (leather rocking chair, repaid) and Sarah Teather (beyond reproach).

Philip Davies (£303 paid back for hotel bills) asked about the government's various schemes to help people who can't pay their mortgages. So far only two families have been helped. Why don't they just cut out the middleman and stand for parliament?

'Name them!' cried Fabricant. What a guy. You can see why we willingly pay his £700-£900 mortgage bill every month. Let's hope he's never repossessed.

Then we heard from Jacqui Smith, the *pro tem* home secretary. This too had a certain poignancy, since one of the reasons she is going is because of her husband's rental of a porn film, *Raw Meat III*, charged to the taxpayer.

She came up against Desmond Swayne (squeaky clean) who was in rumbustious mood. Swayne, unfairly I am sure, looks rather like the chap who never tells the gels his surname just in case they complain to his commanding officer. The Speaker, also *pro tem*, called the borders, citizenship and immigration bill. 'Why?' boomed Swayne.

'Secretary Jacqui Smith,' said the Speaker. 'Why?' bellowed Swayne.

'This bill introduces measures...' she began.

'This is an entirely content-free bill!" shouted Swayne.

The Speaker called for quiet, but Swayne would not be deterred. 'This bill!' he began, but before he could continue, the home secretary snapped, 'He's just had lunch, but he didn't have coffee!'

This neat and wholly parliamentary means of implying that he was as overwrought as a newt, got a huge laugh. It may be the biggest laugh Smith ever got in the Chamber. Or even the only one.

Hazel Blears duly resigned, allowing one MP to accuse the cabinet of trying to re-shuffle itself. Next day John Hutton, the defence secretary, also resigned. Ministers were disappearing faster than we could keep up. It began to look as if the rats were leaving the sinking ship, leaving only the captain.

But the show must go on, and new parliamentarians had to be created. The latest was Alan Sugar, 'Srallen' of *The Apprentice*, who has become 'Lorshugger' and will work as the government's Enterprise Tsar. Gordon Brown's economic strategy may be to get teams of ambitious if unpleasant young persons to sell us over-priced bling on television.

Tories leapt into action. They found a letter he had written to the *Financial Times* in 1992 when he was plain Mr Sugar. 'I have noticed with disgust the comments of a Mr Gordon Brown who has accused me of doing well out of the recession,' the letter began. Well, at least he's got his resignation speech ready.

Just before noon we heard that David Miliband and Alistair Darling were to stay, even though Gordon Brown wanted them to move. This is becoming like the dinner party from hell, in which guests refuse to accept the hostess's *placement* and won't budge from where they have chosen to sit down. And they refuse the food. 'Kindly have the butler bring me my pizza when it arrives from Domino's.'

Local election results poured in. They were uniformly dreadful for Labour. We learned that Alan Johnson was to become home secretary. This has not proved a good career move for previous home secretaries. It's rather like marrying Bluebeard; there can only be one outcome and it's not pretty.

Bob Ainsworth was to become the new defence secretary. Who? Somehow I doubt that telegrams flashed to all our armed forces telling them that 'Bob is back!'

Finally, an extraordinary press conference. Gordon Brown, as always, accepted all the responsibility but none of the blame. Ministers were still resigning, but Glenys Kinnock was to be parachuted into the Lords, offering hope and comfort to the resistance.

The new cabinet, we were told, was full of people of strength, experience and resilience. 'They are not the kind of people who walk away when the going gets tough,' Brown said bitterly, without naming the names who must have been on the tip of his tongue. Nor would he walk away. 'I never believe in walking away ... I will never waver, and I will never walk away.'

He made it sound like a soldier in the first world war, liable to be shot for leaving the trenches. Then – aaargh – he smiled.

11 June 2009

Things became more demented. Peter Mandelson was appointed 'the right honourable Lord Mandelson, First Secretary of State, Secretary of State for Business, Innovation and Skills, and Lord President of the Council', making him the only person in Britain whose job title is too long to get into a tweet on Twitter. The parliamentary Labour party held a packed meeting addressed by Gordon Brown. It was so full that MPs were literally hurling themselves at the door in the hopes of getting in, even though the room inside was as full as a rush-hour Virgin train on a Friday night.

Some readers may recall that Peter Mandelson was 'intensely relaxed about people being filthy rich', though many Labour MPs felt that they were also intensely relaxed about people who were dirt poor. So Gordon Brown tried another strategy.

His great new idea is constitutional reform. That'll win the next election. You can imagine the scene on the doorstep.

Canvasser: I'm here on behalf of the Labour party. Can we count on your support?

Voter: Your lot have done nowt for us, nowt. As for that Gordon Brown...

Canvasser: What if I told you that he was considering whether to table a motion giving greater independence and authority to parliamentary select committees?

Voter: Is he, by heck? Now you're talking...

The scene in the Commons was more desperate than ever. Labour MPs were certainly relieved that the bloodbath seems to be over, for the time being at least. But they had the air of survivors in a *Mad Max* film, desperate to grab any crumbs of comfort they could find in dustbins, nuclear waste tips, etc.

159

Whereas the Tories were beside themselves with glee. They were like a sackful of ferrets that had forgotten to take their Ritalin. If they had been schoolchildren, the Speaker would have threatened to keep them in for an hour. As it was, he promised the opposite – expulsion, because he still can.

This is how mad it was. When Labour's Shona McIsaac asked a creepy question about economic growth, Michael Fabricant shouted out, 'Love the hair!'

Having Mickey Fab praise you for your hair is like having Jordan congratulate you on the size of your bosom – it might not be real, but you are getting plaudits from an expert. And they do both have magnificent blonde locks. No working-class roots to be seen. And if they both decided to sell their long, shiny tresses, they would keep the My Little Pony factory in business through to Christmas.

The Tory glee was largely due to the fact that Gordon Brown was still there. They cherish him as their best hope of a landslide election victory. Meanwhile, the prime minister was taking us all for fools, claiming that he hadn't want to sack Alistair Darling as chancellor. Just as he wanted us to believe he hadn't called an election in 2007 because he was sure he would win it.

I don't suppose that the countryside was ever really idyllic, but it must once have been a more agreeable place than it is now. Every month, agriculture questions in the Commons opens a window on a world of misery, in which farmers battle with falling prices, rising costs, EU bureaucracy, rapacious super-markets, bizarre diseases of livestock, and to cap it all, Defra.

I wondered vaguely how a memoir of a country childhood, written perhaps in 2050 but recalling the present day might go. All the jargon could be heard in yesterday's exchanges.

'It was the year of our Lord 2009, and my carefree days seemed to be filled with endless sunshine. I was a merry young lad, working on a train-to-gain apprenticeship at the old call centre in Farmer Pettigrew's converted barn. Kelly Braithwaite was my girl, and at weekends she and I would roam over the hill sheep farming sector, seeking out nitrate vulnerable zones, for with all our kissing and canoodling we were generally too late for the day-rate vulnerable zones.

'Sometimes we would take a can of extra-strength Irish cider and sit under a black plastic-covered hayrick as the sun went down. Afterwards I would throw the empty can into a copse, and Kelly would give me a tongue-lashing to remember. "Do not be a silly ha'poth, my girl," I would tell her. "I am merely participating in the 'recycling on the go infrastructure', as outlined by the new under-secretary of state, Dan Norris!"

'Soon we were on our way back home, and paused by Farmer Catchpole's set-aside. We would play a simple game, spotting indicator species – birds, insects and invertebrates. As country folk said round our way: "Find a ladybird afore your tea / You'll have a viable measure of increased biodiversity."

'One night Kelly and I were walking hand-in-hand through the gathering dusk. I nipped off to empty my bladder of the recycled cider and to light a fag, boldly defying the government's stated opposition to "slash and burn" policies. Then, out of the darkness we saw an eerie figure clad all in white. Kelly grabbed my arm. "It must be the ghost of old Ned Sowerbutts, who was ruined by the collapse of the Dairy Farmers of Britain, with the consequent reduction of milk prices to 10p a litre, and who fell in his drunken state into a vat full of slurry, forgetting that the new regulations on slurry storage do not apply until 2012!" she gasped.

'"No, that is no ghost!" I cried. "That is old Amos Flowerdew, the government trial badger culler," I told her. "He means no harm, except to badgers, though if he offers you a whiff of what he has in that spray can, you would be wise to refuse."'

Gordon Brown was in Italy for the G8, as a guest of Silvio Berlusconi. It was a dank day in London, and we were about to be harangued by Harriet Harman. No wonder one's thoughts drifted towards the sun-dappled jewel of the Mediterranean.

I imagined our prime minister being greeted by his host. 'Ah ha, my fren' Gordon, eet is good to see you!' (Berlusconi, as well as sounding like Chico Marx, also bears a passing physical resemblance to him, though Chico, unlike the Italian premier, was more or less sane.) 'I 'ave, 'ow you say, a leetle surprise waiting for you in your room!'

At Westminster Ms Harman was exchanging with William Hague more or less the same ludicrous figures that Brown and Cameron swapped a week ago. Hague asked if she would put into plain English what Brown had meant when he said that total spending would continue to rise, and that the rise would be zero per cent in 2013.

She replied: 'The shadow chancellor says he spends 40 per cent of his time thinking about economics; it's amazing that he spends all his time thinking about doing absolutely nothing.' Hague snapped back: perhaps she would spend 100 per cent of her time answering his question.

Back in L'Aquila, Gordon goes up to his room, looking forward to a quiet hour with some world output figures. Instead he is greeted by a young woman in a babydoll nightie who, it appears, is not the chambermaid. 'Meeser Berlusconi – 'e send me! To make you 'appy!'

'Nooo,' says Brown. 'I am a son of the manse, and have nothing to do with happiness. Be away wi' ye!'

Back in London, Harriet was explaining how a reduction in public expenditure from £44 billion to £42 billion was actually an increase. Hague said that was exactly the kind of statement that damaged the credibility of all politicians.

In L'Aquila, the young woman in the babydoll has rushed downstairs in tears. 'Meester Brown, 'e send me away! 'E make me vair, vair sad!'

The Italian premier is enraged by this rejection of his well-intention gift. 'OK, so these Inglish, these Scottish Inglish, 'e insults zurr mos' beautiful Italian women! 'E will not get away with ziss!'

Back in the Commons there is a strange silence. Normally the exchange of meaningless statistics would call forth much excitable cheering and mockery. Instead everything was greeted by a mild, sullen chuntering, like commuters who've just learned that the 7.49 is running 10 minutes late.

Vince Cable asked if Harriet had suggested that Gordon take some of her progressive views on gender equality to Berlusconi, which evoked some laughter.

In Italy, Gordon slips gratefully into bed after a long day instructing world leaders on the need to follow Britain's shining example. His foot meets something wet and warm. It is only when he pulls back the sheets that he sees the horror of the horse's severed head.

Now and again there is no one topic that demands attention in parliament. But modern technology can usually come to one's aid.

Time for another Twitter! Once again, events of great moment rub shoulders with things that don't matter at all.

12.44 Son texts to say 'it is all over', i.e. England has won Test against Australia. Celebrate with meal at All You Can Eat Gourmet Chinese Buffet, £5.20.

14.38 Sir Alan Sugar introduced into House of Lords as baron, so that Srallen has become Bronnshugger.

14.39 As in Rolling Stones song.

14.41 Observe that he is swathed in lashings of ermine. Tempted to lean over balcony and shout, 'You're furred!'

14.42 Clerk says that Bronnshugger has been given new gig 'by warrant of Queen's sign manual'. Cannot believe Queen giving sign manual to anyone.

14.43 Sugar favours clerk with the kind of look he gives a spotty whippersnapper who has failed to sell more than £7.35-worth of dried flowers in an afternoon.

14.53 Go to favourite toilet in House of Lords. Comfy.

14.55 Buy stamps at Commons post office. Two books first class, one second class. Result!

15.02 Notice a notice saying hacks now allowed back on Commons terrace, from which I used to bowl wine glasses into Thames in my youth.

15.03 But only during the recess, thus cannot talk to MPs, who'll be on holiday. So what's the point?

15.09 Culture questions. Peter Bone points out that last time England beat Aussies at Lords, 1934, Labour govt was in financial crisis, Tories won election following year. Hmmm.

15.11 Minister Ben Bradshaw asked about very high pay for BBC executives. Refuses to interfere.

15.12 He adds: 'The BBC has enough managers at senior level who are well enough paid to make these decisions for themselves.'

15.13 This seems to mean, 'Because they get such fabulous salaries, they must be capable of judging whether the salaries they get are fabulous enough.'

15.20 Bradshaw says he went to two festivals at weekend, Latitude and 'the wonderful Tolpuddle Martyrs'. Anyone heard of that group?

15.34 Health secretary Andy Burnham statement on swine flu. We have enough vaccine for the entire population, and that's not to be sneezed at.

15.39 Government obsessed by alliteration. If you think you have swine flu, you can call a number and get a code, then send 'flu friend' to pick up medicine.

15.40 So will we have 'measles mates' and 'chicken pox chums'?

15.41 Or 'arthritis associates'?

22 September 2009

The party conference season began with the Liberal Democrats. Vince Cable, still at the height of his popularity, made a controversial speech.

The Lib Dem deputy leader described a new tax, on people whose houses are worth more than £1 million. For every pound their house is worth over the million mark, they'd have to fork out half a penny, averaging £4,000 a year.

This mansion tax would certainly make life difficult for estate agents, who would need to execute a swift U-turn and start telling people how awful the properties they're selling are. 'Some restoration required' would turn into 'serious deterioration needed'.

Instead of just saying 'with many original features', they would have to add, 'which can easily be ripped out'. 'Set in 10 acres of rolling parkland' will become 'hideous prospect of bombsite covered in toxic waste'. 'Two hundred yards of excellent fly fishing' would appear as 'serious flooding danger'.

Potential buyers will be shown the original Adam fireplace and told, 'But you can easily replace it with a coal-effect Cosyglow with Formica surround.' Dinner party conversations will swivel too: 'The people two doors away paid one and a quarter mil last year, but they demolished the conservatory, painted the outside puce, and they've managed to get it down to 900K!'

'That's marvellous. Our friends have a lovely Queen Anne house, but they dumped a rusty old Volvo in the front garden, and it took nearly a hundred grand off. We're planning a colony of bats in the guest room.'

I can't say the conference was enthralled by Vince's speech. If other orators give you a large gin and tonic, or a bracing glass of champagne, Vince gives you a glass of chilled apple juice: tasty, but slightly sour and good for you.

Some, however, produced Bloody Marys with extra Smirnoff. One woman was cheered when she said that we didn't need a block of flats for those cheating MPs. 'We need a prison ship on the Thames!' Chris Davies, an MEP, lost control of his voice when he talked about the expenses fiddling that went on in Brussels and Strasbourg. 'I hate the dirty, cheating bastards,' he raved. 'I want them exposed! I want them thrown out!' The conference, normally ruminative cud-chewers, loved this rare example of Lib Dem fury. If Vince was serving apple juice, Mr Davies was giving them worm-wood and gall with ice and lemon.

23 September 2009

The Liberal Democrats do tend to retreat to a world of their own.

Dozens of schoolchildren trooped into the conference centre yesterday to hear the end of the Lib Dem debate on Afghanistan. Youth! Genuine young people of the type every political party wants to grab and to keep. What an opportunity!

Whether the party made the most of it is difficult to say. Ed Davey, their foreign affairs spokesman, was defending his statement that it was time 'to take tea with the Taliban'. What he had meant, he said, was that we should negotiate, and in that neck of the woods, tea was the tipple of choice for negotiators. And indeed, in Northern Ireland we could have a pint with the Provos, or in Pakistan, 'a quick one with al-Qaida.' It's a very Lib Dem notion that we could sit down with our enemies, and find the path to peace over a chinwag accompanied by an appropriate beverage.

None of this mattered. Thousands of miles away soldiers are knee-deep in blood and sand, death waiting behind every rock, alongside every road. Corrupt politicians, fanatical terrorists and drugs profiteers are their constant companions.

However, we were not in Helmand, but in Libdemland province, a world far from explosions and gunfire, a world of committees and steering groups, motions and amendments. As the debate clanked to an end, the chairman declared: 'We shall now consider the reference back. First I will read to you the statement of reasons for the reference back. Then there will be a vote on whether we would like to have a mini-debate on whether there should be a reference back, with speeches from a mover and an opponent ... if the first vote is passed, we will have the mini-debate on the reference back, but if the first vote falls we will move straight to the summation for the main motion. Can I now see those in favour of holding a mini-debate?'

Up in the gallery, the schoolchildren looked blank, perhaps longing for their computer games, or Facebook pages, or even a daytime TV show about a couple who want to buy a two-bedroom flat with off-street parking in Montenegro.

Later Duncan Brack, a Lib Dem who sits on more committees than all the people you know combined, announced: 'It's unusual, not to say unprecedented, for the movers to amend their own motions.' But why unprecedented? As in every party, the Lib Dems disagree with each other. But only in the Lib Dems do members disagree with themselves.

By this time the young persons had left, possibly to do something more interesting, such as collecting matchbox labels, or drugs.

Nick Clegg strode out to make, yet again, the most important speech of his life. Oh well, can't win 'em all. He was in a dark suit with a shiny yellow tie, and looked as if he were about to hop up as the decoration on a wedding cake.

It wasn't a bad speech. It aspired to the condition of OK. At times it soared to the heights of the not bad. The audience was a little slow to respond, though they got there in the end. But it was meant to greet a new political dawn in this country, in which the old, weary usages would be shredded and replaced by the revolutionary and the cleansing.

So why was it a traditional leader's speech of the type that could have been delivered more or less verbatim, at any time, by any leader in the last half century? It was full of breaches of the law of reverse intention, which I have made up, and which states that if the exact opposite of a statement is plainly nonsense, then it probably wasn't worth making in the first place. For example, 'I want to change our country for the good!' (I want to change our country for the worse.)

Or, 'I want to live in a country where prejudice, insularity and fear are conquered by the great British traditions of tolerance, pluralism and justice!' (I want to live in a country where liberalism, compassion and fairness are replaced by those great British traditions of prejudice, terror and xenophobia!)

There are the embarrassing faux-populist jokes. 'Labour is like the *Big Brother* house, located away from reality, arguing about trivia – and like *Big Brother*, they are about to be taken off the air.'

There is the occasional false modesty. Leaders love to list their faults that, on examination, turn out not to be faults at all. 'Occasionally I am a bit too blunt in interviews – but at least you know I'm not spinning you a line,' which translates as, 'If I have a failing, it's that I'm sometimes too honest.'

There is the ersatz candour. 'I'll be straight with you. There are no easy answers.' This is a line you hear in speeches roughly as often as 'the answer is perfectly simple.'

There were artful new clichés, such as his favourite, 'progressive austerity', which means cuts, but cuts 'driven by generosity of spirit'. Which will be a lot of comfort when you lose your job, or the local clinic closes.

There are the wildly improbable tributes to colleagues. He mentioned Chris Huhne at the Home Office, demanding change, being balked by technocrats. 'He'll produce volumes of statistics showing he's right, and look sternly over his glasses until they cave in.'

(Somehow I don't think that the mandarins of Whitehall will give up so easily. It's not like *Are You Being Served?* in there. 'Oooh, I was getting on so well, then he gave me that really stern look over his glasses, and I went all shivery!'

There were moments when he sounded as if he'd left the ancient template at home, and the audience responded with genuine enthusiasm, as when he accused Labour of betraying 'the best hopes of a generation'. But then we learned that the Lib Dems now 'carry the torch of progress', and we were once more in the past, borne back ceaselessly into the future.

For ages, the Labour party had held a deep mistrust of Peter Mandelson. But something changed when he turned up to rescue Gordon Brown. He spoke at their party conference.

It was a modern miracle, the scene we thought we would never see. The Labour party rose, not just to applaud Peter Mandelson, but to cheer him, to whoop at him like Texan cheerleaders, to adore him. Tony Blair famously said that his project would not be complete until the Labour party has learned to love Peter Mandelson, and as he said yesterday – in a rare moment of self-deprecation – 'perhaps he set the bar a little too high'.

Not high enough, as it turned out. On yesterday's form he could have cleared 12 feet without a pole. The same people who resented and mistrusted Mandy, who used to listen to his speeches in near silence, interrupted only by an occasional disgruntled noise, like a frog stuck in a bucket, sat entranced and then inflamed.

No matter that the speech was bonkers. The business secretary was by turns coy, kittenish, camp and crazed. Occasionally his voice rose to a squeak. His facial expressions were, frankly, weird, and now and then he slowed down alarmingly, as if his carburettor had cut out. Half the time he was like one of those people who shout at strangers on buses; during the other half he resembled a slightly creepy uncle reading a bedtime story. Sometimes he ranted; sometimes his voice descended to a sinister murmur.

But why did they love him? Perhaps it was his unwonted self-deprecation. Normally we would associate Peter Mandelson with self-criticism in the way we associate Victoria

Beckham with particle physics. False modesty is generally the only kind he knows. But yesterday he produced humility with added welly.

He talked about his shock and surprise when Gordon Brown invited him back into government, and his apprehension – 'returning to the goldfish bowl of British politics – and all my fans in the media!' He reminded us of his two resignations. He admitted ignoring people's susceptibilities: 'I made enemies, sometimes needlessly. I was sometimes too careless with the feelings or views of others.

'But please accept this … I was in a hurry to return this party to where it should be, in government.' So it was a politician's apology: 'If I have a failing, it is that I am too keen on our party winning.'

He had been born into the Labour party. 'So it is in my blood, and in my bones,' which made him sound like a mummy excavated from an ancient tomb. 'I love this party, and those who work so hard for it – even if, at times, perhaps not everyone in it has loved me.'

But what they liked best was the way that he offered them at least a sliver of hope. They were in the fight of their lives. They were the underdogs. 'But if I can come back, we can come back!' There were an awful lot of references to himself, but then that is a subject on which he can speak with real passion.

By the end he was yelling and shouting, raving at the Tories. Deep in his gut, he had known the result of every election before it happened, even in 1992 when he had expected Labour's surprise defeat. 'But this time it is not cut and dried. This election is up for grabs!'

No wonder they went berserk for him. Any kind of hope is preferable to despair, and a false dawn is better than no light at all.

The dreamlike atmosphere persisted with the leader's speech.

Brown came on to a storming ovation, which must have been a relief. But then the Labour conference loves Sarah, and she loves Gordon. 'I know he's not a saint,' before revealing that is exactly what he is. 'He's messy, he's noisy ... but he wakes up every morning and goes to bed every evening thinking about the things that matter ... intense, serious and gentle ... always takes the time for people ... and that's why I love him as much as I do ... my husband, my hero!'

I tried to imagine Denis Thatcher saying a similar thing about his life partner, but then my synapses started to make popping noises.

'It can only go downhill from here,' said my neighbour, as the paragon himself appeared on stage. In fact it started out quite well, with a highly selective list of Labour's 'achievements', some real enough, some dodgy, some downright dubious. But then we had just been shown a video in which the party appeared to take credit for JK Rowling's success.

The speech ended with a mad flight into the vague and intangible. 'Dream not small dreams, because they cannot change the world!' he said, misquoting Goethe. 'Dream big dreams, and watch our country soar!'

Good Lord, how big do our dreams have to be? I resolved to start dreaming enormous dreams, economy-sized dreams, dreams so huge they'll need a forklift to get me out of bed.

'Never, never stop believing!' he raved. 'Now is not the time to give in but to reach inside ourselves for the strength of our convictions!'

('Doctor, I have these terrible stomach cramps.'

'Hmm, looks as if you have the strength of your convictions blocking the lower intestine. We must operate fast. July 2012 any good for you?')

But there was a dreamlike quality to the whole speech. The gist of it was, that after 13 years, Labour wants a crack at government. Having constructed a short, sanitised version of a past that did happen, he launched into a future that probably never will: whimpering bankers flee from the wrath of the British people, grateful old folk get care at home, sinister sounding 'action squads' will sort out trouble-makers on problem estates, no more hereditary peers, a plebiscite on PR, and a strange Victorian notion of an institution for fallen women – a barracks for single teenage mothers. There will be 'family intervention projects' for the 'most chaotic' families. 'Blimey, it's the FIP man at the door. Put that spliff out, and get the dog out of the baby's tea.'

The whole fantasy, that Labour needs another term to get round to everything it didn't think of in 13 years, pleased the conference mightily. They are now going to go away and dream massive buy-two-get-one-free dreams and reach deep inside themselves, like the monster from *Alien*.

Afterwards I bumped into an MP for a now marginal seat. He was as gloomy as I've ever seen him. 'Go back to your constituencies and prepared to be...' at which point he described something very rude indeed.

As ever, the Tories followed Labour.

David Cameron has finally turned into Tony Blair. It's a project he's been working on for years, and now it's come to fruition. Oh, he attacked him all right – he has to – but it was brief, and some of us remember that this was the man who led the standing ovation when Blair walked out of the Commons for the last time.

We had the same breathless Blair build-up, with offstage voices and throbbing music, as if we were attending the launch of a mid-size family car. There was the on-screen appearance of Bono, obligatory now for all party conferences, sporting extraordinary eyewear that may have been Pierre Cardin welding goggles. There was the same somewhat limp delivery – Blair was always happier on a sofa than at a rostrum. If Barack Obama tried to get his audiences 'fired up, ready to go!' Blair and Cameron had them calm down, ready to catch the train home.

There were the same vague wish lists that didn't amount to promises. Whereas Blair conveyed a fuzzy, feelgood mood through verb-free sentences, Cameron used the formula: 'I see a country where ... [fill in benign aspiration without either a pledge that it will happen or the means by which it might].'

We had the almost subliminal pop culture references. 'There aren't many reasons to be cheerful' (Ian Drury). 'But there are reasons to believe!' (Rod Stewart). 'If we come together' (The Beatles), 'if we work together' (Canned Heat). This was rhetoric for people who still remember when music came on records rather than in downloads.

Actually, you could tell how the speech was going by watching the shadow cabinet, who were seated behind him, and able to admire his back. The ones immediately behind him appeared on the giant screens, so we could get a good look at the expressions on their enormous faces. Andrew Lansley was trying to look hard and determined. Chris Grayling and Liam Fox seemed puzzled. Ken Clarke, however, looked bored. The oyster eyes were narrowed, and at times he gave the impression of a man having a short kip.

And who can blame him? He must have heard dozens of these speeches, and you could tell he'd rather have been at Ronnie Scott's, in a hide by some bird-festooned fen, or propping up a bar – just about anywhere rather than where he was. At the big clap-lines – whenever the leader mentioned poverty the claque at the front rose to lead a mini-standing ovationette – the other ministers in waiting would clap energetically. Clarke by contrast would pause, then two hands would make brief and flabby contact. It was like two tired plaice engaged in foreplay.

As for Cameron himself, he did seem a little tired, unable perhaps to excite himself and so thrill the conference. Maybe the mood was set by the one personal reference, to the death of his son. 'It's like the world has stopped turning and the clocks have stopped ticking … you think about what you believe and what sustains you.' Hard to rouse a rabble after that.

Finally it was over, and he was joined by Samantha. The music struck up the Monkees' 'I'm A Believer', including the lines, 'What's the use in trying? All you get is pain. When I needed sunshine, I got rain…'

Not exactly the message the speech was trying to convey, but you can't blame him if he thinks that's what he's in for.

We later learned that Ken Clarke's main strategy for coping with long, dull speeches was to slip into the arms of Morpheus. In 2011 he napped through part of the Chancellor's budget speech, and during Barack Obama's address to parliament.

Meanwhile, the expenses scandal continued to drag on.

All round the Commons, MPs were trying to find ways to wriggle out of paying back their expenses. Many of them were outraged. It was, they said, 'against natural justice' to have to cough up money they'd received legitimately, in accordance with the rules.

And they are right. It is against natural justice. If I went round to someone's house and they said, 'Come on, mate, have a drink! Have loads of drinks! Sup up!' I'd be jolly offended if, months later, he put in a bill.

On the other hand, if you were being finicky, you might argue that it was against natural justice to expect taxpayers to fork out for your food, gardening, bath plugs, blue movies, moat-cleaning, hanging baskets, wisteria-stripping, laundry and mortgages, whatever the rules apparently said. But most MPs don't seem to agree.

Yesterday, in one of the many magnificently ironic moments that have marked this gruesome affair, Michael Martin, the former Speaker who presided over the whole farrago, and did his utmost to stop it from coming under the public gaze, was promoted to glory, or at least to the House of Lords.

Normally this is routine for any Speaker. But Mr Martin was the first Speaker to be forced out of office for 300 years, and the House of Lords Appointments Commission, which looks at all nominations for peerages, had told Number 10 that his arrival might damage the house's reputation.

No matter. Gordon Brown waved the objections aside, like a diner dismissing an unwanted bread roll. We all assume that the peerage was part of the tempting package that finally persuaded Mr Martin to quit.

You might have thought, to misquote Groucho Marx, that he wouldn't want to belong to any club that didn't want to have him as a member. But Mr Martin is clearly plated with the sheet metal that he used to work with, so yesterday afternoon we trooped in to see him, clad in ermine robes, shuffling towards the table of the house to hear the ancient, time-encrusted words: 'Elizabeth II, by the Grace of God of the United Kingdom … [the clerk somehow manages to pronounce the capital letters, which are used for every mention of Her Maj, rather like Jesus, or God.] Know ye, that We of Our especial grace, certain knowledge, and mere motion, do advance, create, and prefer Our trusty and well-beloved Michael John Martin…'

On and on he went. And this was the recent, short, New Labour version. '… And also that he may enjoy all the rights, privileges, pre-eminences, immunities and advantages to the degree of Baron…'

Now he was talking. Rights, privileges, pre-eminences, immunity and advantages! That's the kind of language Michael Martin understands.

Meanwhile, Helene Hayman, the Lord Speaker who sits on the Woolsack, maintained a distant glare. This was not a facial expression that cried 'Welcome!' She seemed an unhappy bunny, right up to the moment when the new Baron Martin walked past her and she managed a smile that might have lasted almost two seconds.

There was a sort of cheer from some of the lords and ladies, but it was polite and formulaic, quieter than any cheer I can recall for a new peer.

In October of 2009, the Guardian revealed that some pranksters had persuaded the tabloids to run several news items about celebrities that were completely untrue.

The story about the researchers who forwarded fake celebrity gossip to the papers struck a chord with me. But, I wondered, why did anyone think it was so new? It's been going on in the Commons for ages.

For example, someone rang the papers to say that Gordon Brown was going to crack down on the banks, to make them stop paying ridiculous bonuses and start lending money to businesses instead.

It should have been easy to check that was nonsense, but nobody did. It was picked up and run by papers all over the country. Another practical joker tried to claim that Harriet Harman was committed to cleaning up the parliamentary expenses scandal. If editors had the faintest interest in confirming the facts, they'd have known this was just another crazy invention!

As was proved yesterday. MPs had several sessions in the morning, including a lengthy slot in which they discussed their own affairs. This is usually a favourite topic, but yesterday it was anything but.

They considered whether deconsecrated churches could be turned into lap-dancing clubs. Sir Stuart Bell, who speaks for the church commissioners, deployed Ezekiel in support of the church's decision to concrete over 300 acres of fine agricultural land in Sussex, against the presumed wishes of the Archbishop of Canterbury, who wants us to be self-sufficient in food.

'They shall keep my laws and statutes,' said Sir Stuart, quoting God. 'We propose to keep our laws and statutes.' Sir Stuart is particularly fortunate among politicians, since he can quote the Bible, which gives support to almost everything, including slavery and stoning to death for wearing the wrong clothes.

It was fully 92 minutes before Douglas Hogg uncoiled himself and declared that Sir Thomas Legg's decision to rewrite the rules and demand money back from MPs was 'a denial of natural justice' and would be overthrown by the courts. He then slumped, eyes hooded, half in his seat, half falling towards the floor, looking in the end like a large fish that has just choked to death in a filthy moat.

The place fell very quiet. Harriet Harman, the leader of the house, umm-ed and ahh-ed. She recognised that the system had become discredited. But, she said, it all depended on the standards that had obtained at the time. 'To do anything else would be arbitrary'. And MPs had three weeks to appeal against any decision.

So it's all up in the air again. Making us think that she was going to take firm, decisive action was just another cruel spoof.

11 November 2009

During the 2009 Labour conference, the Sun *came out in favour of the Tories, for the first time in four elections. Desperate to justify its position, the paper kept dredging up fresh anti-Brown stories. They were not hard to find.*

It was excruciating. You would have needed a heart of Kevlar not to sympathise with Gordon Brown yesterday as he used his prime ministerial press conference to try to portray himself as warm, caring, capable of grief and fully hooked up to a human nervous system.

The prime minister has been caught in a ghastly trap by the *Sun*, which on Monday printed a letter he had written to the mother of a soldier killed in Afghanistan. It was full of spelling mistakes, apparently including her name – though this was difficult to tell since he has handwriting like a spider suffering from existential angst.

On Sunday night he had phoned the woman, Jacqui Janes, and contrived to use a call meant to express sympathy and regret to embroil himself in an argument. Mrs Janes told the newspaper: 'It sounded like he was trying to put me right, instead of making me feel better.'

Those of us who have followed Brown over the past two years know how she felt. But why do we connive to inflict such torment on our leaders? Watching him twist and turn in the gales of artificial rage from newspapers was awful. He is no good at soft, empathic, emotional. At least not in public. You sensed that some awful consultant had been drafted in and had told him to let it all hang out, Gordie baby. Let them see the real you, the egg inside the sausage meat!

So he did, or at least tried to do. 'I feel for a mother's grief. I understand the pain of her sadness. I understand very well the sadness that she feels, and the way she has expressed her grief is something I can clearly understand.'

He apologised for his handwriting, not just to Mrs Janes, but to anyone who had had to read it.

But how many ways are there of saying the same thing? 'I wanted to say, but couldn't because I did not know her, that when there is a personal loss it takes time to recover, that loss can never be replaced. You've got to take every day at a time,' he added. What he wanted to say, I assume, is that he had known similar grief when his infant daughter Jennifer died. But he could not say that, because more ordure would have been dumped on him.

There is no comparison, they would have said. No one is blaming you for her death. She didn't die because you declined to pay for that piece of equipment that might have saved her life.

Every answer came back to the same answer, the one he had to give, time and again. Had it anything to do, he was asked, with the general view the country held of him? Was it his unpopularity, the questioner meant but did not say, that was making people so cynical about the war in Afghanistan?

'I am a shy person,' he said – news to us – 'but I try to go round the country and debate about Afghanistan issues.' Then back to the leitmotiv: 'But I also do feel the pain of people who are grieving. I understand the sadness and anger sometimes of people who have lost loved ones...'

The whole thing was awful. He's not good at doing it, and we shouldn't make him do it.

Every year the Spectator *magazine hands out awards to various parliamentarians. The event is usually held at a posh hotel.*

Lord Mandelson was yesterday's big winner. (I wasn't a judge this year, so I'm not to blame. Others know who they are.) He received his award for politician of the year from Boris Johnson.

It was, said his lordship, a great honour. He was the first winner since 2006 not to have been a member of the Bullingdon Club. Then he added, 'This is another to add to the list of things I have in common with Boris. We both spent a long time in Brussels. We both had very public resignations. And we both have an overwhelming ambition to do everything we can to undermine David Cameron.'

From his right came a great sound of harrumphing and denial. 'Humph! No! No! harrumph!' cried Boris.

This protestation might have been slightly more convincing if it hadn't been for Boris's own speech a short while before. This took the form of a mock-heroic address to MPs, who had created a 'magnificent catastrophe' to distract the voters' attention from the banking scandal.

'How proud I am!' he said, addressing MPs, his former colleagues. 'I want to give you the most massive plug – but unlike Jacqui Smith I would not dream of claiming for it – for the chaotic, shambolic handling of the expenses scandal which has brilliantly directed media and public anger away from the financial services of London!'

Warming to his theme – and Boris never cools to any theme on which he has embarked – 'you resemble Leonidas and the

Spartans, or Clint Eastwood in *The Bodyguard*, standing in the path of public rage. You have taken the bullet for the bankers!'

Why, he said, it was marvellous that MPs should win all these *Spectator* awards. They would each need a trophy cabinet to display them all! This would go on their additional costs allowance. The cabinet might be so full that it could damage a wall. 'So,' he went on, 'it would be necessary to add a wisteria trimmer to the bill.'

Did he mention moat cleaning, or duck houses, or flat-screen televisions? No, he mentioned only wisteria trimming. And who is the only MP to have claimed for wisteria trimming? David Cameron. You would not need to be obsessed by politics, or even the control and maintenance of climbing plants, to understand what he was getting at. But we knew. That is Boris's genius. He always gets it both ways.

Most other award winners were just happy to get their gong and go. Ken Clarke, named with irony as 'newcomer of the year', said the judges had made an old man very happy. The Tory peer Lady Warsi was moving. She said she had also been voted sexiest member of the House of Lords, 'but in light of the fact that I still have my own teeth, that is not so extraordinary.

'But I am the daughter of a Pakistani immigrant mill-worker, and I ended up in the House of Lords!' We all applauded madly what a wonderful country she still thinks this is.

19 November 2009

It was Labour's last state opening of parliament.

I've been going to state openings, on and off, for decades. And they get weirder all the time. Obviously the Queen is a little older each year, and yesterday she seemed to have a sore throat, so her catchphrase, 'My lords, pray be seated,' was almost inaudibly whispered. But she's a trouper that girl, and the show always goes on.

The whole thing has a dreamlike, phantasmagoric, fairytale quality. The setting is out of some impossible fantasy, all red and gold, shimmering candelabras, scarlet and ermine, the vast double throne magnificent, gold-encrusted, yet curiously theatrical, as if they had bought it from Ikea and painted it.

What is Sir Alan Sugar, now Lorshugger, doing there? Why do the law lords sit lined up bottom to bottom? Lady Thatcher arrives, looking scary now, and you half expect her to hold out a rosy red apple to Snow White. The heralds and the pursuivants stand in a gaggle to one side. Their embroidered tabards are strangely flat and two-dimensional, so there's a temptation to shout, like Alice, 'You're nothing but a pack of cards!'

Familiar figures arrive for unfamiliar reasons, bearing unfamiliar titles. Harriet Harman is the lord privy seal. I once caught a radio item suggesting that Lord's cricket ground might sell its name to the highest bidder. But if Lord's, why not the Lords? She could be the Investec privy seal. Next to her was the RBS president of the council, or Peter Mandelson as we used to call him.

Next Her Majesty arrived and sat on the Habitat throne, her train flowing down the steps like the result of a terrible accident in a Bloody Mary factory. The Commons arrived, having been summoned by Black Rod. They were led by Gordon Brown, in his popular role as Baron Hardup. Back in 1997, the newly elected MPs sounded like a football crowd arriving at a match. Now they are quieter, perhaps bored or fearful. Jack Straw, the Tetley's lord high chancellor of England, knelt before his monarch, a position he has probably yearned to adopt since his days as the fiery head of the National Union of Students.

Then the speech, written as if with a shovel dipped in ink. It was a collection of wearisome clichés and clunking constructions, bunged together by a blind brickie. 'Ensuring individual entitlements'; 'sustainable paths'; 'introducing transparency in the workplace'. They say that if 100 monkeys had 100 typewriters, they would, in the course of eternity, produce the works of Shakespeare. This sounded as if 100 hippos had worked on it for all of 10 minutes. She reads it all out in a voice that goes beyond neutrality to a resonant distaste.

Mercifully the speech was short, though it too was dream-like. The deficit would be halved by law. Anti-social behaviour and gang crime (or 'geng crime' as the Queen pronounced it) were for the old heave-ho. And the maddest dream of all: the government would 'build trust' in parliament itself.

Suddenly it was all over, a fantasy Queen's speech packed with fantasy legislation. 'See you again in six months,' said an attendant, since a new government will need a new state opening, and a brand-spanking-new load of fantasy legislation.

David Cameron gave a press conference. Gosh, he is a perky person these days, now he can assume a good result in the coming election. Perky, perky, perky – and never once pinky. We are in line to have the perkiest ever premier. He gurgles and bubbles, like a coffee perky-lator. He perked his way to the front of the room and started talking about 'modern, progressive' Conservatives. In short, a perky party! 'We can make change happen!' he cried.

How would he do that? Well, there wouldn't be any vacuous pledge-card promises. Instead there would be top priorities. 'We will not be drowning in day-to-day fire-fighting!' he declared.

Or being burned to death by a 40-foot wave, he might have added.

Would he still hold a referendum on the Lisbon treaty if it had been ratified by all the EU nations when he came to power? That was a tricky one. But his perkiness did not desert him when he needed it most. 'If a new set of circumstances exists, then we will have to consider that!' he said. The Tories' new battle cry: 'Give us time to think!'

Then we got another exciting new word. He was asked several times if he supported Tony Blair for the new job of president of Europe. No, he didn't. They didn't want a president of Europe in the first place, but if they had to have one, they didn't want Tony Blair. The new president, he said, should have a 'chairmanic role'. A what? It almost rhymed with 'Germanic'. We stared wonderingly at each other. 'It means going mad, but in a seated position,' said my neighbour.

And why not Tony Blair? 'We don't need an all-singing, all-dancing, [brief pause] all-acting president,' he said. Then he repeated it. I could understand that. Who would want to become prime minister, and after all that time and effort, discover that Tony Blair is still more important than you? Gordon Brown found that out the hard way, and look what happened to him. And Gordon Brown these days is as perky as a natterjack toad dropping off to sleep.

'Europe seems to be heading in the direction of statehood,' Cameron said, 'and I think El Presidente Blair would be going in that direction.'

His tone on Europe, he insisted, was not a hostile tone. Just a hostile to Tony tone, it turns out. And with that, perkier than ever, he left us.

One of my favourite MPs has always been Sir Peter Tapsell, a man of immense grandeur whom I have always suspected of wearing three-piece pyjamas in bed. Sir Peter's interventions are always greeted with great cheers from the Labour benches, partly because they like the way he is quite prepared to attack his own frontbenchers, but mainly because they adore his magnificent style of speaking, as if at dictation speed for a team of monks who are illuminating his words as they are uttered.

I have just heard the gladsome news that Sir Peter Tapsell has been re-selected as Conservative candidate for the seat of Louth and Horncastle. It will be his 15th campaign, and he will probably be 80 years old. You can almost hear the huzzas ringing down from Lincolnshire!

What makes his victory especially unique is that as part of his 45-minute speech to the local Conservatives, he read out part of one of my sketches. This was from 2006, shortly after Tony Blair had claimed that God would judge him on Iraq. At the time I compared listening to Sir Peter speak to relishing performances by Alfred Brendel and George Best. I was tempted at the time to rework the old Tommy Cooper joke, and say that unfortunately George Best was a lousy pianist and Alfred Brendel can't play football. Luckily I didn't.

At the time Sir Peter had arisen in his pomp. A small foundry in Birmingham got to work preparing to cast his words in bronze for the enlightenment of future generations. He asked the then prime minister, Tony Blair, 'Will he tell us which archangel is now beckoning him towards southern Afghanistan?' No wonder, with questions like this, that even in this youth-crazed world, Sir Peter was re-selected.

Yesterday he was in his place listening to yet another statement on Afghanistan. Sir Peter believes that we should not have gone there in the first place, and that since the Soviets could not hold the place with 300,000 men, the extra 500 we are sending will not make the slightest difference.

Gordon Brown's statement required a certain understanding of metaphysics. The gist seemed to be that since our military intervention had been so successful we needed more troops to make it even more successful. And we should send extra men now, so that our boys could come home earlier. And the fact that several nations were threatening to take their troops out of Afghanistan meant that even more nations would be represented there soon. Hmm.

You can always tell when politicians are in trouble, because they start coining new clichés. 'We need a military surge, complemented by a political surge, which is essentially an Afghan political surge,' he said. Try picking the sultanas out of that cake.

Sir Peter did not arise straight away. Instead, he deployed body language, the Esperanto of the Commons, to express his deep dissatisfaction. He rested his hands on his lap, but in a very aggressive fashion, if you can picture that. He leaned forward and scowled. At one point he leant back, folded his arms, and looked, quite simply, furious.

The prime minister ploughed on regardless, deploying more of his weird pronunciations. 'Mastiff', the armoured car, turned into 'mas-teef' as if it rhymed with the French *canif*. Al-Qaida is not longer 'Alky Ada', the drunken old aunt at the party. She has become Al, Kay, Ada, a music-hall trio of the interwar years.

Finally Sir Peter erected himself and, to our disappointment, asked a question about Pakistan rather than Afghanistan. But his fans didn't mind. Our cup of joy was brimming already.

Gordon Brown went on a morale-raising, or possibly morale-lowering, visit to our brave lads.

There were two arresting pictures in yesterday's papers: Silvio Berlusconi, with bloodied face after an attack by someone brandishing a model of Milan's cathedral, and Gordon Brown in full armoured kit for his overnight visit to Afghanistan. Our prime minister appeared to be wearing two helmets, and looked extremely uneasy, proving once again that politicians should always be wary of donning military gear.

On the other hand, it would be a brave madman who attacked him with a souvenir building while he was clad in so much protective clothing. I wondered which ecclesiastical structure a British assailant might select. Salisbury Cathedral has the longest, thinnest spire, so would work as a stiletto. Westminster Abbey, with its square towers, would inflict blunter but still very unpleasant injuries. King's College Chapel is the weapon of choice for gangs, who favour the four sharp but shallower wounds it creates. And of course a 'St Mungo's Kiss' is street slang for an assault by Glasgow Cathedral.

Some MPs gave the impression yesterday that they would willingly attack Gordon Brown with almost any souvenir, even something labelled 'My prime minister went to Helmand province, and all I got was this lousy flak jacket.' Nick Clegg asked a perfectly good question. What, he asked Brown, did he make of his predecessor's announcement that he would have invaded Iraq even if he'd known there were no weapons of mass destruction?

Did he get a straight reply? Don't be daft. Brown didn't even try. There was an inquiry sitting, it would report, and that was that. The temptation for Clegg to lob over a scale model of Stonehenge, or even the real thing, must have been great, but was resisted.

David Cameron complained that Brown had wasted good time trying to get Tony Blair elected president of the EU, yet we had wound up without one British representative in an important economic position.

The prime minister did what he always does, which is to sit on the bench muttering imprecations, in the manner of one of Macbeth's witches working on a new recipe before trying it out on the other girls. 'Perhaps,' said Cameron, 'he can answer my question when he has finished chuntering from a sedentary position!'

But Mr Brown will never stop chuntering to himself. In decades to come, MPs will say, 'Gordon Brown must be chuntering in his grave at that news!'

The most savage attack came from Paul Flynn, a Labour MP, who described how 300 Afghan soldiers had fled from seven Taliban, having no motive to risk their lives for a corrupt, ballot-rigging president. Did the prime minister imagine that a security service could be built on these collapsing foundations?

This was the equivalent of getting York Minster, Blackpool Tower, Buckingham Palace and the London Eye right in the kisser, all at once.

Labour MPs returned from the Christmas recess with one important question on their minds: which was their favourite Miliband brother? Was it Ed, the one who looks like the manager of an upmarket Indian restaurant? Or David, who resembles Gavin from the TV series *Gavin and Stacey*? Could there be a mystery third brother, possibly Gummo Miliband, who left the act and went into agency work?

It is possible that none of these people will get involved in a putsch against Gordon Brown. But if they did, an important participant will undoubtedly be Lord Mandelson. We piled into the House of Lords to catch him.

It turned out that he was discussing the Queen's diamond jubilee, due in June 2012, when, it is fair to say, she is much more likely to be in charge than Gordon Brown. It seems that, *pro tem*, Mandelson has been put in charge of the festivities. You must wonder how they picked him.

'Look, chaps,' someone must have said, 'it's a big national celebration. We need someone with real flair, and a terrific capacity for organisation. How about that fellow who ran the Dome? What was his name?'

For the event, Mandy had transformed himself into a courtier – not a very great stretch. His voice simultaneously softened and rose half an octave. Words like 'seemly', 'gracious' and 'confer' slid off the Mandelson tongue. Sir Alan Fitztightly could hardly have sounded more deferential. 'Remarkable achievement … celebrating with great pride Her Majesty's 60 years on the throne…'

There was to be a jubilee medal. There would be a competition to find a new city, or rather to give city status to some place that had not already been citified. Greenwich in south-east London would become a 'royal' borough, which brings no money or even a new hospital, but was 'an exceptional mark of royal favour'.

There would be no link between the jubilee and the Olympic Games. For the Tories, Lord Hunt said that the jubilee was 'of sufficient moment in itself'. This courtier-speak is infectious. A pity about the missing link; the Queen taking part in the beach volleyball would have been a high spot for thousands of us.

Lord McNally for the Lib Dems was misty-eyed. He told the lord president, 'In the midst of the cold winter, you are a little ray of sunshine,' a phrase that I can guarantee has never, ever, been used about Mandelson before. Or will be in the future.

Then Mandy finally lost it, and disappeared forever up some imaginary royal fundament. It had been an extraordinary reign. 'As far as any human being can possibly be, she has been as near perfect during every single moment of that reign as any member of the human race could be!'

And covered in this velvet, hand-stitched duvet of royal admiration, we fled.

12 January 2010

The election campaign is well under way. The parties are rivalling each other by promising the most savage cuts. Alistair Darling has said that there will be grief on a scale beyond which none of us can imagine. David Cameron says no, the Tories will be much worse. It's the opposite of any politician's normal strategy, the equivalent of going around slapping babies.

Yesterday Nick Clegg joined in with a bonfire of Lib Dem policies. His pledge was to tear up all the party's previous pledges. Free childcare? Forget it! Scrapping tuition fees? No way! Citizens' pensions? Sayonara.

The problem with Mr Clegg is that he is adept at coining phrases that are so vivid that they stop you attending to the rest of the speech. It's like trying to go for a walk with a dog snapping at your shorts. 'Shopping lists and pledges just don't wash any more!' he said, and you find yourself disentangling that while thinking, 'No, Pledge is furniture polish, not washing powder.' The other parties, he said, were trying to buy favour with 'cheap trinkets'. But if they were cheap, we could afford them. Didn't he mean expensive trinkets? 'We must upend the status quo!' he announced and we pondered what that could possibly mean.

The only politician who isn't promising to pile misery upon misery is Gordon Brown. I caught up with him at a huge international educational conference in London. The prime minister was greeted by that throbbing electronic music which usually presages New Labour promises. It accompanied meaningless slogans projected on to giant screens. 'World-class teaching'; 'Enabling regeneration'; 'Re-imagining education'. It was a *son-et-lumière* version of a Tony Blair speech, all vague verb-free promises, accompanied by that throbbing 'plung, plung, pling' noise.

Gordon Brown seemed to go berserk. The prime minister announced that, thanks to the leadership shown by Britain (i.e. himself), Britain could now offer itself as 'an education super-power'. He went on, inexplicably, 'Already the UK sells more brainpower per capita than any other country in the world!' It sounded like the grit we need for our roads: urgent brain-power was being exported around the world.

But Lord Mandelson spoke entirely in jargon. At one point he denounced 'the lump of digital innovation fallacy'. What? That'll save the election for Labour. 'Good evening, sir, can we count on your support?'

'Not as long as you Tories continue to promulgate the lump of digital innovation fallacy.'

For much of 2010, the Chilcot inquiry took evidence from the leading players in the decision to go to war in Iraq. Among the most influential was Alastair Campbell, Tony Blair's mouthpiece and consiglieri.

Alastair Campbell looked taut and nervous when he arrived to give evidence to the Chilcot inquiry yesterday. Not for long, though. The guy is a pro. He's been doing this gig for years: the Hutton inquiry, the Butler inquiry, various House of Commons committees. You'd think he might still get stage fright, but if it does, it evaporates after the first exchange, to be replaced by an affable, fellow-me-lad camaraderie – with an underlying hint of violence.

Campbell is the modern version of those grandees who used to be known as 'the great and the good'. These days, politicians require someone to do their dirty work for them – the great and the bad – and he fits the bill perfectly.

By now he has evolved various techniques to stymie the committees before whom he is hauled. One is to talk at immense length, which is why yesterday's session lasted nearly five hours. Some of his answers were 300 or 400 words long, as if he was trying to bury the whole inquiry under verbiage, like a mountain of nutty slack. Ronald Reagan used to tell a story about a boy waking up on his birthday, to find a vast pile of manure in the yard. He starts digging gleefully through it, explaining, 'With all this dirt, there must be a pony!'

If Sir John Chilcot and his team can find the pony inside Campbell's evidence, then they will have done a magnificent job.

As I say, like all top performers he has strategies. You couldn't call them crowd-pleasers; more like question-shredders. There is the innocent 'who me?' appeal, accompanied by an opening of the arms, as if to show that he has nothing to hide.

This tactic is linked to his belief in the saintly figure of Tony Blair, who did nothing wrong, and probably could never have done anything wrong. He was 'someone of deep conviction and integrity, making the most difficult decision of his premiership'. Had he tinkered with the evidence to persuade the British people to follow him and George Bush to war? Absolutely not! He had hoped to avoid war right up to the moment it broke out.

Or take the September 2002 dossier with its notorious 45-minute warning. This was not a shameless piece of propaganda, or 'communication' as Campbell prefers to describe spin, but 'a genuine attempt to take the public into his confidence'. Had it been doctored? Heaven forfend! 'We did not question, override, rewrite, let alone the ghastly "sexed-up" phrase, the intelligence assessments in any way or at any time.'

Why, no one had paid any heed to the 45-minute claim until 'misleading reports' had emerged. Sir Lawrence Freeman, one of the inquiry members, pointed out drily that some tabloids had greeted the claim at the time with huge headlines, such as 'Brits 45 Minutes From Doom', so it had attracted at least some attention beforehand. But Sir Lawrence was the only inquisitor who sounded consistently sceptical. We know Sir John Chilcot doesn't want to turn his inquiry into a bear pit, but Campbell must have felt he was being interrogated by a teddy bears' picnic.

One of his most effective ploys is to condemn the media, with extravagant scorn, for even suggesting that he might have been mistaken.

14 January 2010

Business in the Commons went on much as usual, though the more dramatic events of the Chilcot inquiry were taking place in a modestly sized room in the nearby Queen Elizabeth Conference Centre a two-minute walk away. Around the same time the Tories unveiled a portrait of David Cameron that appeared to show him with the most astonishingly smooth skin. This in turn led to Steve Bell drawing him with a tightly fitting condom over his head. The condom, and the 'teat' or reservoir at the top, caused much displeasure to the opposition leader who told Bell 'you can push the condom too far, you know', which is good advice in life as well as political cartooning.

Prime minister's questions got off to a bad start, then went bonkers. A Tory, Bill Wiggin, started by saying that we in Britain had one of the largest budget deficits of any first world economy. 'Does the prime minister regret that?'

'No,' said Gordon Brown. It was a 'have you stopped beating your wife?' question, unanswerable on its own terms. What he wanted to say was, 'No, because we have the second lowest debt of any G7 country.' This is pure creative accounting, like saying you're not in debt at all – except for the £250,000 mortgage, which doesn't count.

David Cameron asked two questions about preparations for the freezing winter to come. Mr Brown replied at interminable length. I was reminded of Nye Bevan, who said, approximately: 'This island is made largely of salt, and is surrounded by sand. Only an organising genius could create a shortage of both salt and sand at the same time.'

The prime minister replied that there were now depots where salt could be obtained. These were known as 'salt cells', rather like 'pepper grinds' or 'ketchup botts'. People laughed, disbelievingly. Things were turning surreal.

Mr Brown mocked the new poster of David Cameron. Admittedly this does look as if a small boy had been playing Mr Potato Head with a piece of veal. 'You look very different from the poster we see,' said the prime minister, adding that the Tories had the posters, while Labour had the policies.

Mr Cameron then pulled a stunt that no MP should have fallen for. 'When it comes to Labour members' election addresses, who is going to put the prime minister's picture on the front?'

This is technically known in the trade as a heffalump trap, as in *Winnie the Pooh*. It comes clearly marked with a flashing neon sign, saying 'Heffalump Trap'. Four Labour members, all with less common sense than Pooh bear, fell into the trap and raised their hands. Huge mistake.

Mr Cameron gloated. 'Six of them don't want him in the cabinet, and just four are going to put his picture on their election addresses! He is being airbrushed out of the campaign.'

The Tory leader wound up by saying that the Labour party were 'too disloyal to support the prime minister, but too incompetent to remove him'.

The last, feeblest and wettest reply came from Gordon Brown. 'I must say that your airbrushed poster had better lines on it than the lines you are delivering.'

The rest of what he said was drowned by happy Tory jeers.

Yesterday the prime minister admitted that he had got something wrong. It was amazing. And slightly embarrassing. The prime minister doesn't do errors. Like Dr Johnson's woman preacher, or a dog standing on its hind legs, the picture is neither convincing nor appealing.

The rest of us spend our lives acknowledging that we've miscalculated or have been misinformed. ('I am sorry; when I said it was the 73 that went past Marks & Spencer, I meant the 37. Silly mistake. I hope it didn't delay you too much.')

And of course when he does get it wrong, he has to find a way of saying that it's not *wrong* wrong, more a sort of right wrong. ('You will have noticed that, while the digits were in the reverse order, they were the correct digits. The opposition should stop complaining about such trivial matters and ask questions about their constituents' concerns.')

The startling moment came when a Tory backbencher asked why he had said that, under him, defence expenditure had risen in real terms every year when the House of Commons library – a source which MPs regard as being as wise as the Oracle at Delphi and a good deal more reliable – said it wasn't true.

Mr Brown had his reply ready, but he wasn't happy reading it out. He can't stand eating his own words, and wouldn't even if they were to be washed down with a magnum of Dom Perignon. He assumed the low, confidential mumble he has used ever since he was accused of bullying. But he stuttered a lot, threw in plenty of 'ers' and had to repeat the words 'I do accept' as if to convince himself.

The Tories were thrilled, not least because Brown had given the wrong information to the Chilcot inquiry, and has had to write to Chilcot to set the record straight, at least straightish. But even when our prime minister gets it wrong, he needs us to know that, deep down, he has got it right. Defence spending had indeed risen every year in cash terms. 'Because of operational fluctuations in the way the money is spent … in real terms it is 12 per cent higher, but I do accept that in one or two years defence spending did not rise in real terms.'

In other words, what he had lost on the roundabouts, he had gained on the swings. He was eating his words in the way that a child might eat broccoli – with some difficulty and much resentment.

David Cameron leapt down his throat. In three years of asking questions he had never heard the prime minister make a correction or a retraction. (And you won't hear another in a hurry, I thought.)

But then the Tory leader blew it. He called upon British Airways cabin crew to march through the picket lines and keep the airline flying. Suddenly we were back in 1926 and the General Strike, when thousands of public schoolboys manned the buses and dustcarts. Cameron and Osborne, in morning dress, will be pushing the Bolly trolley down the aisle and apologising if the lobster and caviar option is not available. Instead of instructing 'doors to manual' the captain will say, 'All right, chaps, time to sport your oak!'

7 April 2010

Finally the election was upon us.

You can tell something important might be happening when College Green, the patch of grass opposite parliament with a view of Big Ben, becomes a tent town, rather like an Italian city after an earthquake. You half expect Silvio Berlusconi to appear and tell everyone they're having a camping holiday.

The tents are for the broadcasting organisations, who will spend the next month pumping out predictions, judgments, rambling guesswork and a small dollop of what might loosely be called information. There are scores of tourists too, wandering round taking pictures of people they don't recognise but who might turn out to be important.

In fact they're not – they are journalists, pollsters, political aides and MPs, all waiting their turn at the makeshift steps that could be leading up to a gallows. There are kindly young women with clipboards, whose main job is to stop you from running away. 'I'm afraid Mr Pierrepoint is rather busier than we expected today, but he's got just one more hanging before you, so we'll have you out in a jiffy. Promise!'

All round Westminster politicians and cameramen are chasing round after each other like puppies, the politicians afraid of missing the TV and the TV afraid of missing them. None have the faintest idea of what, in the event of either party winning, their policies will be. Or if they do know, they're not letting on, for fear the public will be frightened.

So they speak very cautiously and use as few words as possible. The words they dare to use are 'hope', 'future', 'fairness' and 'change'. Especially 'change', a word they can use over and over again in a single speech without having the least notion of what it might turn out to mean.

The Liberal Democrats have a slogan, 'Change that works for you'. If it were possible, the Tories have one that means even less: 'Vote for change'. Labour is, for obvious reasons, wary of asking for change (though two and a half years ago Gordon Brown walked into Downing Street saying, 'Let the work of change begin.' Now his unspoken slogan is, 'That's quite enough change for now, thank you very much.')

But Brown does have a new book out, a collection of his speeches entitled *The Change We Choose*. It is not a rattling good read.

David Cameron launched his campaign from the balcony of the old County Hall, just across the river from Westminster. 'Vote for change' banners streamed in the sun. Mr Cameron had arrived equipped with a wife and a selection of sparkly new clichés. 'Let's get off this road to ruin, and get on the path of prosperity and progress! Let us win this election for the country we love!' (Possibly by that he meant Belize, where one of his party treasurers is domiciled.)

The word 'future' lodged in his brain like a wasp in a jam jar. 'It is about the future of our economy, the future of our society, the future of our country!' What, no mention of change? 'Real change can take place!'

In Downing Street Gordon Brown was flanked by a couple of dozen people described to us as 'the cabinet'. Some we recognised; others might as well have been passing tourists.

Earlier Nick Clegg had appeared in front of the cameras. He told us what inspired him. Was it tax breaks for the wealthy? Was he trying to attract voters who believed that everything was already for the best in the best of all possible worlds? Apparently not. 'People want fairness and real change … We will bring about that real change Britain needs, change that works for you. Our change is change that will make a difference.' As opposed, I suppose, to change that changes nothing at all.

In a nearby alley I found a beggar. I feared he would ask for some 'change that works for you, mate.' I gave him one penny. It was the least I could do.

(Sorry, old joke. Actually I gave him 50p.)

It was the crucial press conference for Gordon Brown. The Tories were making the running with their claim that national insurance increases would lead to lost jobs. Things were this bad: the prime minister told us that he loved his wife. It took some doing. In fact it had to be dragged out of him like a recalcitrant tapeworm. So at least there is one vote in Downing Street that's in the bag.

We assembled under Labour's new poster. This shows the sun coming up over a flat field of wheat. It is no doubt meant to symbolise warmth and lush prosperity, though it reminded me of the field in *North By Northwest*, where Cary Grant is strafed by a crop duster.

Gordon Brown arrived. He was smiling that terrible smile, the one that says: 'This is going to hurt me more than it hurts you, and you're not going to like it either.'

He was introduced by Lord Mandelson, who was on chirpy form. The Tories claimed they could cut £12 billion in public spending, 'just like that!' It was the old Tommy Cooper line. 'I can't recall your name, but the fez is familiar.'

Alistair Darling, the chancellor, hurled statistics at us. I felt like Cary Grant as the figures flew past. One of them was 10.5 billion. Another was 381,000. There was a slight air of desperation about them. Somehow they hope against hope, if they can hit us with enough facts and figures, we will work it out for ourselves. They handed out a leaflet. It was full of statistics and graphs that candidates will be encouraged to use on the doorsteps. Thus: 'DCFS, DECC and FCO are all saving millions by outsourcing back office services. And MoJ is introducing a new shared service centre for HR, finance and procurement transactions. Think on't before you vote.'

'You can't spend money twice,' the chancellor intoned. Why not? Gordon Brown did it for more than 10 years.

The recovery, Brown said, was 'robust but fragile'. What, like a plastic Ming vase? Or a filigree breezeblock? How could it possibly be both?

Then came the question that almost stumped him. Why was his wife playing almost as much part in the campaign as he was? He hadn't expected that. 'My, my, my wife Sarah and I are travelling round the country together. I made a statement to that effect.'

'A statement to that effect.' Not since Prince Charles asked if he was in love and replied 'whatever love is' has anyone sounded less romantic in public. The prime minister realised that something was missing. 'I really enjoy the fact that Sarah is with me. She is the one who warns me not to smile at people.'

No, of course he didn't say the last bit! I made that up, but it would be very helpful if it were true.

The hacks were determined to get some kind of confession out of Mr Brown. David Cameron had called Samantha 'my secret weapon'. Was Sarah his? Finally we extracted it. 'She is the love of my life,' he said. But immediately he must have felt that he had gone too far. He started to row back. 'We work well together. And we are enjoying the campaign.'

Before it could get any worse, Peter Mandelson interrupted. 'There you are,' he said, 'isn't that nice?'

14 April 2010

The Tories launched their manifesto in the now semi-derelict Battersea power station, site of the Pink Floyd album cover with the flying pig. They have put a glass-topped atrium inside the old building. You look out on a desolate scene, the crumbling structure held up by props and girders, looking as if one of the great chimneys might collapse at any moment, killing off half the party. It has a melancholy grandeur, as if someone had put a conservatory inside Tintern Abbey. Pigeons dive-bombed us, narrowly missing the glass.

The Conservatives had assembled dozens of ordinary people on stage and sprinkled members of the shadow cabinet among them, so that a member of the public might find him or herself sitting next to a household name, such as Theresa Villiers, or Owen Paterson, or Jeremy Hunt, or that other bloke. How thrilling to be able to go home and say: 'I was chatting away only this morning to – Grant Shapps!' and get the delighted reply, 'Who?'

Sam Cameron arrived and was cheered for just being her. But there is something about the Tories. They don't do excitement. The audience – media on one side, party members on the other – were up for inspiration. What they got was the shadow cabinet. By the end you could almost hear the groans as another well-meaning functionary rose to burble on, or they announced yet another dreary video, about schools or national insurance rates.

There was a video. Julie from Llandudno was depicted making her breakfast, just like David Cameron in his first Webcameron broadcast. They even had a close-up of her dashboard as she drove her children to school, to prove she was inside the speed limit. Former Labour voters for safer roads!

What is this patronising nonsense? Are we supposed to say, 'Gosh, she's just like us – a housewife, mum, charity volunteer and careful driver. It's the Tories for me this time!'

George Osborne spoke. I have finally worked out who he sounds like. Close your eyes next time you hear him speak, and it's Ann Widdecombe. Try it next time he's on TV.

Finally David Cameron introduced the Conservative manifesto, which is a dark blue hardback and looks like a tombstone. The theme is that the next government can save money by getting people to do the work themselves, whether it's taking planning decisions, holding elected representatives to account, saving local pubs and post offices, appointing the chief constable, checking wasteful public expenditure online or founding new schools. This is to be known as the Big Society.

'It's about we, the people!' said Mr Cameron, with great conviction but terrible grammar.

Gosh, life is certainly going to be busy if the Conservatives win the election. Luckily their campaign against waste means that there will be mass sackings. Otherwise nobody would have time to do everything the Big Society demands of us.

8.00am   Get up, discover that transport department has spent £40 on 'consultancy'. Write furious letter.

9.30am   Support Mr Patel at post office by buying premium bonds and Romanian wine, two for £3.99.

11.30am   Picket police station, demanding resignation of chief constable.

1.00pm   Lunch. Help keep local pub open by eating Ginster's microwaved steak pie washed down with five pints.

2.30pm   Smash Mr Patel's windows as warning to him not to serve booze to under-16s.

3.30pm   Establish new school.

4.30pm   Veto council tax rise online.

6.00pm   Break to watch *Eggheads*.
7.30pm   Sack local MP, just for the hell of it.
8.30pm   Stand for mayor.
10.00pm   Have second thoughts about local MP. Unsack him.
10.30pm   Bed.

The scariest moment came when Andrew Lansley, the shadow health minister, said: 'You want to be your own boss, and you can with us.'

What does this mean? Do-it-yourself operations? 'The procedure you need at the time you want it. All you require is a sharp knife and a mirror...'

15 April 2010

Vince Cable referred to himself as the Elephant Man yesterday, which may have been a mistake. The original Elephant Man was hideously ugly, led a life of unrelieved misery, and was jeered at by boys in the street. Of course, this is true of most MPs, though not, on the whole, Vince.

The Lib Dem economic spokesman was speaking at the launch of their manifesto in the UK headquarters of Bloomberg, the financial news service. It's a startling building, with floors lit from beneath in fluorescent colours, computer screens everywhere, and conference halls with glass walls.

Through one of these I observed the real British economy, as a dozen or so young persons gazed at a PowerPoint screen on which appeared messages in a language faintly reminiscent of English. 'AIM is fully pre-populated with Bloomberg data and integrated with core Bloomberg functionality and analytics,' it read. 'Client site functionality released weekly to all clients ... comprehensive audit trail...'

The last three words made a sort of sense, and it was the theme of the launch. The Lib Dems are trailing their comprehensive audit of public spending. It is as woolly as only a party that has little hope of taking power could produce, a sort of ImpotencePoint presentation.

Vince spoke first. He is playing the role of wife to Nick Clegg, since he is his constant companion, and like Sam and Sarah more popular than the chap he's with. He said that government finance was the elephant in the room. You couldn't banish the elephant; you had to confront it. 'I guess I'm the elephant man,' he said. This had the air of an impromptu joke that he might live to regret.

213

There was another beast to be confronted – the mouse in the aircraft hangar, perhaps. The party's cost-cutting programmes amount to surprisingly vague aspirations matched to improbably precise figures. For example, 'cutting economic cost of mental health programmes through better treatment' will save £425 million next year. 'Prison reform' will save £845 million in 2014-15. And best of all, 'cutting cost of politics' will save £635 million in 2013-14. Not £600 million, not £650 million! You just know that some teenager with a computer has crunched a whole set of fantasy figures together and totted them up.

Why not add 'nicer behaviour by everyone', saving £865 million? Or 'more fruit and fibre in diet improves nation's health, saving £1.283 billion on NHS bill'? Or even 'neighbours rescuing pets from trees enables less expensive fire service'?

If Labour or the Tories had tried this on, they would have been torn apart like a wounded elephant being attacked by a hungry lion.

Nick Clegg addressed us. He stood in a curious way. For some of the time his right hand was waving through the air to emphasise what he was saying, while his left hand stayed firmly in his pocket. So there was a line down the middle. Half of him might have been Lenin haranguing a crowd, the other half waiting his turn at the snooker table.

It was all about fairness. 'Four steps to a fairer Britain ... so you know what fairness feels like.' He made it sound like a fabric softener. There was one curious omission. If we had a hung parliament, would he back the party with the most seats or the most votes? This could be important.

Mr Clegg may be all in favour of candour and transparency, but he wasn't answering that. 'Both,' he replied, before he scurried off to Oldham.

We now know the answer to that last question. Of course once the Lib Dems did get their feet under the cabinet table, most of their promises evaporated, of necessity.

This election was the first in which the party leaders debated with each other on television. The first debate, held in Manchester, was the start of that brief phenomenon, Cleggmania.

In the end, the debate was livelier than any of us had the right to expect. After a start as stiff as a starched dress shirt, the three men got stuck into each other, talking over each other, chipping in and barracking, so that the poor moderator, Alastair Stewart, trying and usually failing to shut them up, sounded like a racing commentator: 'Mr Brown, Mr Cameron, Mr Brown now, Mr Nick Clegg! Briefly, Mr Brown!'

All three were wearing dark suits with the appropriately coloured ties. They looked like the villains in a Quentin Tarantino film, lined up in the bar after the heist.

The first historic question was asked by Mr Gerald Oliver, a retired toxicologist. I hoped it would be 'what's your poison?' but instead it was about immigration.

Delicate stuff, but Gordon Brown moved in confidently. He talked about a chef he had met somewhere or other, the first of dozens of people they've encountered in the campaign who, wonderfully, reflect their policies. 'Let's be honest with each other,' he said, which is politician-talk for 'let's all agree with me.'

Nick Clegg's strategy was to make the two big parties sound drearily identical. 'The more they attack each other, the more they sound the same!' he remarked in a pre-digested and regurgitated soundbite.

But he was the one who spent most time gazing straight at the viewers rather than the audience in the hall. He looked mournful, as if appealing for news about his children's missing puppy.

He said that immigrants should be allowed only if they worked in regions where they were needed, and didn't move elsewhere. David Cameron riposted with the historic first joke. 'Will they have border posts on the M62?' he asked.

At this point the audience, expressly forbidden to cheer, jeer, clap or even laugh, was looking somewhat stunned. Viewers at home could switch off or over. Or even go to the loo. But this lot had spent hours queuing to get in, and now they were stuck.

Then law and order. Clegg said that short sentences turned prisons into colleges of crime. Cameron said that his mother had been a magistrate and had dished out loads of short sentences. So Clegg was attacking his dear old mum! Things were turning nasty, which was hopeful.

At this point, Brown deployed a battery of soundbites, each of which had the smell of a spin doctor sprayed all over it. 'David, I'm grateful to you for putting up all those big posters because they show me smiling. So I'm very grateful to you – and Lord Ashcroft.'

Cameron shot back with a question. 'This is not question time, it's answer time, David,' said Brown. 'You can airbrush your answers but you can't airbrush your politics,' another line that might have sounded better if it hadn't been so obviously microwaved.

By now they were getting tired, as if they had all switched onto autopilot. In the media room, the spin doctors were at the back, telling us how dazzling their man had been before he had even finished being dazzling. Brown tried another little joke: 'At least, we weren't up against *The X Factor* or *Britain's Got Talent*!' Of course they weren't; they're on ITV too.

We clustered round the television to discover the result of the instant poll. 'Gassy material being ejected high into the atmosphere – and it could go on for days!' said an expert. It turned out to be the Icelandic volcano.

Then the result: Clegg was the clear winner with the public. But still no news of that missing puppy.

Cleggmania began to cool down almost as soon as it had begun, no doubt helped by some extraordinarily vicious 'reporting' in the Conservative press. The second debate was in Bristol.

The three party leaders threw themselves into last night's debate as if competing in the Olympic luge. They didn't talk; they gabbled. They weren't debating so much as downloading. Brown and Cameron had clearly been told to gaze into the camera in the same soulful way that Clegg had done last week. They did so much gazing that it became fairly clear that they weren't actually listening. Like pub bores, they were just waiting for their turn.

Exactly seven minutes after the debate was over, we had the instant poll: Cameron was the winner, Clegg came second, and Brown was, as before, last. Meaningless, of course: you might as well decide a football match by the result of the fans' votes.

Brown kicked off with a fine display of fake abnegation. He is the peacock of false modesty. 'If it's all about style and presentation, count me out!' he said. (Translation: I am too straight, too honest.) 'Like me or not, I can deliver!' (Tr: everybody hates me, I don't care.)

But the two big party leaders are in a bind. Clegg is simultaneously the most liked and the most reviled man in Britain. ('Kiss goodbye to your kidneys if Clegg wins power' – Tory press, *passim*.) Yet they couldn't assail him head-on because they would look like bullies. So they attacked him ferociously by the cunning stratagem of being nice to each other. 'I never thought I would utter these words, but I agree with Gordon,' said Cameron. (Tr: we are distinguished statesmen, able to agree over the head of this callow schoolboy.)

But none of Brown's advisors have got rid of that ghastly smile. He wagged and dipped his head, while putting on that truly ghastly grin, as if he were channelling the Joker.

Cameron has clearly been told that his favourite phrase, 'the Big Society', isn't working, because nobody knows what it means. So last night it became 'the big and strong society'. Tomorrow it may become 'the big, strong and very long society', because, like Andrex tissue, it does an important job without actually hurting you.

There were moments of hilarity, none of them intentional. Clegg had to show that he was no Euro-patsy. He had to find ways of doing the EU down. Why, he said, it had taken them 15 years to find a definition of chocolate. It could be a new insult: 'You frog-eating, goose-stepping, chocolate-defining Europhile!'

But it was Brown who uttered the first real porkie. Cameron wanted to repatriate the social chapter. 'That's what gives us paid holidays,' he announced. Cameron let the implication – Tories would abolish holidays – whizz past his head.

First pre-planned gag: Brown said of the other two, 'They remind me of two young boys squabbling together at bathtime!'

'That sounded better in rehearsal,' said someone, perhaps Clegg, but we didn't really care.

First double entendre: Clegg said we had clout in trade talks because the EU was the world's largest economic bloc. 'And to coin a phrase, size does matter!' (Roy 'Chubby' Brown, your job is safe.)

First attempted use of embarrassing demotic: Brown said on Trident, 'I say to you, Nick, get real!' Cameron must have liked that, because he too told Clegg to 'get real'. But in a very caring way.

Most heart-tugging story: Clegg had discovered pensioners who use their free passes to spend all day riding on a bus, just to keep warm. And as Brown pointed out, the Tories have not guaranteed to keep free bus passes, so pitching these old folk out on to the freezing streets.

There was a spat about some Labour leaflets that Cameron suggested were full of wild exaggerations of Tory policies. But it flew past. They had no time to waste on discussion – this was a debate!

Most enigmatic remark: Clegg on the crisis in the Catholic Church: 'You can't keep a lid on sin.'

Cheekiest claim: Gordon Brown demonstrating his green credentials by pointing out that during the election campaign he had taken only one plane. So was that why the airspace is closed? And neither of the other two picked him up, because nobody was listening – just talking.

The nurses Gordon Brown was addressing must have felt as if they were being hosed down with maple syrup. And added treacle. I know the prime minister needs every vote he can get, and he seems to be aiming to win them with a combination of flattery, praise, acclamation, eulogy and thick whipped cream.

He was at the Royal College of Nursing annual congress in Bournemouth, addressing the most wonderful people in the known universe.

He started slowly: 'The work you do expresses to the world not only the greatness but also the goodness of our country.'

He cranked up into second gear. 'I am here with Sarah to say from the bottom of my heart words not always associated with politicians, the two most important words in the English language: "Thank you."' He liked the sound of that, so he said it again: 'Thank you.' Then once again, presumably from underneath the bottom of his heart, just above his liver.

Next came some heartwarming stories about folk who had been ill, and were now cured. 'The parents whose children have been tended by loving nurses, who treat their precious child as if it were their own.' A Tory had attacked the NHS and millions of people had gone on the internet to say: 'We love the nurses of the NHS!' Yum! Raspberry sauce!

'I am here with Sarah not just to say thank you from our family, but thank you from millions upon millions of families.'

He became lyrical. The speech had clearly been written by a frustrated poet, or a junior employee of Hallmark Cards. 'You make the difference not just between sickness and health, but also between pain and comfort, between loneliness and friendship, sometimes between despair and hope.'

I have to report that some nurses began to look a shade uneasy at these encomia. But we Gordon-watchers had an idea of what was coming, and it did. 'We have been in the presence of angels dressed in nurses' uniforms.' Angels! Cherubim and seraphim flying round the wards, performing 'amazing works'. By now they must have felt they were squelching their way through Tate & Lyle's finest, topped with chopped nuts and chocolate sprinkles.

I feared he was going to burst into song, and he nearly did. 'I asked Lesley Garrett to Downing Street and that evening, in front of nurses who had served the NHS all their lives, she sang "The Impossible Dream" … "to right the unrightable wrong",' he added (though not the line about 'to be willing to march into hell' – that comes on 7 May).

The prime minister continued: 'The truest measure of the society is not the size of its wealth, but the width of its generosity, the breadth of its humanity and the depths of its compassion.'

The saintly compassion of nurses caused him to thump the podium. Everything the government had done, every penny spent, would have been worth it 'just to keep one person alive. Because if you save one life, you change the world.' (Not very good value for all those billions, perhaps.)

'You are our country's heroes. And you are mine!'

The standing ovation was a while in coming – around two-thirds finally stood up – and there were some embarrassed grins.

But by then they must all have felt extremely sticky, covered with ice cream, honey and meringue.

Cleggmania was short-lived.

Nick Clegg spoke to students at Oxford Brookes yesterday. They seemed a bright and eager bunch. You could look around the hall – it was packed with hundreds of undergraduates, with scores of them standing round the walls – and know for an absolute fact that not one of them will ever be recruited for the Bullingdon Club.

They really wanted to love the Liberal Democrat leader. When our dazzling bus pulled in (it also has standing room only: the party expected a handful of hacks but now reporters have come from all round the world) they lined the path and cheered him. The ones in the hall cheered too. But not for very long.

He has a terrific gift for sedating people. If you were bitten by a snake and had to lie still until the serum arrived, he could save your life by telling you his thoughts on banking regulation.

He likes to cover all the bases. Some politicians offer nothing but sound-bites. Clegg serves you an all-you-can-eat sound buffet.

He has been compared to Barack Obama. But I have seen Barack Obama perform and there are key differences. For example – inspiring Barack Obama slogans: 'Yes, we can!' and 'Fired up! Ready to go!'

Inspiring Nick Clegg slogan: 'Now if I may make a third point here...'

The American presidential candidate he most reminds me of is Michael Dukakis, who also appeared to assume that the voters were taking notes. If the students were expecting an exam paper on, say, Lib Dem policy concerning the murderous exploitation of raw materials in the Congo ('alert the world to what is going on … have media highlight the plight of people … bring pressure to bear through the EU…') they would have sailed through.

They were begging to be uplifted. And he started well. 'How many of you are registered to vote?' Almost every hand rose. 'That's a North Korean-style election!'

That got a laugh. 'Our manifesto, great bedtime reading, it's so stimulating that you won't be able to go to sleep!' That got a faint titter.

There were good lines: 'the industrial-scale destruction of our civil liberties' or 'it's only a small cross next Thursday, but it's a big opportunity'; 'how can debt be the answer to debt?'

But most of the questions led him on a random ramble. Asked if a Lib Dem government would compensate Iraqi widows and orphans, he couldn't say 'Now? Are you mad?' so he said that he hadn't actually put money aside for the purpose.

Suddenly we were off down memory lane, how the Lib Dems had opposed the war, why he didn't like the Chilcot inquiry, how it was only because of him that Gordon Brown had given evidence … You could almost hear the air hissing out of his balloon.

On the NHS he wouldn't shut up, finally saying that you could save money on managers. Ten minutes earlier he had said it was a 'fantasy' that you could save cash on bureaucratic waste. So which was right?

One courteous young man remained standing while his question was being answered. 'You're staying standing because you're so dumbfounded by that reply!' Clegg said, and that got another laugh. But it was a little close to the bone.

224

While Clegg was in Oxford, Gordon Brown was in Rochdale, where he was bearded by one Gillian Duffy, a local housewife, who asked him about immigrants 'flocking over here'. He got back into his car, not realising that his mic was live and he was broadcasting to the world a private conversation in which he called Mrs Duffy, a Labour supporter, 'that bigot'. When the tape was played to him during a radio interview he buried his head in his hands and promptly went round to Mrs Duffy's house to apologise in person. The apology lasted one hour. One theory was that he had thought that instead of saying 'flocking' she had said 'fucking', so making a reasonable inquiry sound like a racist rant.

It was widely assumed at the time that this one remark had cost Labour the election. But in the event Labour recaptured Rochdale from the Lib Dems. They know Mrs Duffy's type up there – stern, determined spunky old ducks, and know very well they can take a lot worse than Gordon Brown dishes out.

The day after this event, the third and final debate took place in Birmingham.

There was one question when the last debate began yesterday: how would Gordon Brown get out of his Gillian Duffy moment? Would he bring her on stage and give her a big old hug? Hardly. Perhaps he would make a self-deprecatory remark. Nah. Gordon doesn't do self-deprecatory.

What he does is faux candour: 'There's a lot to this job, and as you saw yesterday, I don't get all of it right. But I do know how to run the economy, in good times and bad.' The message was clear. I may go round insulting blameless old ladies. But if you don't want this country to be like Greece, with mobs attacking the police and burning cars, then you must vote for me.

The atmosphere was nerve-snappingly tense. The spin doctors, who last night were mostly frontbenchers – I even recognised some of the Tories – looked tired and drawn. They all knew this was their last chance. It was as if the cup final were to be decided a week before the match. 'Wasn't David/Nick/Gordon brilliant? Oh, sorry, that's my brief for afterwards.'

All three leaders were staring straight into the camera, the trick that did so well for Nick Clegg in the first debate. It was alarming to watch. Each one was trying to create a sort of golden glower. But what makes Clegg look good is his air of melancholy pathos. It's as if he's saying, 'When I took that candy from the baby, it was an error of judgment which I freely acknowledge. And anyway, babies don't like the purple ones.'

His strategy was clear – a plague on both your mansions. 'Let's move away from these party political points!' he cried, to snickers from the media centre. It's the old declension, 'He is a liar. You make party political points. I lay out the facts as they are.'

Clegg scored a hit, when they let rip against the bankers. Birmingham is the home of Cadbury's, now sold to the Americans. 'When you lent money to the banks, did you know they would use it to destroy British jobs?'

The end, thank heavens, was near. All three were desperately trying to make the other two sound barking mad. 'This is the old style of politics, making misleading claims,' said Clegg, as if no Lib Dem had ever uttered an untruth. Then the final statements, which were almost identical. But British politics has changed forever. Why tour the country and risk bumping into other Gillian Duffys when you can do it all on TV?

The instant polls after the debate showed that Cameron had 'won' by a narrow margin over Clegg, but the clear loser was, for the third time, Gordon Brown. He was not down and out, however.

5 May 2010

On the eve of the election, Gordon Brown held a mass rally.

I don't know what they are putting into Gordon Brown's cocoa – malt whisky, monkey glands, V-power unleaded – but it seems to be doing the trick. If he is heading for an almighty crash tomorrow, he's so high that he may not notice.

He was at a rally in the Granada studios in Manchester. It was supposed to be Gordodammerung, the twilight of the grump, but it was more like the fateful Sheffield rally of 1992, when Labour thought they were going to win. He was performing in front of 500 crazed Labour supporters. Suddenly he was a rock god!

Celebrities, some not even from *Coronation Street*, lined up on video to razz up the crowd. Bill Bailey! Tony Robinson! Prunella Scales! Someone else you had vaguely heard of! Jo Brand said Labour had done things that made her angry. But they didn't matter, because 'Cameron is a knob!' Or possibly a nob . It's all the new politics. ('Mr Attlee, will you tell the voters why you believe people should vote for the Labour Party?' 'Because Mr Churchill is a knob.')

Our MC was TV's glamorous Gloria de Piero, who is the Labour candidate in Ashfield, an old mining seat of the type where they generally weigh the Labour vote rather than bothering to count it. Her accent grew flatter and more northern by the minute, as if someone was driving a steamroller over it. 'Wurr not Tories, an' we doan't tekk people for grunted,' she said, to huge cheers. It was getting like a revival meeting, or possibly Alcoholics Anonymous. Voters were wheeled out to confess that in the past they had voted for other parties. But they had been saved! By Jesus! Or at least by Gordon. The audience whooped and yelled, like drunken Texans at a rodeo.

Connie Huq of *Blue Peter* confessed that she, too, had voted for other parties in the past. But she had seen the light! The audience went berserk. She began to meander. 'I saw Iceland go down, I saw on the news all those banks collapsing. And I thought, "oh my gosh," and I was expecting Armageddon, I couldn't afford to live where I'm living with interest rates at 15 per cent!' If it hadn't been for Gordon, she'd be living in a Toshiba box. Ms de Piero suddenly reappeared on the stage, possibly hoping to cover her mouth in sticky-backed plastic.

But nothing was going to calm the audience down. When Brother Brown arrived, at the climax of his travelling salvation show, they gave him a standing ovation. Then they sat down. Then, feeling that they probably hadn't done enough, they gave him another standing ovation, all before he even opened his mouth.

He recited a list of Labour's achievements, 55 of them, but nobody could hear a word because they were all praising Gord so loudly. We could make out one or two of them, such as 'the right to book into a bed and breakfast'. Presumably he meant for gay couples, but it did sound weird. Did he mean that the Tories would force everyone to sleep apart? Or only in chain hotels where the sin of Sodom is actively encouraged?

He joined in the chorus of praise for himself. He even had applause for his own dishevelled look. 'If you want the guy whose hair is always perfect, whose tie is always straight, you have a choice – the other two!' he said.

'Come home to Labour!' he yelled, and like one of those manic talk-show hosts, he plunged into the audience.

7 May 2010

Election night, and the main broadcasters held parties. The BBC's was on a boat moored on the south bank of the Thames.

The mood was set by Andrew Neil, addressing the revellers on the BBC boat, or 'ship of fools' as someone called it quite early on. 'The Dow has fallen by 1,000 points, and the gilts market is opening early,' he announced. 'Enjoy yourselves!'

ITV was in the less exciting surroundings of the old County Hall, home of the Greater London Council. Whispering Geoffrey Howe arrived, relishing the fact that soon after Margaret Thatcher had tried to abolish democracy in the capital, large parts of the vast hall had been converted to a luxury hotel.

ITV had the politicians – Roy Hattersley, plus Geoff Hoon, the former defence secretary who was caught in the cash for consultation scam. I thought it took some top brass neck for him to turn up at all. They also had union grandees, such as Bob Crow, Britain's best-loved hate figure, and Charlie Whelan of Unite. Bob can stop the tubes more or less by snapping his fingers, so you're too late for your plane, but that doesn't matter because Charlie has got British Airways cabin crew out on strike. It's a full service arrangement!

Bob Marshall-Andrews, who has stood down as an MP, said sarcastically at midnight, 'Look, we've won three, and they haven't won any! We're unstoppable!'

Over at the BBC it was celebrity heaven. Slebs love being with other slebs, and lost no opportunities to schmooze with each other. The celebrated psephologist Bruce Forsyth was there. He was the first person to be interviewed about how the election was going.

229

Arguments broke out. Was Martin Amis the most famous person there, or was that Piers Morgan? Stars of stage, screen and BBC 24-hour news kept bouncing down the gangplank. Britain's top atheist, Richard Dawkins! Maureen Lipman! Joan Collins! Christopher Meyer, the former ambassador to Washington, who first told the world about Tony Blair's 'ball-crushing trousers'. Top historians such as David Starkey and Simon Schama, Ben Kingsley, Nicholas Parsons, presenter of the in-depth current affairs programme *Just A Minute*, Jeanette Winterson, Mariella Frostrup, John Sergeant, and Alistair McGowan, who could be any one of those if you asked him.

Every now and again, three of the celebrities would be seized by one of Andrew Neil's satraps and hurled into the bilges, where they would be punished by having to sit on comfy sofas and to stop drinking for five minutes. And say how they thought things were going, as if they had any idea, since nobody was paying attention to anything that was going on in the election. The exit poll came at 10.01pm, and hardly anyone bothered to look up.

This year's Portillo moment was provided by Michael Portillo, now the caring, sharing voice of *bien pensant* TV documentaries. But still they kept coming: Julian Fellowes, Clive Anderson, Gerald Scarfe and his wife Jane Asher, Diana Quick, plus famous peers such as Cathy Ashton, the EU's foreign minister, and likely to be Britain's most powerful Labour politician by this morning.

A few Lib Dem supporters did notice the bad news from the exit poll, but sighed and resumed chomping on the canapés. Then we heard the scandal of the disenfranchised voters, unable to get into the polling stations on time, and we needed a feta cheese mini-salad to sustain us. And a seventh glass of Chilean Chardonnay.

The election gave no party an overall majority. The Tories had failed to get anywhere near the huge number of seats that had seemed likely a year before, and even though the Lib Dems had lost several constituencies, they did hold the balance of power. Labour seemed certain to be thrown out of office, but the results had been far from the 1997-style landslide they had feared.

A frantic few days of horse trading, wheeler-dealing and negotiation began. Smoke-filled rooms of legend had become rooms equipped with bottled water and nutritious organic snacks.

It was the craziest day in British politics for some time, perhaps ever. It began with news of the voters who had stormed the polling stations, trying to get in before voting ended. It was becoming third world. The prime minister announced that it was his 'duty' to provide Britain with strong, stable government. He was firmly lodged at Number 10, probably not tying coloured labels on the furniture for the removal men.

You can imagine how it would be reported abroad. 'General Brown declared that the so-called popular vote had been "an error". He would remain in office as head of a national government of unity and reconstruction. To inspire confidence, opposition leaders would be jailed.'

So the man who had lost the election was staying put, but for his own good. He was trying to put together a government of losers.

News came that Nick Clegg had arrived in the capital from his power base in the northlands. TV cameras got a lock on his car and followed it from St Pancras to Westminster, like OJ

Simpson being pursued across Los Angeles, though Mrs Clegg was, we were told, still alive.

He arrived at Lib Dem headquarters, where he was cheered as if he were someone who had actually won more seats than his predecessor. Clegg was in the ghastly position of being both the wallflower at the ball and Cinderella, forced to choose between the two ugly sisters.

I counted 13 camera crews, a heaving, pullulating, media mass – what American reporters sometimes call a 'goat fuck'. A security helicopter thrashed overhead, so it was almost impossible to make out more than the occasional word: 'Disappointing ... more votes than ever before ... real change...' Somehow we got the impression that he would be seeing the Tories first.

On the foreign exchanges, the pound spiked upwards. Traders are like nervous grannies trying to sleep. They hear a noise and assume it's burglars. Then a voice says, 'It's all right, Nan, I kicked the cat,' and they go back to sleep. Until a floor-board creaks.

So the graph on the screen looked as jagged as the iceberg that sank the *Titanic*. Exit polls suggest a hung parliament, and it crashes down. Nick Clegg has warm words for the Tories and it leaps up again. Esther Rantzen loses humiliatingly in Luton – actually that didn't have any effect, but it's worth celebrating just the same.

The whole of Westminster was a fevered manic mass. TV satellite vans zoomed around the streets looking for any politician, or failing that, any hack. College Green, the patch of grass in front of parliament, was covered in tents and tall wooden platforms for the TV crews and presenters. It was Glastonbury for political anoraks, without the mud. Gangs of tourists wandered round, gazing up at people who must, to them, have been as unfamiliar as the Belgian foreign minister's press secretary might be to us.

Gordon Brown came out of Number 10. He had his sombre face on, the one that looks as if he has just been wrestling with the Giant Serpent of History. There was an economic menace. Alistair Darling was attending to it, somewhere in Europe. The implication was clear. How could we protect jobs and sterling without Alistair in charge? This was the man he had been trying to sack a few months before.

It was right, he said, for Clegg to speak to Cameron first. But he had something more to offer – economic stability, far-reaching political reforms. It was like the old Shirley Bassey hit, 'I Who Have Nothing'. I might not be able to offer you riches, or even sufficient seats to form a stable government, but I LURVVV you!

Finally we heard from David Cameron. His equivalent to Brown's sombre face is the tilted head. The greater the angle of tilt, the greater the sincerity. This was no time for party political bickering, grandstanding or cheap point-scoring. He outlined the many wonderful policies he and the Lib Dems had in common.

I realised what this reminded me of. Brown and Cameron were too embarrassed to talk to Clegg. They were like a teenage girl getting a friend to tell that fit boy that if he asked her to the school dance, she might think about it. We, the media, were meant to pass the message on: 'He really, really likes you!'

10 May 2010

The talks continued over the weekend.

So this is what a constitutional crisis looks like. In some countries, rival mobs would be fighting each other in the city centre, the police trying to hold them apart as petrol bombs fly through the air. Here we have a handful of bored photographers, some reporters, and a handful of tourists standing in front of a door. In some capitals, they would be marching on the presidential palace. Here we have policemen saying, 'Move along please, nothing to see, it's only a door.'

In copper-speak 'nothing to see' generally implies a gory scene. Though in fact there was only a door, the door to the Cabinet Office in Whitehall, unless you could picture the British constitution lying dead on the ground with a chalk line drawn around it. All morning politicians were filmed leaving for church, or coming back from church, all wearing what passes for smart casual clothing, or what we used to call Man at C&A. They may be the only people in the country who iron their pullovers. They looked as relaxed as if, under their jumpers, they were wearing whalebone corsets and cast-iron Y-fronts.

At 11am the party negotiators turned up at the door. The Lib Dems – Chris Huhne, Danny Alexander, David Laws and a man called Stunnell who you may not have heard of, arrived like bank robbers in a fleet of black people movers. They were carrying yellow folders, possibly left over from the last hung parliament in 1974.

The Tories looked more formal, with George Osborne and William Hague in suits and ties. Oliver Letwin was in an open-necked shirt – knowing him, he had probably given his tie away to a beggar.

William Hague was very optimistic. The talks had been 'very constructive, very positive, very respectful of our positions'. Yes, it was as bad as that.

Outside, the tourists were told they could stay if they didn't get too close. It didn't look much like fun, but at least it was free, unlike most things in London. The press, cold and bored beyond reason, fell to discussing the colour of the door. Turquoise? Petrol blue? We settled on 'teal'. They were hammering out a teal deal. We were told they had broken for lunch. Was it a meal to seal the teal deal?

Back in Downing Street, Gordon Brown and his family arrived back from Scotland and went in by the back door. It was brave: a squatter seldom leaves the squat for fear it might be possessed by someone else. He would have known that down the corridor the men at C&A were trying to work out a means of evicting him from the house. He was like a squatter coming back to find that another bunch of squatters had taken over the extension and were arguing about who got the best bedroom.

At Number 10 itself, there were gathered the legion of the lost: Ed Miliband, Peter Mandelson, and later Alastair Campbell, the people who had buried New Labour and were now trying to dig up the corpse and plug it into the mains.

In the street, a Kuwaiti reporter was attempting to disentangle the situation for his viewers, who were no doubt concentrating on which was the best method of proportional representation, the single transferable vote, or the D'Hondt system.

I bumped into a Labour MP and asked him how long Gordon could stick it out. 'My grandmother worked in a laundry,' he said, 'and she used to say that there was nothing more difficult than getting shit out of a blanket.' And with that runic thought he scampered away.

After six and a half hours, William Hague emerged to say that the talks had been 'positive' and 'productive', so we were absolutely none the wiser.

Next day the febrile atmosphere became more demented.

The prime minister announced his resignation, and it seemed like just another development in a day of crazed developments. Mr Brown, who had been doing his reverse Captain Oates act – 'Gentlemen, I am staying put. I may be some time' – changed his mind. The man who had survived more assassination attempts than General de Gaulle had decided to abolish himself, only five days too late.

The unelected prime minister offered to stand down and make way for another unelected prime minister, possibly so that an unelected deputy prime minister could join him. He was the mate of a praying mantis, willing to be eaten in order to preserve the line of praying mantises.

Brown looked calmer, more at ease than at any time recently. Gone was the grump who abused Mrs Duffy, and gone was Brother Love at his salvation show. Instead he looked like a CEO announcing slightly disappointing figures for this quarter's sales.

And those poor Liberal Democrats! For decades they have been more or less ignored. If a seaside pony broke wind on the beach during one of their conferences, the press room would empty as reporters rushed to cover the story. Now, suddenly, they matter! The media were clustered round them, like vultures spotting a lion fighting a wounded gnu. They were not in Seventh Heaven, but 177th heaven, on Cloud 99! Then Gordon Brown spoiled it all by resigning. Suppose it was your 21st birthday party, and your big sister announced she was engaged to Prince Harry. You'd be furious.

The media were gathered outside the Grand Committee Room where the Lib Dems were meeting to discuss the Tory proposals for a deal. Mike Hancock of Portsmouth North, whose name is largely unknown, even in Portsmouth North, was first to emerge. He was immediately set on by a crowd of cameramen, reporters and snappers. Mr Hancock tried to move away to meet some constituents, but he didn't really want to. So the laws of physics caused him to swirl, first to the left, then round to the right, then back to the left, surrounded by the pursuing hordes. And he had nothing to say.

There was a poignant moment when Lembit Opik, who had lost his seat, walked into the hall, alone, and straight past the reporters. In past times nothing would have caused him to do this. It would be like Billy Bunter avoiding a bag of dough-nuts. But all was well. Moments later, he was back and giving an impromptu press conference.

The Lib Dem negotiator David Laws came out. Mr Laws, who has the air of a coffin bearer for very small corpses, had anti-climactic news. He said that the Lib Dems were not disposed to accept the package offered by the Tories. Of course they weren't! They are back in the headlines, every day! No more need they bang on about secondary drinking or the preservation of independent cinemas. They are currently the greatest sideshow on earth.

By the evening, the Tories had arrived for their meeting. What was amazing was that even the newcomers looked as if they had been there for years. They were every bit as plump, glossy and confident. Maybe it's because they've lived in Gothic or neo-Gothic buildings all their lives: home, school, Oxbridge, the law courts. Some were wearing the green badges that identify a new MP like pictures in a private art gallery. Red means 'sold', green means 'for sale', so no change there, then.

On live television, Alastair Campbell almost got into a fight with Sky's Adam Boulton. They squared up to each other, threatening to rain karate chops down, over the question of whether Boulton wanted Cameron to become prime minister.

Then to complete the lunatic day, William Hague appeared on TV offering a referendum on the alternative vote. Plus a country house and 20 acres with fishing rights for every Lib Dem MP. Of course I made the last bit up, but it wouldn't have been any madder than anything else that happened yesterday.

12 May 2010

The Tories and the Liberal Democrats managed to put together their coalition, and Gordon Brown finally announced that he was going for good, straight away.

To resign once in two days may be thought regrettable; to have to resign three times in the same period – he quit instantly as Labour leader last night – can only be humiliating. Gordon Brown emerged from the black front door of Number 10 with his wife, Sarah, who looked blank-eyed and tired. Her husband wished the next prime minister well – I expect she wished him haemorrhoids, or at least a lot of rebellious backbenchers.

One had the feeling that if the public had seen the side of Gordon Brown that he finally managed to drag out of himself, like a benevolent monster in *Alien*, they might have felt fonder about him. He had learned a lot about human frailty, he said, 'including my own'. He had gazed into the eyes of our armed forces. He would never forget those who had died in honour and those whose families lived in grief.

Then he turned to Sarah, whom he thanked for her unswerving support as well as love. He thanked their two boys for the 'love and joy they bring to our lives'. I gather that the staff in Downing Street began to tear up at this, even those who had had staplers thrown at their heads. But he had one final assault on their tear ducts. 'As I leave the second most important job I could have had, I cherish the first, as a husband and father.' At this even cynical old journalists began to snarl.

'Thank you, and goodbye.'

At this, they brought their two boys out, sweet, smiling, puzzled, at last with their parents after hardly seeing them for weeks. We haven't seen them at all until now, their faces fuzzed out on TV. Now they emerged, blinking, to a great 'Aaaah!' from the nation.

Earlier he had come back from the palace. We assumed that he didn't climb back into the car and say, 'That woman is a bigot!' Then to Labour HQ, where he was applauded wildly. He had failed, he said, and 'the fault is mine'. Again, you felt that if he had managed to talk like a real human being over the past three years, he'd still be in office. Even the smile looked real, not operated by a cack-handed ventriloquist.

Then it was Cameron's turn. The husband of a PR woman had been replaced by a PR man. And he knows which knobs to twiddle. He paid tribute to his predecessor. 'Compared to a decade ago, this country is more open at home, and more compassionate abroad.'

That's how we do political change here. Lots of noise – cheers, helicopters thundering overhead, and street shouts of 'Tory scum!' But little violence.

Except, that is, earlier in the day when Boris Johnson appeared at Westminster tube station with Mike Bloomberg, the mayor of New York, who was here to check out the CCTV security. But as cameramen forced their way into the station control room, fights broke out between the British snappers and aggressive American security men. Half the TV crews were fighting, while the other half filmed the fight.

I walked down the colonnade from the station, and was passed by Nick Clegg, pacing, pacing. They have learned to pace from watching *The West Wing*. It doesn't matter where they're pacing to, but they have to keep moving, flinging remarks back towards their posse, in mid-pace. A minute later, Cameron appeared, also pacing at top speed. You could just make out hair vanishing. If he starts pacing in Number 10, he'll bang his nose against the wall.

Labour MPs seemed glad it was all over, desperate not to join a legion of the losers. Now it's the Tories who can cope with the greatest economic crisis for 80 years.

Commons officials have, with amazing speed, produced a booklet containing pictures of all MPs. Some of the newcomers are scary. As Dave Barry says, anyone who looks like their passport photograph is too ill to travel. These guys look as if they could use an embalming. I did an ethnic count: 14 MPs from various Asian backgrounds, 8 black people, and 27 people who appear to be Vulcans.

The coalition was consummated in a short but moving ceremony in the garden at the back of 10 Downing Street.

'This is what the new politics looks like,' said Nick Clegg, as he stood in the sun-drenched garden. It looked more like a civil marriage. This is a press conference that would have been illegal in 45 American states.

There were trees in the bright green colours of early summer, a trimmed lawn, the happy couple in their smartest clothes. All it needed was a band, a marquee and a table for the presents.

All the guests marvelled at how delighted they looked. And they have so much in common. The groom is from Eton and Oxford, whereas the groom is from Westminster and Cambridge. They handed out copies of the pre-nup, or 'coalition agreements reached document' as they call it.

Earlier they had posed on the steps of Number 10. They might have been conjoined twins. You had the feeling that if they ever fell out, they would have to go to Great Ormond Street hospital to be surgically separated. The man who had told us we had to vote Conservative to avoid the horrors of a hung parliament, was full of the joys of a hung parliament.

It was going to usher in the new politics, in which the national interest was more important than party. It was a historic, seismic shift! By contrast, St Paul might have spent years changing his mind.

Apparently it had nothing to do with electoral arithmetic. It was all inspiration. 'We did both have a choice,' said the new prime minister. 'We looked at minority government, and we thought, "This is so uninspiring".'

He was asked how he felt the morning after the night before, hooked up with someone he barely knew and had hardly spoken to. 'I woke up thinking, "This is so much better than the alternative!" I had a great sense of inspiration and excitement!'

It turns out that Clegg will take prime minister's questions when Cameron is away. It will give him something to do during those long, lonely days when Cameron is in Washington, or Brussels, or Witney. 'I'm looking forward to a lot of travel!' said Cameron, while Clegg smiled happily.

They'll be sharing accommodation, of course. 'There's a corridor connecting Number 10 with where I am, but I don't yet know where I am,' said the deputy prime minister, with an air of the existential angst that must come to anybody who doesn't yet know where he is.

Things got more metaphysical. 'This will succeed through its success,' said Cameron. Suck on that one.

Inevitably there was a bad fairy at the wedding, who pointed out, 'When you were asked what your favourite joke was, you said "Nick Clegg".'

'Did you?' asked Clegg.

'I'm afraid I did,' the prime minister replied.

'Well, I'm off!' said his deputy, again with a merry smile. All the happiest partners recall the time when they couldn't stand each other. It's utterly romantic, like *The Taming of the Shrew*.

All too soon it was over. 'Bye, and thanks for all your lovely gifts, especially the fondue set and the hostess trolley!' No, of course not, but they did look awfully happy.

The new parliament assembled, following the Queen's instructions. She had formally demanded such an event, due to 'arduous and urgent affairs'. She could have said that again. The following day Nick Clegg outlined the work he had planned for the complete over-haul of our constitution, such as it is.

It was billed in advance as the most important speech since the Great Reform Act of 1832. But in fact it was much more important than that. Apparently it was the most important speech for more than 400 years, or so the spin doctors told us. Compared with this speech, the Gettysburg address was little more than a polite cough and a word of thanks to the vicar. Henry V at Harfleur was the mayor's wife declaring the flower show open. And it was to be delivered by Nick Clegg.

Clearly it would have to be delivered in a venue worthy of the occasion. The royal robing room in the House of Lords, perhaps. Or the O2 Arena. Or Wembley. In fact he chose a further education college in north London.

I decided this was precisely because, in the past, any speech delivered by a Lib Dem leader would have attracted an audience that could have fitted into the upstairs room of one of the many kebab shops that constitute the local economy in this part of the capital. If they had put him in a bigger room, he might not have been able to cope. He'd have been like a pet falcon, released into the wild, and then torn to pieces by the other falcons.

The hall, if medium-sized, was packed. Students love Nick Clegg. Or rather, they love the idea of Nick Clegg. The reality, as always, was a bit of a let down. He outlined enormous changes. The Lords would be reformed, civil liberties restored, evil MPs fired, CCTV cameras torn down like statues of Lenin, and everyone would have authority over their own lives – not only on election day, either. 'You will exercise your voice and your power, every single day!'

This was Tony Benn's view: a citizenry that took charge over every decision, all the time, whether on war and taxes, or the siting of a new bus shelter. Who would have thought this batty idea would become received wisdom in a Tory-led government?

The bad news is that councillors are about to get more power. Frankly, I would rather trust our own moth-eaten parliament than some councillors, who can be as petty and tyrannical as any third world dictator. 'Recentralise power!' That should be a true reformer's battle cry. The students listened in near silence, as people normally do when listening to Nick Clegg.

As he left, I noticed him switch off his microphone. Like survivors of some terrible car crash remembering their seat belts, all politicians now make certain they won't suffer the fate of Gordon Brown in Rochdale. If they were even brighter, they might leave the mikes on, and say something magnificently non-incriminating, such as: 'That woman had some really interesting ideas. Thank you so much for bringing us together!'

A new government always means a new Queen's speech.

For once the speech was written in a language approximating to English. During the New Labour years it appeared to have been inscribed in crayon by the bastard child of Alastair Campbell and a corporate mission statement. Yesterday's wasn't exactly mellifluous, containing lines such as: 'addressing serious international concerns posed by Iran's nuclear programme' and 'allowing new providers', but at least you didn't feel you had to wince along with Her Majesty while she read it out.

But the ancient, traditional flummery remains the same. An elderly lady, rather stooped these days, dressed in her finest threads, entered the Chamber and was guided gently to her seat. All eyes swivelled.

Yes, the arrival of Margaret Thatcher brings the level of hubbub right down, as people marvel that she is still there – and mobile. It was a slow progress to her seat, as she was passed from one attendant to another, like a child being evacuated to a strange place during the war. Her face is a deathly white these days, so she looks like Miss Havisham on an unexpected day out.

She sat next to Tom McNally, who used to work for Jim Callaghan, but who is now a Lib Dem minister in a Tory-led government. He was in chatty mood, turning round to speak to the former prime minister. She closed her eyes. Feigning sleep is a useful shield, though of course old people do tend to drop off, at random intervals.

It was bling heaven. Tiaras glittered off the TV lights, and sparkled against the gold fitments. Ken Clarke, the new lord chancellor, arrived looking grumpy, though he told me later he was just hot, in heavy robes that looked rather like the curtains in *Abigail's Party*.

Various heralds, including Fitzalan Pursuivant Extraordinary (real name: Al Bruce) and Maltravers Herald Extraordinary (Jack Robinson, I promise) shuffled in and stood as if waiting for a bus. Lord Strathclyde arrived wearing the Cap of Maintenance, so allowing me to reprise my annual joke about Queen Beatrix and the Dutch Cap of Maintenance.

Suddenly, the Queen was amongst us, the Imperial Crown radiating like a spangly disco ball. She was about to address us, for free, not charging half a million quid like some fringe members of the royal family I could mention. She sat in the ancient, twitch-free silence, while the Commons shambled towards the peers. For the past 13 years they have sounded rather like a football crowd. Now they are enthusiastic but quieter – the White's Club annual outing to Goodwood, perhaps.

Her Maj read the speech then handed it back to Ken Clarke. He followed the modern tradition of walking away with his back to her, and as always he rolled off like a man who is late for an urgent appointment with a pie and a pint. Lady Thatcher snoozed on regardless of it all.

11 June 2010

Eric Pickles yesterday answered his first questions as secretary of state for communities and local government. What a tale lies behind that simple fact, a story worthy of JB Priestley, Roy Hattersley or even Jeffrey Archer.

Come back with me to Bradford in 1887, when young Obadiah Pickles – bored by the bland food of the day – began to marinade baby cucumbers in vinegar and spices, cooking his recipes in an abandoned pigeon loft.

At first he gave them to friends and family, who were delighted by the crisp crunch of the vegetables, and the fragrant tang of the flavourings. Obadiah then hit on the idea of sending his son Zebedee to stand outside fish and chip shops, offering slices of the delicacy to customers as they left the shop.

Before long, the public was clamouring for the Co-op to stock the treat, and soon Pickles was doing a roaring trade in what he called 'Pickles' Exotic Vegetable Condiment'. Like the relish itself, the title was a mouthful, and soon happy Bradfordians were referring to the savoury morsels simply as 'pickles'.

Within 10 years, a turnover of a few pounds had become a vast half-million pound business. A local advertising agency, Saatchi and Entwhistle, was engaged and they came up with a snappy slogan: 'Plump for Pickles' pickles, the pickles picky people pick.'

Jars were even found in wealthy London homes, introduced by servants who discovered that their aristocratic masters also loved the tasty tracklement. One cunning poster showed a cheeky urchin dressed in Eton clothes, saying: 'Me mam says that foie gras tastes like nowt wi'out Pickles' pickles!'

Within a few years Obadiah had built an 18-room mansion in an unusual Gothic-Palladian style, on the hills overlooking Bradford. 'It's the bits they leave behind on t'plate that paid for this!' he would tell awestruck visitors. When the old man finally died, still in harness, Zebedee took over and brought new ideas with new products. 'Pickles' Piccalilli, the piquant palate-pleaser' was an early success.

But his son, Eric, was a disappointment. He tried a new relish involving sun-dried tomatoes and Bacardi vinegar, but his heart was not in the business, which was taken over by Cadbury, then in turn by Kraft. Pickles' pickles – 'the original and only' are now made in Poland.

Meanwhile, Eric went into politics, becoming leader of Bradford's Conservative group. Unable to find a Tory seat in the city of his birth, he moved to what his grandfather would have called 'the soft south'. In 2006, the party's new leader, David Cameron, tried a pastrami on rye sandwich garnished with Pickles' pickles, and was so delighted by the fact that Eric came from the family that he promoted him to the party's highest levels.

Not that Mr Pickles had much to say yesterday. He cuts a mighty figure at the dispatch box, being the shape of a gigantic gherkin, but he left nearly all his answers to his understrappers, most of whom would not know the difference between balsamic vinegar and non-brewed condiment.

16 June 2010

After 12 years, the Saville inquiry reported on Bloody Sunday, the day in 1972 in which 13 civilians were killed by British forces in Derry. David Cameron's speech on the day the report was published, including the frank admission that the army had got things dreadfully wrong, was regarded as one of his finest.

At 3.29pm the news had been leaked in Derry, and the cheers of the crowd burst from every TV set in the Commons as we dashed to hear Cameron's statement. He, by contrast, was received in a sombre, almost fearful silence. MPs might not have been surprised, but they were certainly stunned.

The prime minister could hardly have done better. For someone who was aged five at the time of Bloody Sunday, it was a poised and almost perfectly judged performance.

And all the more difficult for someone who has had to spend years paying tribute to the British army, to their courage and patriotism. When it comes to our lads in uniform, no politician wants to say anything that is not cut from a template of praise.

'I never want to say anything bad about our country,' he said. He never wanted to call our soldiers into question. They were, he believed, the finest in the world. Clearly an enormous 'but' was on its way.

'But,' he said, 'the conclusions of this report are absolutely clear. There is no doubt. There is nothing equivocal. There are no ambiguities. What happened on Bloody Sunday was both unjustified and unjustifiable. It was wrong.'

The Commons was, if anything, even quieter when he went through the most startling and shattering conclusions. No warning before the soldiers opened fire, which they did before anyone shot at them. Soldiers had lied to protect themselves. Some of the dead had been fleeing, or going to the aid of the wounded. Every sentence slashed through the silence.

'The report refers to one person who was shot while "crawling away from the soldiers". The father who was hit and injured while going to the aid of his wounded son.'

I doubt if the Commons has ever heard a statement so raw, etching with acid into the polished veneer of our nation's image of itself.

For someone of his generation, he said, Bloody Sunday was something learned rather than lived through. 'But what happened should never, ever have happened, and for that, on behalf of the government – and indeed our country – I am deeply sorry.'

He also set the day in context, reminding us of the scores of soldiers – for the most part as innocent as any civilian – shot dead because they were wearing a politically inconvenient uniform. The IRA would never be put on an even footing with democrats. 'But neither will we hide from the truth that confronts us today.'

As Lord Saville had said, Bloody Sunday came as a tremendous boon to the IRA, and made the continuing conflict far, far worse. (Of the 3,500-odd people killed in the 40 years of the Troubles, around one-seventh died in the year following the massacre.)

Various Unionists, such as Ian Paisley Jr, watched from the gallery by his father, pointed out the suffering of many Protestants in Northern Ireland. But this was not their day.

18 June 2010

Alan Sugar had been appointed 'Enterprise Tsar' by Gordon Brown. He made an amazingly self-admiring maiden speech. The baroness sitting beside him was clearly enraged, and looked as if she might spontaneously combust with anger. Or, as Lord Sugar would have put it, 'You're fried!' But he did play a part in many Lords debates.

It was Alan Sugar day in the House of Lords. The show *Junior Apprentice* is over. Now it's *Senior Apprentice*, as Lorshugger was surrounded by ancient yet ambitious persons, most of whom could not sell handwarmers to Inuits, or advocat-flavoured dentifrice to your Nan. He intervened in a question about loan sharks. He's against them, and said so at great length. Tories (Lorshugger sits on the Labour benches) grew weary as his question wound on and on and finally got bogged down. 'You're mired!' was the gist of what they wanted to say.

Next we had a discussion on urban foxes, of the type that could only ever take place in the Lords. Baroness Sharples said she had been walking from Westminster tube station, and had seen a fox stroll from the underground towards the House of Commons. Lord Henley, who appears to be *de facto* the minister for vulpine affairs, said that it clearly wouldn't want to come into the House of Lords. The unspoken implication was that their lordships would be up in hunting pink, on their horses, crying 'tally-ho!' before the poor beast had got past the Pugin tea room.

Lord Lea of Crondall recounted a heart-warming story about the time he saw a fox electrocuted. He recommended this for all foxes, though how you would persuade them to sit on the chair he wouldn't explain.

Lord Greaves said that dogs bit far more children than foxes did. He suggested 'immuno-contraception' which had worked on 'wild boars'. He left open the question of whether it would work on the mild bores of which the upper house is full.

Lord Geddes asked if a repeal of the hunting act would be of any use. It would not help, replied Lord Henley, though I thought it would be fun to see a meet of the Westminster Hunt, with neighs, whinnying, flared nostrils, pawing the frozen ground – and that would be just the baronesses!

George Osborne, for all his undoubted skills, was never entirely popular with his fellow Conservatives. After his first budget, he was hauled before the Commons treasury committee.

The chancellor came to give evidence about his traditionalist, slash-and-burn budget. This was like a traditionalist doctor appearing in front of the BMA in order to explain why leeches are the best way to heal most illnesses, and how skin rashes can be cured by a poultice made from toad skin and hazel blossom, gathered by virgins at midnight. He would not expect to go unchallenged.

And he wasn't. If I were Osborne, I would be worried by the new chairman of the committee, Andrew Tyrie, who is a Tory himself but clearly doesn't believe that Chancellors should be under-grilled just because they are in the same party.

He stared at Osborne coldly, rather like an Oxford don contemplating the first essay by an undergraduate who showed promise at his admissions interview, but who now seemed a disappointment.

Why, he asked, in a voice as chilly as a Scottish summer breeze, had he been content to let the bottom 10 per cent of British earners be hardest hit in the budget?

The chancellor, who had arrived with his usual two smiles – the one open and friendly, the other basically smug – was taken aback. He clearly hadn't expected this. He started flannelling about students, who might be technically in the bottom 'decile' of earners, but are actually not poor. Or poor in the usual sense.

Tyrie wasn't having any of that. His manner became superior as well as supercilious. If there had been an ivy-covered quad for him to stare out at, he would have stared out at it, balefully.

It turns out that it is the middle classes, people earning between £16,000 and £38,000 a year, who are paying proportionally the least. Was that fair?

Osborne made his point about students, again. Tyrie folded his hands under his chin, as if nurturing a sick seagull back to life. The budget included cuts in housing benefit and in disability allowance. Would that not affect lower income groups?

Finally he asked Osborne to come back with charts amended to show the actual effects of the cuts, 'so we can get a more measured view'. This is the equivalent of a don marking an essay *'non satis'* and demanding it be written again.

Nor was the chancellor a huge hit with the rest of the committee. Labour's Andrew Love pointed out that, thanks to sluggishness in Europe, the devaluation of the pound had not increased exports much. Was there are Plan B?

'The plan is,' said Osborne, 'to have confidence in the British economy.' Oh dear, things must be much worse than we thought.

David Rutley, a Tory from Macclesfield, said that the problem was that young British persons didn't want proper jobs. Instead they wanted to be footballers.

Osborne, who sits for a neighbouring seat just north of Manchester, said: 'You are the MP for Wayne Rooney, so I would be careful about slagging off footballers!'

Ah, 'slagging off'! A new term that would not have tripped off the tongue of Sir Stafford Cripps. Mind you, the Labour newcomer, Chuka Umunna, accused the chancellor of producing a 'tabletastic' budget, by which he appeared to mean that it contained several tables. Sometimes this new economic jargon is quite hard to keep up with.

The new education secretary was Michael Gove. His Labour opponent was Ed Balls, who had done the job himself in the Brown government. Balls was one of five people running for leader of the party.

Gove versus Balls! What a magnificent grudge fight! The winner of the Miss Grabitas Prize for Debating up against the school bully.

Mr Gove doesn't really speak; he squeaks. You can't call it gabbling, because he enunciates each word very clearly but very quickly. Half a second of Gove, squirted down a phone line to his spymasters, could be extended with the right equipment into an entire speech. 'Tovarich, standards in British schools have declined precipitously over the past 13 years. The Kremlin must know this!'

Ed Balls cannot bear to simply sit there and take it. So he has developed a line in ultra-expressive face and body language. His face was rigid. His eyebrows hooded. The mouth half-open, as if frozen on its way into turning into a full Munch-type scream. The effect is of a huge but silent snarl.

Now and again he shook his head in despair, rather like the rest of us do while watching *The Weakest Link*, when a contestant, asked what 'B' is a yellow fruit, replies 'beetroot'. Or else he flares his nostrils, and when the Balls nostrils are dilated, they stay dilated. If the wind changed, he would go through life looking like a very angry horse. Sometimes he hugged his knees, as if afraid that, were he to let go of them, they would jerk randomly and he would kick everyone in sight.

Mr Gove had to pull out all the debating skills he had acquired while he was training for the Miss Grabitas prize.

With his academy schools, he said, he was only extending what Tony Blair had tried to do in 2005. 'He wanted every school to have academy status ... All I see on the Opposition benches are people who have betrayed the Messiah, or at least the former prime minister, and now that the cock has crowed three times...'

As they say on the *New Yorker*, 'Block that metaphor!'

Ed Balls got his chance to respond, which he did by accepting every intervention from a Tory or a Lib Dem. This enabled him to conduct several fights at once, rather like a chess grandmaster playing a dozen opponents simultaneously, except that he ends each game not by winning but by overturning the board.

He was so enraged that he hurled each page of his speech down in a fury, any which way, so they landed like giant's confetti, as if his anger at the Tories had deprived him of hand-eye co-ordination. But he is running for party leader on the platform of never knowingly being out-seethed.

20 September 2010

The Liberal Democrats held their first conference as a party in power.
Things didn't seem to have changed all that much.

The former Lib Dem MP David Rendel explained the principle
of the coalition to his party's annual assembly. 'If I disagree
with my wife about which film we want to go to, it doesn't
mean we go to separate cinemas!' he said. Actually that seems
to me a perfectly sound idea, especially if she wants to see a
chick flick and he's more excited by *Saw IV*.

But that wouldn't be a very Liberal idea, and in any case
they are not at all sure what they want. They may be a party
in power for the first time since the war – if then – but nothing
much has altered. As always, any inspiration runs into the
sand. The excitement isn't so much pent up, as dribbled out.

On the Andrew Marr show Nick Clegg had said, 'We must
take ownership of the now!' It isn't much of a battle cry. 'The
now is ours! We must seize the now, now!'

We heard Danny Alexander, who is now the minister in
charge of cuts. Since most Lib Dems hate the cuts, he had a
difficult sell. He managed it with a typically Lib Dem rabble-
soothing speech. He praised them for agreeing with him, even
when they didn't. 'We didn't do things because they were
easy! We did them because they were right!' he told them,
many times.

Mr Alexander used to be press officer for the Cairngorms
national park. His tactic was to make his speech marginally
less interesting than a PowerPoint presentation to other
tourism executives. 'We inherited a country in the danger zone,
and we have taken it into the safe zone,' he said, in the manner

of someone saying: 'A new seven-minute orientation video has led to a 13 per cent increase in take-up at the visitor centre.'

'Some people think that not paying their taxes is a lifestyle choice. Not true.' ('A wider range of cakes and pastries has increased revenues in the refreshment facilities.')

He addressed the unions directly, in particular those who were spoiling for a fight. 'We don't want to take you on. We want to take you with us,' he said, or possibly mumbled. ('Anti-littering signage has decreased recovery rates by over 21 per cent in the last six months…')

By the end, the conference had had any rebellious thoughts squeezed out of it. His peroration consisted of him muttering, 'Together we can make it happen, thang yew.' He then received the kind of slow, half-hearted standing ovation that means: 'Oh well, could have been worse.'

21 September 2010

Nick Clegg tried to set the conference on fire, but not very hard.

The Lib Dem leader is morphing slowly into Tony Blair. There was the shiny-eyed gaze towards the future. 'Britain in 2015 will be a different country. Strong, fair, and full of hope again!' Yeah, right. He even adopted Tony Blair's verb-free sentences, the ones that suggest much but promise nothing. 'Tough on the welfare cheats and tough on the tax cheats!' he declared.

'It's not a smaller government I believe in; it's a different kind of government, a liberating government!' It will certainly liberate a lot of wage slaves who might otherwise have to go to work. Instead they'll be liberated to watch *Deal or No Deal*.

Tony Blair had a device he often deployed at his party's conference. He would take obscure themes that he knew were popular with Labour members, and imply that they would also be a huge hit with the voters. The reconstruction of Maputo docks was one example. Clegg combined this strategy with the word 'imagine', as in the [John] Lennon song.

'Imagine what you will say to people when you knock on their door at the next general election,' he said.

'Imagine how it will feel to say that the Liberal Democrats have restored civil rights, scrapped ID cards, and got innocent people's DNA off the police database!'

Or it might go like this: 'I've been out of work for four years now, and you're banging on about a DNA database? Gerroffit!'

But nothing would stop him. He went on: 'Imagine how it will feel to visit home after home, that our green deal has made comfortable and affordable to heat!'

Well, we could all imagine that scenario. 'Shut that bloody door, will you? The price of gas just doubled, and my dole cut...'

260

Liberal Democrats discussed intimate same-sex relations yesterday, and for once it wasn't about Cameron and Clegg. Evan Harris, the former MP, said he had been listed as the party's only 'out' gay member. 'And I'm not even gay!' he said. This proved, once again, how eager the party was to demonstrate diversity.

The motion was to let same-sex couples have proper marriages, in church if they wished, instead of mere civil partnerships. Fred Dunsford, a wheelchair user, was against the idea because most voters wouldn't like it. Facing one member of an oppressed and ignored minority opposing the wishes of another oppressed and ignored minority, the conference didn't know which way to turn. So they compromised and gave him a light sprinkling of applause anyway.

Liz Williams talked about 'all my lesbian, gay, bisexual and transsexual friends' in all of whom she 'sees the same grace'.

Blimey, I thought, she must have some terrific parties.

Sara Bedford was not gay, but was treated with the same reverence as if she were. She described her typically Lib Dem wedding anniversary, which she had spent at a Lib Dem meeting while her husband did the ironing at home. She recalled taking her daughter to a Gay Pride march and telling her that some people didn't approve of gay relationships.

'Mummy,' the little girl replied, 'surely love is a good thing? People should be allowed as many hugs and kisses as they want!' This heart-warming tale brought loud applause.

A former prison chaplain described how he had 'happily made friends of murderers, rapists and paedophiles, and you can't get more inclusive than that!' Well, you could always support the rights of paedophiles to marry underage children in church, I thought (but would not have dreamed of saying).

Ed Fordham of north London had been asked by a woman what his 'dear wife' thought of politics. 'I said, "My dear wife – he's over there." She replied, "In Hampstead, as long as it's not animals, we don't mind."'

Things were getting more surreal. Jenny Barnes announced: 'Liberal Democrats are different, and as a transsexual I welcome that. There is obviously a huge impact on a transsexual's partner when they realise that their partner is not of the gender they were assigned at birth.

'I have a friend who is fully transitioned, and wants to stay in her relationship, so it's very confusing for her and her wife.'

She went on to explain that she couldn't marry in a church because she wasn't recognised as a woman, and she couldn't marry a woman, because that would be a same-sex partnership. But help was at hand. 'Luckily I'm an atheist, so I'm not bothered.'

You can be sure nothing as interesting as all this will crop up at either the Labour or Conservative conferences. Brian Paddick, the former policeman who ran as the Lib Dem candidate for mayor of London, described his fully legal wedding to a 'gorgeous' Norwegian man in Oslo. He had been deeply moved, as we all were. 'We really feel, my husband and I – that's husband and husband – really equal.' The conference passed the motion by a huge majority, as if you needed to ask.

Just before the Labour conference began, it was announced that – by a very narrow margin and to everyone's great surprise, not least that of the candidates – Ed Miliband had beaten his brother David to become leader of the party.

Ed Miliband faced his first rite of passage yesterday, being interviewed by Andrew Marr. He looked as nervous as a young man at his first job interview. You could imagine his mum brushing the dandruff from his shoulders and straightening his tie. His legs were apart, and his hands were clasped between them.

In short, he looked like a geek. He did have some good news for the middle classes, but they will probably beware of geeks bearing gifts.

Ed had a tough task ahead. He had to spend an hour talking about absolutely nothing and giving nothing away. Except how much he loved his brother. 'He has shown the most extraordinary generosity to me,' he said, several times. 'He is a fantastic person.'

Almost everything he said was in accordance with the law of the nonsensical reverse. For example, Ed said that he was 'passionate about Britain'. Had he said he was passionate about Bolivia, we might have paid attention. He felt we should have great respect for nurses. ('I despise nurses with every fibre of my being.') He thought strikes should always be used as a last resort. ('Get the lads out, and only then talk to management – that's my plan.')

He was, he assured us, his own man. ('I am a puppet, ready to be manipulated by whoever can grab my strings.') He represented the change that Labour needed. ('No real problems in our party. I plan to put my feet up and leave well alone.') Unity would be his watchword. ('Let's keep fighting each other – it's always fun!')

Their new leader might be embracing change, but the Labour conference continues as it always has for more than 100 years. The event is actually run by the Conference Arrangements Committee, a terrifying backroom body that resembles the old Soviet Politburo trying to rewrite the Talmud.

At the start of business, Margaret Wheeler, a handsome woman with a flat but mellifluous voice, recited the latest bureaucratic horrors that the CAC has devised.

She describes, in a tone that might be apt for thanking Mrs Prendergast for the loan of the tea urn, details that only someone with a feel for four-dimensional mathematics could understand. 'We have adopted the contemporary issues process to enable supporting statements to be treated as motions. These appear in CIC1 and will be composited this evening … your submission is not accepted as contemporary,' she told some poor bastard who had challenged an unimaginably obscure ruling.

Compositing is an ancient Labour tradition which has nothing to do with enriching garden soil. It means, roughly, combining several motions as one, usually neutered so that the leadership isn't put to any trouble. A man with so much hair above and below his face that you could scarcely make out his nose came to the podium and raised a point even more arcane than the earlier arcane points.

He got a crisp elucidation from Ms Wheeler. 'The constitutional amendment is laid before you as an appendix, closed after other rule amendments had been finalised, and the NEC is not subject to the three-year rule.' Touché!

I don't suppose more than two per cent of the people in the hall understood a single word. But they understood one thing – you don't mess with the CAC.

28 September 2010

At first the Miliband brothers seemed to be getting along. It wasn't to last.

The brothers can't stop being nice about each other. They are spraying each other with fudge, whipped cream and caramel sauce. They keep on finding nice and nicer things to say. As that earlier fratricide, Cain, remarked: 'Am I my brother's creeper?'

David spoke to the conference on foreign affairs. Perhaps he would describe a historically acrimonious separation, like that of the comedians Mike and Bernie Winters, when Mike went off to America and Bernie got control of Schnorbitz, the loveable St Bernard which, like the Labour party, was big, fluffy, well-meaning and easy to trip over.

'We have a great new leader!' said David, 'and we all need to get behind him. I am really, really proud. So proud of my campaign, so proud of my party, and – above all – I am proud of my brother.' This was just throat-clearing. Soon he returned to his original refrain. 'Ed is a special person to me,' he said, and, liking the sound of that, repeated: 'Ed is a special person to me. And now he is a special person to all of you. And our job is to make him a special person to all the British people!'

There were hints that not all might be well in the D. Miliband heart. Nobody, he said, should go into politics without being 100 per cent committed to winning. But, 'You should never go in without being reconciled to the prospect that you might lose.' So you have to be desperate to win but delighted to lose. 'To those of you who have been coming up to me – don't worry, I'll be fine!'

Thank heavens. We had feared he might break down sobbing. But there had been one bad moment. 'A guy came up to me at a party and said, "Ed, congratulations on your victory." I can do without that.'

The party should stick together. It could go inwards and backward, or it could go outwards and forwards. This was sounding like the hokey-cokey. It could go leftwards and right-wards, upwards or downwards, or it could shake it all about.

They rose to a standing ovation. He was no longer Supernerd. If he had made that speech two years ago, he might be leader now.

29 September 2010

Ed made his first conference speech as party leader.

'Vote for us! We're rubbish, but at least we admit it!' That was the rallying cry from Labour's new leader yesterday. The party, having chosen the spare Miliband, was fearful that he might be appalling. The fact that he wasn't bad brought them stomping to their feet after a speech that sloshed and sprayed his predecessors with scorn.

Gosh, the last (Labour) government had been a disaster, it seems. The City was allowed to run amok, immigration was ignored, they thought they could end boom and bust, and as for Iraq, don't get him started.

It was Labour's first chance to get the measure of their new leader. He blinks a lot, roughly once a second, and in time to his hand movements, so it looks as if his eyelids and wrists are connected by a gossamer thread. Like his brother, he has an asymmetrical mouth; the right side makes an O, while the left side remains closed, so he gives the appearance of a man who has just spotted half a maggot in the apple he is eating.

More than ever, he resembles a newly promoted maître d' in an upmarket Indian restaurant, possibly one with an ambitious menu of Goan food. He started off by signaling to the audience as if to tell us that our table was ready. He looks determined, but the determined look is perilously close to a scowl. The panda eyes are hooded.

'Your table is ready. But I cannot promise you that you will like your table. Nor can I pledge that you will like the food. And you most certainly will not like the bill. But, I implore you – follow me anyway! And your waitress will be along in a moment to take your drinks orders.'

He began with the predictable encomium to his brother, 'an extraordinary person' who had made 'an inspiring speech' the day before. But the faintest note of bitterness crept in. There were those who said he was more leftwing than David. 'But on the day I stole his football, he was so angry that he nationalised my train set.'

We learned an important fact from that: he simply can't deliver a joke.

My own most vivid memory of the Labour conference was a trip to a genuine upscale Indian restaurant, where I made the mistake of having a curried sheep's trotter as a main course. It was horrible, being fatty, bony and woolly and entirely lacking in meat. Leave that sort of dish to those travellers who explore the Hindu Kush alone and rely on the hospitality of the simple mountain dwellers. All of whom would prefer a decent steak and chips anyway.

The Tory conference was held in Birmingham, where there are many first-rate curry houses.

The Conservative party is back in power, and the good news is that they are as bonkers as ever before! At the start of their conference, David Cameron sat in the body of the hall, along with all the real and semi-real people. Why? Possibly because the arrival of such a young man brought the average age of the audience down by months if not years.

As he sat there, the aisle nearest to him was jammed with photographers and TV cameramen. This meant that the poor fellow had to look interested in what was being said on stage – often a difficult job. He tried to keep awake by jabbing a finger in his cheek (from the outside, of course) but it must have been difficult at times, such as during the speech made by Charlotte Leslie MP, who began to recite a large part of the plot of the film *Ghost* in which Patrick Swayze tries to throw a mug at the man who killed him, but can't because he's a ghost. Apparently that's what life was like under Labour. No, I don't understand either.

The party logo of an oak tree, which has been compared (by my colleague Steve Bell) to a urinating elephant, has been retouched as a Union Jack, which is also weird; he should be named Percy the Patriotic Pissing Pachyderm.

So the whole day had the feel of a post-waking dream. Events and images followed one another with no apparent connection.

Baroness Warsi spoke. Being youngish, working class and brown of complexion, she was as unlike the vast majority of the delegates as it is possible to be. As well as being joint party chairman (no 'chair' or even 'chairwoman' nonsense for the Tories), she is minister without portfolio. She said she didn't know what that meant. She should: you get a lovely red and gold portfolio, marked 'Minister without Portfolio'.

Next there was an unexplained display of Indian dancing. The gorgeous silk robes, the sinuous, hypnotic music, the languorous, curling curves! None of this recalled the days of Edward Heath or Sir Alec Douglas-Home.

A pause. Then for some reason the sound system began to play Ringo Starr singing 'Gotta pay your dues, if you wanna sing the blues,' or in the Tory version, 'Gotta pay your dues if you wanna reserve tickets for the annual dinner dance and raffle.'

Lord Young next appeared, to talk about health and safety and how he was going to stop all that rubbish. Did you know there were restaurants where they won't give you a toothpick because it might injure your mouth? And he had heard of an Italian restaurant 'where you have to set light to your own *osso buco*!'

Perhaps he meant Sambuca, the liqueur that is traditionally set alight. He got a loud cheer anyway. But what could be crazier or more dreamlike than this Tory nightmare of a restaurant where you have to take charcoal briquettes and a blowtorch in order to incinerate your own veal stew? Who said the new government wouldn't make a difference?

George Osborne made his first conference speech as chancellor. As before, David Cameron sat in the body of the hall. It was hard to spot him at first. He should have been wearing a red and white striped sweater, like in the *Where's Wally?* books. 'Look, darling, Wally's at the Conservative conference now!' Your toddler would be asleep in minutes.

Mr Osborne was preceded by three of his understrappers, who were clearly put on to be so dull that the chancellor would seem interesting. This calming-down process was necessary, because they had been preceded by Boris Johnson, who is adored by the conference. He made his traditional attack on the party leadership, this time covertly accusing Osborne of starving London – 'the great motor of the British economy' – of badly needed funds.

But he surrounded this lightly disguised assault with plenty of Borisovian jokes and wordplay. He planned a cable car across the Thames, 'and we will name it by honouring the sage of Twickenham, Vince Cable!' He also praised Barclay's bank for funding his bike loan scheme, 'to the tune of 25 million smackeroonies!'

Perhaps the delegates would have been keener on George Osborne's speech if, when he told them he was going to cut child benefit for some of them – at least the few with children under the age of 35 – he had pointed out that it would save one billion smackeroonies.

The absence of smackeroonies was the important theme of the speech. We were paying £109 million every day on servicing the structural deficit – smackeroonie meltdown! But as so often with an Osborne speech, there were more subtle messages interwoven into his theme, like the barely audible double bass in a jazz riff. Lower taxes for the poor! Capital gains tax up! No retreat on the 50p top rate of income tax! Whole chunks could have come from the Labour manifesto.

As for the Lib Dems, people had said that he and Vince Cable would knife each other in the back. 'What do they think we are? Brothers?'

A good gag, right on the smackeroonie.

7 October 2010

David Cameron used his speech to flesh out some of his vision of the Big Society. It is going to be even more hectic than we thought. Yesterday the prime minister told us we were going to have to start a great project in our neighbourhood, launch a business, demand a new school, patrol the streets against crime, and root out waste in government.

There won't be a spare moment in the day. At 6am, we'll be up, tramping the streets, marching drunken revellers off home. By 8am we'll be working on a spanking new community project, possibly building a life-size model of Percy the Pissing Pachyderm for the park. By 9am we'll be founding a new business, possibly cold-calling people in India and asking if they have all their insurance needs. This will leave a few minutes to eradicate waste in local government, by Tazering a minority self-esteem co-ordinator, grade II? Then we will demand a new school. The prime minister wasn't clear how we might do that. Perhaps we'll stand outside Michael Gove's house bellowing 'We demand a new school!' until a patrol of local vigilantes bundles us into the back of a van and makes us paint old folk's homes for 180 hours.

This, we were told, was 'the Big Society – blasting through!' It demanded 'big citizens'. So amid all those foot patrols there will be huge people, blasting through. What happens if they meet? Won't there be a fight?

So life is going to be very hectic.

And the same is true of all of us, apparently. 'The British people are not passengers – they are drivers.' Back-seat drivers for the most part. 'Look out, there's a giant micturating elephant straight ahead!'

The defence cuts mean that much British history will have to be re-written. A modern Shakespeare would have written, 'Once more into the breach, dear friend ... or close up quite a small part of the wall with our English dead.' Churchill would have stirred everyone by saying, 'This was his finest hour!' Wellington would have announced, 'I don't know what he does to the enemy, but by God, he frightens me.' And Drake would have declaimed, to no one in particular, 'There is plenty of time to finish my game of solitaire, and thrash the Spaniards too.' Nelson: 'Kiss me, anyone. Anyone?'

All right, it isn't quite that bad. There are to be two new aircraft carriers, but no aircraft to put on them apart, perhaps, for an advance squadron of stealth paper darts.

Ed Miliband made a nervous reply, repeating 'I also welcome...' three times. But if the prime minister thought his problems were over, he was wrong. For there arose Sir Peter Tapsell, a panjandrum's panjandrum, and someone who makes even other double-breasted MPs look like Norman Wisdom stepping on a banana skin at the top of a marble staircase.

Hansard writers stood by. They knew that Sir Peter's words would soon be carved and gilded upon a mighty limestone memorial in or near Whitehall, so that every word would be preserved for generations yet unborn.

'Is the pwime minister aware [Sir Peter has a slight speech impediment] that there will be many who view with gweat concern the decision to postpone the vital decisions on the future of the Twident nuclear detewent until after 2016, after [he thumped the word 'after' as if it was a hooligan who had attacked his daughter] the genewal election, when! For all we

274

know! The Lib Dems! [he pronounced the name of that party as if referring to the lice that live under stones] may still be there in the cabinet, lifelong opponents of the nuclear detewent, who will continue to twy to veto it!

'This decision looks like the subordination of the national interest to political expediency!'

Once you have been rolled over by Sir Peter you generally stay rolled over, though in this case David Cameron picked himself up and, like a cartoon character who, flattened by a train, gets up and runs away, brushed himself off and disappeared.

3 December 2010

The expenses scandal continued.

Snow had fallen over London yesterday, which is perhaps why there was only a light sprinkling of MPs on the green benches, even though the topic was always a favourite – themselves.

They were pondering the bodies that now have control over their financial affairs. One of the things that bothered them was that some opponents at election time invent spending scandals purely in order to be able to report them on the lines of, 'My opponent is being investigated for his outrageous claims.' Many of these allegations disappear in a puff of smoke as soon as the election is over.

But how can you judge some of the claims published yesterday? Obviously none of us can begrudge Gloria de Piero MP, who claimed £1 for cleaning gloves – which of us would expect her to handle her constituents' mail with rough, raw, washday hands? Can anyone jib at Bob Russell claiming £83.13 for toilet paper in his constituency office? Do we expect him to cut up copies of *Lib Dem Focus* for the same purpose?

Another problem was the suggestion that MPs should also log what they do in their spare time. Bernard Jenkin was furious. 'If we go on holiday to paint water colours, we would have to log that!' Mr Jenkin was perhaps being a trifle disingenuous, since rather than being a water colourist, he is better known as parliament's most celebrated nudist. (A friend of mine has a house in Scotland near the Jenkins. Once, sailing round a loch, he discovered the entire Jenkin family, from Lord – 'brush your teeth in the dark' – Jenkin down to the youngest, disporting themselves nude by the waterside. Not a sight anyone should have to register.)

Round about this time, Jim Naughtie on the Today *programme acci-*
dentally called the culture secretary Jeremy Hunt, Jeremy Cunt. The
phrase was soon adapted to 'you stupid Hunt' or 'those Lib Dems
on tuition fees, what a load of Jeremys!' Andrew Marr made the same
mistake in a later programme the same morning, and it turned out
to be infectious.

Labour attacked the police minister, Nick Herbert, who is rela-
tively new and a little nervous. Especially as the coalition is
cutting its spending on the police, so many forces will have to
reduce their numbers. Mr Herbert insisted that there was no
link between public spending on the police and the incidence
of crime.

Labour MPs fell about in heaps. Greater Manchester alone
is to lose 1,400 officers, at a time when the government is planning to spend £100 million on electing independent police
commissioners – cash that could pay for real coppers, not
politically chosen commissars.

Mr Herbert is a nice, thoughtful man, but he was rattled at
all this barracking. When a Labour MP asked him what his
constituents would make of the reductions, he lost it. As if we
were watching Oliver Hardy taking charge of a piano, or Larry
David trying to make an apology, we could only dare to
glimpse through our fingers.

He tried to reply. 'I accept that those cunts…' he began, and
there was a one-second pause while everyone turned to his or
her neighbour and asked, 'Did he really say that?' Then they
realise that he had, and the place collapses. Mr Herbert tried to
leave the Chamber with what shreds of dignity he had left, but
cries of 'Seven per cent cunts!' echoed from the walls behind him.

10 December 2010

The great political struggle at the end of the coalition's first year was over university fees. Students demonstrated several times, with some of the marchers turning violent. There was a particularly large demo the day that the Commons debated the fees.

It was a Masque of the Red Death moment, as outside demonstrators hurled metal fencing and snooker balls at the police, while the mounted coppers charged against them. Inside, oblivious, MPs were debating in something close to carnival mood. Three protesters got into the public gallery and began chanting before being bundled out by attendants – though since the thick glass screens that protect MPs from the voters are sound-proof, nobody could hear anything, so the event resembled a fight between two fish in an aquarium.

By the end it was the coalition that looked miserable. Labour MPs, who knew there was no chance of their winning the vote against the fees, let out a huge cheer as the government's majority was quartered and more than half the Lib Dems either abstained or voted against.

David Cameron chewed a fretful lip. Vince Cable stared straight ahead and Nick Clegg looked miserable, but then he always does.

A great prolier-than-thou fight broke out between those from humble origins who had only got an education because they hadn't had to pay fees, and those from equally humble origins, who thought that the new system would actually make it easier for people from poor backgrounds to go to university.

Gareth Thomas wound up for Labour, calling Cameron and Clegg 'Britain's premier loan sharks'. David Willetts marshalled both his brains to try to calm the situation. No luck. Nick Clegg walked in to loud and sarcastic Labour cheers. They are so happy to see the hated Lib Dems imploding.

At last the vote, and several Lib Dems, headed by their deputy leader Simon Hughes, sat ostentatiously on the bench, refusing to join the kettled Tories as a whips' push forced them into the aye lobby.

A few more victories like this and the coalition really will be in trouble.

The last prime minister's questions before Christmas, and inevitably it had a pantomime theme. Ed Miliband accused David Cameron of being good at the broad brush and the air brush, but useless at the details.

Cameron was as ever quick on the uptake. 'For a moment I thought I was up against Basil Brush!' Did half the Chamber go 'boom, boom'? Need you ask?

The row was about spending on the NHS, and I won't trouble you with the details, except to say that once again they proved that you can demonstrate anything with statistics.

Miliband said that Cameron was leaving the hard work to Nick Clegg, who was 'the back end of the pantomime horse'. 'It's about time that the front legs take some of the responsibility!'

To which the prime minister quite niftily replied, 'If he wants to talk pantomime, it won't be long before he is hearing, "Look behind you!"'

But it was all so predictable. Why can't we have fresh metaphors from the world of theatre? Given the national situation they might be best coming from tragedies. For instance, 'Like Hedda Gabler, he is stuffing the memories of his own incompetence into the wood-burning stove of the electorate's forgetfulness!'

Or, 'The honourable member reminds me of the characters in *Who's Afraid of Virginia Woolf?* pretending to themselves that they have had the baby of economic success, when in reality the child was never born.'

Maybe, 'Is the chancellor aware that, like Gloucester in *King Lear*, his eyes have been put out, so he is blind to the gaping hole he has left in the nation's accounts?'

Things would perk up if we had more references to Jacobean revenge tragedies. 'As in the last act of *The Duchess of Malfi*, the stage is strewn with the bloody corpses of the cabinet's political reputations. Will the right honourable member agree with me that, in the words of John Webster, he and his colleagues are "merely the stars' tennis balls, struck and banded which way pleases them", and that this is no more evident than in their handling of the education maintenance allowance?'

It would make a welcome change.

The other source of clichéd metaphor is always the fate of the Titanic. *Almost invariably the stock phrases roll out: 'they are re-arranging the deck chairs on the* Titanic,' *or 'like the band on the* Titanic, *they appear oblivious to the fate that awaits them…' Why not 'as the ship of state steams towards disaster, they are down in the first-class lounge, painting nude pictures of Kate Winslet…'?*

After Christmas we had a press conference given by Ed Miliband. These events tend to be slightly embarrassing.

He did not look at ease. The dark eyes stared fixedly at the back of the room as if he had seen something terrible there, something he could never cope with. North Korean storm troopers? A woman he had once loved but abandoned? His brother? Or more likely, TV cameras. It is hard to concentrate on someone who looks as if he wants nothing more than a speedy escape by a side door.

Then he talks. And talks. But it all sounds rehearsed and memorised. 'In their politically motivated desire to propagate a myth about the last Labour government, they are ignoring the real lessons…'

And several more like that. He was like one of those old talking dolls. Pull a string and they went, 'Can I have a hug, mummy?' over and over, except that this doll has an incredibly long string, and says less winsome things, such as, 'It is this deceit about the past that is causing them to make the wrong decisions,' so that not even the most obsessive child would pull the string twice.

Sometimes the mechanism inside doesn't have an answer. He was asked if the word 'deceit' wasn't a bit strong. 'My mother told me never to call anyone a liar, so I won't. But I think they are practicing a deceit,' he said to laughter, because he meant, 'I would never call anyone mendacious, but they are fibbing.'

13 January 2011

David Cameron cares a lot about his appearance. This is something I learned at the Tory conference when he approached me and Steve Bell, the Guardian *cartoonist, during a party. Steve always draws him with a condom over his head, and had previously explained to the prime minister that this was because he had remarkably smooth skin. At first he had pictured him covered in cling film, then decided the condom served even better.*

I explained that the paper had asked for the condom, and its teat, or 'reservoir', to be removed. But there had been so many complaints from readers that it went right back again. 'Well,' said Cameron, 'you can push the condom too far,' which struck me as good advice for life as well as political cartooning.

This particular session followed the discovery that the nationalised banks were actually paying the same huge bonuses to the people who had caused them to be nationalised in the first place.

The first prime minister's questions of the year, and we craned forward so as to miss nothing. David Cameron's bald patch is still there! Yet – and this seems to me almost incredible – it has moved! Last summer it was on the left of his head, as you see it from behind. Now it has shifted to the right. How is this possible? Is he getting an Elton John weave that's gone wrong? Or is it just because he combs his hair in different directions?

Politicians would say that this is an entirely trivial matter. They can't be bothered with such silliness when there are important things to be done. In their case, trading personal insults.

Ed started off fairly well, pointing out silkily that Cameron had promised that in the banks owned by the public, nobody would get a bonus of more than £2,000. 'Can the prime minister update us on progress in implementing this promise?' Cameron insisted, mysteriously, that this was all the fault of the Labour government.

Then he decided to be rude, specifically about Alan Johnson, the shadow chancellor. 'I know he can't do the numbers. There is no point in Wallace asking Gromit about that one.'

This line smelled of late nights by aides and speechwriters in fuggy rooms, and sessions fuelled by coffee and Diet Coke.

The PM came up with another one-liner. 'That was such a long question, he should be thinking about a TV career and getting his brother to run the Labour party.'

So Ed described John Redwood as a 'Vulcan', a reference to *Star Trek* in which the intrepid voyagers are always landing on planets where the atmosphere is similar to Earth's, and the inhabitants all speak a version of English, but look truly weird, and so all in all are very similar to the House of Commons.

Cameron finished off by producing another sweat-stained line: 'We've got a shadow chancellor who can't count, and a Labour leader who doesn't count ... he is the nothing man!'

And with that he swept out of the Chamber, possibly for an appointment at the Michael Fabricant Trichology Clinic (first consultation free).

Much of the time Cameron speaks in grandiose sentences which mean less than appears at first. 'Teachers nurture the human capital that will create enterprise,' he said about this time, and I found myself thinking of some poor sod levering himself out of a staffroom armchair, saying 'I suppose I'd better go and nurture the human capital that is Year 9.'

He also became celebrated for changing his mind. One of the earlier flip-flops came with the plan to privatise the nation's forests.

I've worked out what it's like – the government resembles the dodgems at a funfair. Ministers all sit in their own cars, driving in a random direction. They press the accelerator: sometimes the car moves forward, but often it goes back or nowhere at all. Swing the wheel to the left, and the car goes right. Or vice versa. Drivers crash into each other, and sparks fall from the roof. The difference is that the spectators are having fun while the drivers are close to despair.

Yesterday's fender-bender, or bumper-thumper, was the plan to sell off forests. Caroline Spelman, the environment secretary, whose bill it was to be, had to announce its demise in the Commons. She had already been royally shafted by David Cameron, who had killed it off in question time. Mr Cameron is a PR man, and he can spot a disaster looming. Privatising trees was the equivalent of trying to sell 'Mr Snotty' brand toothpaste, or calling a rock band the Kiddy-Fiddlers.

So it was a humiliation for the government, which makes it a normal day. Mrs Spelman had decided that her best defence was frankness. She took complete responsibility. She had boobed. Got it all wrong. And she admitted it, at enormous length.

It might have been slightly more convincing if she had spent a little less time proclaiming her own shining virtue. She averred, not once but twice, that she always told her own children that honesty was the best policy. I wondered what teatime might be like in the Spelman household.

'Mummy, I have done a bad thing.'

'I am so glad you want to tell me about it. Now, get it off your chest, darling, and let Mummy know what happened.'

'I promulgated a policy that would have raised considerable sums, but which failed to take into account the strength of public feeling, Mummy.'

'Why, you little bastard! Take that!'

She told us about her own great integrity in the tone of voice you might use for saying that, if the weather were inclement, the fete would take place in the village hall. It made life slightly difficult for Mary Creagh, her Labour opposite number, who might have expected some credit for the debacle. She had to acknowledge Mrs Spelman's apology. But she had a swingeing attack all ready, and didn't want to waste it. Given that it was like taking candy from a fish, or shooting a baby in a barrel, it wasn't very good, partly because she had to cope with continuous barracking from Tory MPs trying to cover Mrs Spelman's embarrassment, partly because she ended by announcing, 'If they won't stand up for the countryside, we will!'

The notion that Labour was more friendly to people who live in the country delighted the Tories, who shouted 'More!' in a mocking sort of way.

Mrs Spelman continued to praise her own candour, relentlessly. 'It is a good example of how humility is a valuable quality in a politician,' she mused.

'Even if I say so myself!' yelled Labour's Kevin Brennan, so puncturing the most truthful politician since George Washington also chopped down a tree.

One of the new intake best-loved by the opposition is the Honourable Jacob Rees-Mogg, the son of Lord Rees-Mogg, famed as the least reliable prognosticator since the pre-war astrologist who called Hitler 'a man of peace'.

His son, by his accent, bearing, background and lack of self-awareness, is a gift for Labour since it is a perfect reminder of the old class war which nurtured and delighted so many of them. The night after this session, Rees-Mogg Jr appeared in a BBC documentary about class in Britain, and declared himself 'a man of the people'.

Prime minister's questions were about the economy. Later there stood up the Honourable Jacob Rees-Mogg. A great cheer rose from the Labour benches. They love him. Like Cameron, he went to Eton and Oxford. He was conceived in privilege, and nine months later born in privilege. No doubt he wore a three-piece romper suit in Harris Tweed, obtained by his parents from Toffs 'R' Us. Over his head there hovers a phantom top hat, and behind his back you can almost hear the tailcoat flapping. You sense the presence of Nanny in the public gallery, leaning over to make sure he has wiped his nose.

If the middle-class Andy Coulson exists to make the prime minister conscious of the people he needed to reach, then Rees-Mogg is there to remind him of the folk whence he came.

The Speaker silenced the Labour oiks. Rees-Mogg thanked him, in the manner in which he might thank his gamekeeper. 'Is not the lesson from the noble Baroness Thatcher that, once you have set an economic course, you should stick to it?' He sat down triumphantly while, no doubt, David Cameron inwardly groaned. Labour MPs cried, 'More, more!'

Select committees often give us a chance to hear people who would never normally have to answer to parliament.

It was a great occasion. Three of the most magnificent magnificos in British public life were gathered together to speak to a committee of MPs. No more powerful panjandrums exist. All were former cabinet secretaries and heads of the civil service: Lord Armstrong of Ilminster, GCB, CVO, Lord Wilson of Dinton, GCB, and Lord Turnbull of Enfield, KCB, CVO, leading immediately to a mystery: what did Lord Wilson do wrong that he didn't get a CVO, or Companion of the Victorian Order? Why doesn't that bauble dangle from his tree?

These were people who made Sir Humphrey look like the boy from the post room. And they had that timeless skill held by all the greatest and the goodest of saying almost nothing, but in a very prolix fashion. The chairman, Bernard Jenkin, kept begging them to keep their answers short. But they could no more do that than paint their backsides blue and dance on the table.

Take the discussion on the powers of the Crown. Labour's Paul Flynn, the thinking man's Dennis Skinner, pointed out that while the Queen never expresses political views, her eldest son does little else. And some Tory MPs had been fearful that in 1990 the Queen might call a general election after the defenestration of Margaret Thatcher. Shouldn't we define what the sovereign can and cannot do?

Here is Lord Wilson's reply: 'The fact is that by not defining it over the centuries, we have allowed the role of the sovereign to evolve in a very British way, without creating crises. We are lucky to have a sovereign who has such wide experience of political life, and who has met the prime minister of the day weekly, in order to discuss affairs of state. But if you tried to put it into law, you would have trouble pinning down the essence of it. Better to move incrementally...'

In other words, let's do nothing at all. But let's do it at interminable length!

Lord Turnbull was asked whether the civil service had held back radical change. 'Radicalism, I have no problem with. Initiativitis is a different matter.'

And having invented this extraordinary new word, he gave a little shudder.

Environment questions are rarely fascinating events, though they do throw up some jargon you will never hear on The Archers *or read in* Cider with Rosie.

They were discussing the EU's appalling Common Fisheries Policy. My mind drifted to Hemingway's novel, *The Old Man and the Sea,* and how it might have turned out if Hemingway had needed to take account of the new rules. All jargon is from the session.

'The old man's forehead crinkled and above him the sun flamed in the pewter sky like the eyes of a Parisian *putain. Madre de Dios,* he had had bad luck. His mind returned to his youth, when his skin was smooth and the women thought him beautiful, to the lost days before the CFP's broken regulations, based on a centralised, top-down system, had come into force under directive number 687 (B,i[d]). "Local and regional sea-based management," he muttered with his sour breath, before spitting on the stones that lay beneath his feet.

'"Get in the boat!" he said to the boy. "Today we will catch us a marlin, a marlin great as any whale, with skin like a baby's skin, and this we shall sell in the market for many, many pesos."

'"But old man," said the boy, "the market is closed. The government now tells us that it is 'supermarkets who are key in driving forward the fisheries agenda'."

'The old man spat again. "Boy, hear me. None of this will change until the coalition wins the support of the radical end of the EU reform spectrum!"'

(This goes on, in Hemingway's bloated prose, till the old man finally hooks his marlin and spends two days pulling it in.)

'"Fish, you were a fine and noble opponent," said the old man. "And now I shall return you to your ancestors and to your offspring."

'"You cannot do that," cried the boy, "for you will contravene ministerial policy on driving down discard levels!"

'"Imbecile child! I shall do as I please!" And the old man spat once more.

'"But, old man, following the latest catch quota trials, investment incentives and selective netting, we now have statutory on-ship CCTV, which will observe all that you do with an eye as all-seeing as the all-seeing eye of God himself!"

'"Bugger," said the old man.'

The galleries were packed for the first encounter between the chancellor, George Osborne, and his newly appointed shadow, Ed Balls. Mr Osborne was clearly nervous; he had increased the taxes on banks by some £800 million, live on Radio 4, in the morning. This means that the interview costs someone £200 million a minute – surely more than even William Hague can command.

Both sides had arrived with folders full of sound bites. And a host of dubious statistics. The economy generates an immense number of figures, so that you can prove anything you wish with them. And they did.

Mr Balls asked how it was that the chancellor had blamed the slowing of the British economy on the bad weather, whereas Americans had even worse weather and their economy was rebounding. Was it the wrong kind of snow?

Mr Osborne's lip curled even more than usual. 'Now you and the leader of the opposition know what it is to be the people's second choice!' he sneered.

Mr Balls then got his Y-fronts in a twist. The chancellor should have spent less time on the ski slopes of Switzerland and more in the meeting halls of Davos, where he would have been able to hear the US Treasury Secretary explain why Labour was right.

Was there a winner? Osborne, I should say, but by a whisker, and in any case, who cares except them?

Then after hearing the mewlings and squeakings of various underlings, satraps and myrmidons, arose Sir Peter Tapsell.

Immediately a crack team of seamstresses at the Gobelin factory were put on alert to start preparing their latest commission: 'Sir Peter Tapsell Addresses The House Of Commons On The Topic Of Bankers' Bonuses.'

Impoverished women in the stews of Paris wept for joy, for this monumental work would mean their children had food! And shoes!

Sir Peter's assumption of the vertical position was met by loud Labour cheers. He paused for the tidal wave to rush back. Then he spake, thus.

'Why are bankers' bonuses not paid out of pwofits, not wevenue, as they always were by my own very efficient stockbwoking firm?'

It was a very good question, landing a serious blow on the government, so he sat down to even louder Labour cheers.

Prime minister's questions were magnificently ill-tempered. David Cameron seemed to be nudging the very edge of his reason. The Speaker also kicked into teddy-throwing mode. It allowed Ed Miliband to knock off the best insult since he got the job.

Cameron was raving that Labour had no new ideas. 'The tree has been chopped down, and there is absolutely nothing in it!' he said, confusingly. It seemed he was referring to a Labour booklet full of blank pages for party members to jot down their ideas. But they foolishly labelled it 'My fresh ideas', which made it look as if they didn't have any. Another Labour catastrophe, like the time years ago when they asked people to contribute £1 to their new headquarters and in exchange get their name carved on a brick. But it turned out it cost more than £1 to carve each brick.

'Where are his big ideas?' Cameron yelled at Miliband. 'He hasn't got any!' At this the Labour leader said calmly, 'He shouldn't get so angry. It will cloud his judgment. And he is not the first prime minister I've said that to.'

Now this was more insulting than it seemed. For Cameron has always been a great admirer of Tony Blair. But the prime minister Miliband served was Gordon Brown. He was, in effect, accusing the present incumbent of being another stapler-thrower, underling-bawler, back-of-the-seat thumper like Brown is reputed to have been. It must have been like having someone stab you with an ivory letter opener – probably not lethal but certainly painful.

The row was over the 'Big Society'. Nobody knows what this really means, and Cameron may not either, because he hasn't told us. But yesterday a vague shape seemed to be forming. It seems to be along these lines: librarians, and people who work in citizens' advice bureaux and community centres, are to be fired. This will leave them with loads of time to volunteer for unpaid work in libraries, citizens' advice bureaux and community centres.

The arrangement sounds perfect. If there is a flaw in it, the prime minister hasn't yet spotted it.

He mentioned the Big Society Bank. Presumably this is a bank where the cashiers work for nothing, and send out letters saying, 'You have not been charged for this letter.'

As he shouted, the noise level grew. The Speaker cut in, very crossly. 'Oh, oh, these exchanges are unnecessarily rowdy. I must ask members to consider what the public thinks.'

This was greeted by a spell of mild jeering from many Tories. It was the first time I had heard such *lèse majesté*. They can't stand him, but have always thought it advisable to hide the fact, in public at least.

15 February 2011

Perhaps realising that most people were still in the dark about the Big Society, David Cameron held a meeting to enlighten us.

We gathered in Somerset House, London, to discover what the Big Society really was. It was quite exciting, like being invited to hear the true secret of the Da Vinci Code, or learning the recipe for Colonel Sanders' secret sauce.

In the end it was a littler vaguer. I felt as if we had been invited to the end of an Agatha Christie novel and Hercule Poirot had gathered us all together to tell us he hadn't the faintest idea who the murderer was, but he was jolly keen to find out.

There are certainly some fine phrases. 'We need social recovery to mend the broken society, and to me that is what the Big Society is all about!' There were hints about what we might do. Maybe we could band together to start a school, or save our local pub from closing. Or we could set up a 'co-op inside the health service'. You or I could volunteer as brain surgeons – I assume that's what he meant. Or you might be like him, and run a crèche 'very badly' at Sunday school. Fair enough: the Good Samaritan was an early member of the Big Society, and the parable of the talents was about the first banker's bonus.

Businesses could be brought in, he said. Marks & Spencer were doing a marvellous job training people who might not otherwise have work. Possibly they call it the Size 18 Society, or in menswear the XXL Society.

There is a great 'let's roll up our sleeves and get on with it' air to everything the prime minister says. He was surrounded by natural Big Society adherents – the heads of charities, voluntary groups and so forth. Some were enthusiastic, others less so. One man said the problem was medium term – the cuts meant that there was a 'sense of devastation and loss'.

'Let's deal with that devastation!' Cameron cried. We instinctively shrank back, afraid that a prime ministerial finger might point our way: 'You! You there! Go out and *kill* that devastation!'

Nothing would damp him down. He makes Tigger looked like Rip Van Winkle. 'This is my absolute passion! It is about a different way of governing, and it is going to get every bit of my passion!'

One journalist ventured that many of his party didn't know what he was talking about. 'The reason I talk about it is because I am passionate about it!' he said, before dashing passionately away.

As deputy prime minister, Nick Clegg had his own question time. Following the great decline in his popularity, these events could be embarrassing as Labour spotted a victim.

Question time with Nick Clegg was unremittingly awful, grim, nerve-shreddingly ghastly. You yearned for him to wake up, sweat soaking his pillow, realising that it had all been a terrible dream, a mother's soothing hand on his brow.

I wondered if the bullies felt some remorse. Did they ask themselves what it must be like for an innocent, vulnerable man to face such torment? Was there the teeniest twinge of conscience that they had made life hellish for someone so unable to cope with their abuse?

At the same time, do we not suspect that the victim covertly accepts, even welcomes, his fate? On the surface, Mr Clegg seemed quite unprepared for what was coming his way, like someone walking down a railway track who is astonished to hear the 10.40 from Euston approach.

It started fairly quietly. Roberta Blackman-Woods wanted to know about the plan for MPs to be recalled by their voters if they had broken the rules, and if so, how many of them would be Liberal Democrats. The rest of her words were lost in a delighted roar. Mr Clegg said that the bill would deal only with serious wrongdoing. 'Exactly!' yelled a dozen or more Labour MPs.

Chris Bryant joined in the monstering. Who decided who had broken the rules? What about a party that promised 3,000 more police officers, then cut the number by 10,000? Mr Clegg responded with nervous hand signals, the left making a cowpat, the right hand a spider dancing on a hot plate. At one point he called for MPs who could 'speak out, and, er, er, you know, articulate…' Send for Lionel Logue!

A Conservative, Andrea Leadsom, tried to help him. Big mistake. What was he doing to restore the public's faith in politics and in MPs? This time the Labour roar was mixed with shrieking and cackling, as if we were watching a convention of drunken witches. Mob hysteria was taking hold. The Clegg reply, 'Our programme is directed to restore public faith in MPs,' only raised the noise level.

Harriet Harman cruelly pointed out that the word 'Clegged' now meant 'completely betrayed'. And John Mann asked brutally, 'What is the point of Nick Clegg?'

There are many answers to that. He could have said something like, 'The point is fighting for a country that pays its debts, but is fair, just and open. I'd like to know what the point of the honourable member is.' Almost anything would have sufficed, except for the answer he got, which was: 'Err.'

Gleeful Labour MPs must have been tightening their body parts to prevent nasty accidents on the benches. But Mr Clegg continued. He chuntered about how a chief executive is still a chief executive, even when he's abroad, a football manager is still in charge of his team even at an away game. I wanted to lean over and shout, 'Stop digging!'

A Labour voice shouted, 'Only two minutes left!' and bang on the hour, the Speaker ended the misery.

One of the most embarrassing parts of the British operation in Libya was the capture of an SAS group who had been helicoptered into the east of the country and were promptly captured by a bunch of puzzled farmers. They were only released after a phone call to British diplomats.

Mr Hague called the disaster 'a misunderstanding'. It seemed a strange word to use in the midst of all the diktats, warnings and admonitions usually doled out by our foreign secretaries to wayward nations. Clearly he was trying to put the best face he could on the debacle: 'Who Dares Spins', perhaps.

Andy McNab it wasn't. I wondered how the chronicler of so many SAS triumphs would have coped with the capture of a crack unit by north African farmers. 'The first rays of the sun were rising in the east. Suddenly we saw them. They were advancing towards us.

'"Sarge!" I whispered, "They're armed! They've got pitchforks, hoes, bags of mulch. These guys mean business!"

'"All right," said the sergeant, and his calm voice put some bottle back in me. "I've faced a few hairy situations in my time. What we're going to do is put in a call to a top-level diplomat and get him to make a whingeing request to release us. That'll teach these bastards a lesson they won't forget in a hurry!"

'Moments later we were seized and forced to eat a nourishing breakfast. Cereal bungling is what the politicians call it...'

Back in the Chamber, Douglas Alexander, Labour's spokesman, was giving Mr Hague the kind of rubbishing this government's ministers are getting used to. 'Serial bungling,' he called it, spelled that way I suppose. He couldn't understand why the SAS and their party had been dropped dramatically from the skies instead of driving into Libya from Egypt, like other foreign visitors.

If new neighbours came to live in the foreign secretary's street, he asked, would he introduce himself by ringing their doorbell, or would he climb over their fence in the middle of the night? Mr Hague's defence was the usual politician's strategy: yes, he had authorised the operation. Yes, he took responsibility. No, it wasn't his fault.

Mr Hague had been under pressure from several quarters. Heavy hints were dropped when it turned out that he had shared a room with one of his aides. He felt obliged to reveal to the world that his wife, Ffion, had suffered several miscarriages. He seemed generally detached and disaffected. The press had a curious way of expressing the problem.

To Foreign Office questions, to answer the conundrum asked by all the British people, or at least the media: has William Hague lost his mojo? This was not a question ever asked of Lord Palmerston.

I wondered how Sherlock Holmes would have tackled the problem.

'Mrs Hudson knocked on our door. "Mr Holmes, there is a most distinguished gentleman to see you!"

'Moments later, there walked into our rooms one of the best-known men in all of England, a man whose face would have been instantly recognised by an earl or a chimney sweep. It was none other than Sir Peter Tapsell, one of the most celebrated politicians of our age.

'"I perceive," said Holmes, "that you have walked here from parliament on a matter of the highest importance."

'"You astound me," said our visitor. "I had heard of your powers, Mr Holmes, but…"

'"A simple matter. It is raining heavily, and you are soaked to the skin. Clearly you walked since if even a cabbie had known you were consulting me, the news would cause the greatest alarm and agitation in the chancelleries of Europe. Now, let us hear of your difficulty."

'Sir Peter groaned. "I will be blunt," he said. "It is the foreign secretary. He has lost his mojo. His mojo! I need hardly tell you, Mr Holmes, that if the news were to leak out it would bring comfort to our enemies and the most terrible anxiety to our allies. The mojo must be returned, and forthwith! I implore you to assist us in this most urgent enterprise!"

'"Pray tell me under what circumstances it was lost."

'"It appears to have gone missing last year, after he shared quarters with another man."

'"And this is now a crime?" asked Holmes, airily waving at our shared bachelor quarters.

'"Enough of one," said the unhappy legislator, "but the mojo was only discovered to be missing when the matter of Libya came to the forefront of our concerns. A number of horrifying misjudgments occurred. And when we searched for the mojo, it was missing!" He buried his head in his hands.

'"A simple matter, but not devoid of interest," said Holmes after our visitor had left. "Clearly the mojo was lost when the foreign secretary was in the midst of one of his notorious 17-pint drinking sessions.

'"I suspect it will be easily traced in the members' smoking room, possibly in the bottom of a beer crate, where it may have been carelessly thrown by the inebriated minister."

'And so it proved to be. The mojo was swiftly restored, and the greatest in the land were able once more to sleep soundly in their beds.

'A few days later, on 15 March 2011, Holmes and I took our places in the Commons gallery. Our client, Sir Peter, rose. "I have never known a foreign secretary surrounded simultaneously by so many difficult problems. I want to say how much I admire the cool efficiency with which he is dealing with them."

'"A most satisfactory ending," said Holmes. "And now I suggest we return and set about some of Mrs Hudson's excellent devilled kidneys!"'

In the meantime, the Commons had voted to support intervention in Libya. There is a pattern for all these events. MPs complain about what is going on in these foreign hell-holes. The government then proposes a war. It will be a short war, involving little loss of life, ending with victory and the prompt, safe return of our troops. The war then drags on without result. Finally it is hard to find an MP who admits to having supported it in the first place.

Meanwhile a lesser, but still important war was going on across the Chamber as the new shadow chancellor Ed Balls faced George Osborne.

There's a famous *Punch* cartoon from around 150 years ago. It shows a mining village. A couple of miners are glaring at a top-hatted toff who has wandered in carrying a cane at an elegant angle.

'First polite native: "Who's 'im, Bill?"'

'Second ditto: "A stranger!"'

'First ditto: "'Eave 'alf a brick at 'im."'

I was put in mind of this yesterday at Treasury questions when the toff, George Osborne, faced the aggressive local, Ed Balls. Until then, the chancellor had had a fairly smooth ride.

Sir Peter Tapsell had made one of his stupendous interventions, calling for a 'complete sepawation' of commercial and investment banks. But for once, Sir Peter was on the government's side, more or less.

Mr Balls showed signs of behaving like one of the natives, raising his right arm and tugging it up and down, which I took to indicate someone pulling the chain on a toilet.

Finally it was his turn, and his chance to heave half a brick. He had, he said, acquired a document that the chancellor had proposed to publish along with his budget, the following day.

'I read it last night, but the chancellor has no need to worry. I won't be showing it to the press as frankly there is nothing worth leaking.' Except, he added, an attack on paternity rights and enterprise zones.

The toff replied languidly that he didn't recognise the document, and if he did, there was nothing in it about paternity rights.

Mr Balls then found the other half brick and lobbed it over. He quoted Vince Cable who, once again, appeared to be opposed to some important aspect of government policy.

Then we heard from the ultimate toff, the nob's nob, Jacob Rees-Mogg in his phantom top hat. He uncoiled himself from the bench to support, in tones that would have seemed strangulated upstairs in *Downton Abbey*, every aspect of the government's policy.

He is the Dennis Skinner of the Conservative party, there to reassure us that the class war is ready to flare up again at any moment. The two red lines down the Chamber have nothing to do with being a sword's length apart – they are there to discourage brick-heaving.

Two minor oddities: Ian Paisley Jr asked a question about, of all things, VAT on toasted sandwiches. For those who recall his father's glory days, it was something of a letdown.

'Let me smell yurr breath!' his dad would say, never following that up with: 'Ah ha, cheese and onion on Kingsmill! The devil's ambrosia!' And you never see a Belfast mob protesting about the increased price of hot lunchtime snacks.

Finally, fashion notes. Sir Gerald Kaufman arrived in a shimmering light grey suit with a faint square pattern woven into the cloth, a shirt striped in purple and mauve, the whole ensemble topped with a necktie in sky blue, navy and orange.

I have now worked out that Sir Gerald's outfits are woven from the most lustrous saris from Oxfam shops in his constituency.

23 March 2011

Budget day came round again.

It was the paradise postponed budget. Gordon Brown used to tell us every year that we were living in a new Elysium, and compared this happy breed to the miserable wretches who inhabited hell-holes such as Germany, Japan and the US.

George Osborne could hardly do that. Instead, the only people he could say were worse off than us were the Greeks, the Portuguese, the Spanish and the poor old Irish. But that was an ephemeral moment – soon, long before the next election, there will be a new Shangri-La in Britain, the most competitive nation in Europe, if not the world. Our children will wear golden slippers and eat lobster at school dinners. (I exaggerate, but not much.)

There was little else the chancellor could do. Faced with every economic indicator – inflation, growth, unemployment – heading in the wrong direction, he could only promise jam tomorrow. But not any old jam. This would be Fortnum & Mason's rose-petal jam gathered by virgins at dawn on Midsummer Day.

Of course he could still blame everything on the last government. We will know things are genuinely improving when he stops doing that – round about 2016, I would guess.

He did concede that recovery would be 'challenging'. This is the word politicians use to mean 'we haven't the faintest idea what to do about it'.

He zoomed right past the reduction of his forecast for growth. Whoomf! The new figures were left behind, like angry pedestrians ignored on a zebra crossing.

His biggest mistake was to declare, 'We are all in this together,' which Labour takes to mean, 'We are all in this together, except for bankers and rich people generally.' So the opposition jeered and hooted merrily for quite some time, so loudly that they woke up Ken Clarke, the lord chancellor, who had been happily asleep during most of the budget speech.

Ed Miliband made a good reply. Admittedly it had all been pre-cooked, and would have been much the same whatever Osborne said, but as ready meals go it was more Tesco's Finest than Lidl. He is beginning to gain experience, and no longer looks like the work experience leader. 'The chancellor isn't rescuing the country. The country needs rescuing from the chancellor' was one line.

Osborne, according to Miliband, had evoked memories of his more or less successful predecessors, such as Nigel Lawson, who was up in the gallery. Why can't he lick his fingers and gaze seductively into the camera, like his daughter? Well, perhaps better not.

Labour had an extraordinary talent for ignoring an issue where they could clearly attack the Tories, for one that would probably not shift a single vote.

The prime minister told a female Labour MP to 'calm down, dear' yesterday. The horror! The sheer, sexist, chauvinist, patronising effrontery of the man! From Labour's reaction, you would have imagined that he had told her not to bother her pretty little head with such things. Or had ogled her bosom, and said something like, 'Don't get many of those to the pound, darling!' Or accused her of being a paedophile who stole charity collecting tins from pubs.

Anyhow, the Labour Party decided that it was the most monstrous thing Cameron had ever said, and called for retribution. Failing that, for thunderbolts to fall from the skies. The MP in question was Angela Eagle, shadow chief secretary and number two in Labour's Treasury team.

It was a bizarre moment. Ed Miliband had done well, being scornful about yesterday's growth figures, which showed a rise of 0.5 per cent, compared to a fall of 0.5 per cent the previous quarter. This shows, in the jargon, that the economy is flatlining.

Cameron (the bald patch seems to have taken up a permanent position on the top right of his scalp) said the numbers showed that the economy was thriving. Miliband pointed out that it wasn't. The Labour leader was clearly right. Mr Cameron's position is that of a man who has decided to put one leg into a combine harvester, and declared it a triumph because he can still hop.

Having scored a good point, at least one that was likely to make the news bulletins, you'd think that Labour would have let it lie. But they didn't.

Mr Miliband raised the question of spending on the NHS. The government claimed to be spending more on the service, but most of that extra cash was going on unnecessary reforms.

Mr Cameron decided to quote Howard Stoate, a GP and former Labour member who is, we are told, in favour of the reorganisation. The Labour front bench began barracking. The following *causerie* ensued.

Cameron: 'He is now a GP. Calm down, listen to the doctor, calm down! "My discussions with fellow GPs" – calm down! – "reveal overwhelming enthusiasm..."' he said, evidently quoting Dr Stoate. The barracking continued. 'I said, "calm down"!'

At this point he turned to Ms Eagle and added – this was the crucial moment – 'Calm down, dear, and I will say it to the shadow chancellor if he likes.' The noise grew horribly.

Ed Balls, a man whose tender sensibilities to all female persons is a byword, shouted: 'Apologise to her!' The prime minister: 'I am not going to apologise. You do need to calm down!'

And that was it – the greatest political insult since the King of France sent tennis balls to Henry V.

What seems to have got lost in this great froth of pointless rage is that Cameron was quoting Michael Winner from the insurance ads on TV. Mr Winner is indeed patronising. But that is the point of the joke. And Cameron has used the same gag before. Also there is a long history of people humorously quoting adverts, from 'Good morning, have you used Pears soap?' to Budweiser's 'Wassup?' campaign. He might as easily have asked about Labour's NHS record and sung, 'Go compare!' Racist anti-Italian bastard.

5 May 2011

A week later, Mr Cameron again got in touch with his childhood.

He was replying to a question from Kelvin Hopkins, a Luton Labour MP. Did the prime minister not realise that half a million more people are going to lose their jobs in the public sector, and another half million in the private sector? And that this would lead to a collapse in the housing market, which in turn would lead to a collapse in the Tory vote and the return of a Labour government? Would he care to say goodbye to many of his colleagues now?

Mr Cameron replied that he had thought Mr Hopkins came from Luton. 'But it sounds to me as if he is from some fairy-dairy land!'

Fairy-dairy land? What on earth was that? What was he on about? Then a colleague reminded me that this was a quotation from the late Benny Hill's great song, 'Ernie (The Fastest Milkman in the West)'. Those who remember this hit will recall that Ernie had a rival for the hand of Sue, a baker called Two-Ton Ted from Teddington. At the end, he and Ernie have a wild west-style shootout, and Ernie is fatally felled by a stale pork pie. He goes to the milkman's Valhalla, or 'fairy-dairy land', from where he haunts Ted and Sue in their marital bed by rattling his ghostly milk crates.

What is startling is that Cameron chose this song on *Desert Island Discs*, even though he was only five years old when it was a hit. He can perform it as a party piece. Maybe it would help to calm down cabinet meetings, which we hear are growing more vituperative as Tories and Lib Dems attack each other.

Chris Huhne: 'You, prime minister, are a braggart and a liar. You are scarcely better than your chancellor, who is a thief and a scallywag!'

Cameron (singing): 'She nearly swooned at his macaroon, and said, "If you treat me right, you'll have hot rolls every morning – and crumpets every night!"'

Huhne: 'Oh well, since you put it like that...'

It could have been worse. Margaret Thatcher's favourite record was Rolf Harris singing 'Two Little Boys', to which the only possible response is 'Aaargh!'

6 May 2011

On 5 May there were local elections – in which the Tories did better than expected, Labour were almost wiped out in Scotland, and the Lib Dems had terrible results on all counts, losing umpteen council seats and, by a huge majority, the referendum on the Alternative Vote system.

The house was more or less empty, as MPs scattered themselves around the country to support their party in the local elections. Except for a few people who were faintly bonkers – one vote short of an alternative, you might say. It was transport questions.

The first topic was the scrapyard fire that had closed the M1 last month. Apparently it had caused temperatures of 1,000 degrees, enough to make steel reinforcements buckle. It was probably enough to buckle Chris Huhne's self-esteem, if you can imagine such a temperature.

The accident evoked a rant from Labour's Denis MacShane, who said that the real problem with the M1 was people who lived in big cities using the road as 'an urban rat run'. He demanded 'motorway vignettes' – toll tickets, I suppose – 'to discourage urban drivers from using it as an ordinary road'.

I don't know how the police are going to distinguish urban drivers from rural ones. 'Take a look at your shoes, sir? Hmm, Italian loafers, I see. Not quite as rural as they might be, are they sir? Can you show me any mud in your car, animal hairs, evidence of abused sheep?'

Much of the session consisted of MPs demanding more money for transport for their constituents, who for various reasons are all uniquely deserving. Take Crossrail, the boondoggle that will cost a minimum of £14.4 billion, around £700 for every household in the land, whether in Lambeth or

312

Lerwick. Lyn Brown of West Ham almost wailed, 'When will I be able to take a train from Stratford to Heathrow?' To which the only possible response is 'Calm down, dear. Take the tube from West Ham to Green Park, then the Piccadilly Line to Heathrow.' It is not a very speedy journey, but I do not see why the rest of us should stump up billions just so Ms Brown can get to the airport sooner to discover that her flight has been cancelled due to snow, fog, or international terrorism.

Then they got onto screwball fares. Philip Hammond, the transport secretary, spoke about 'crunch points', a very good way of describing the bone-crushing, rib-crunching effect of standing for two hours on a Virgin train, jammed up against your fellow passengers. He pointed out that any train leaving Euston at 18.59 is virtually empty because it is at peak time, whereas the first after 19.00 hours is a mobile Black Hole of Calcutta.

But it's weirder than that. I investigated prices yesterday and found that next Friday, according to thetrainline.com, a standard class single on the 19.20 from London to Manchester would cost £69, whereas a first class single would cost £46. No doubt they have put that right, but it does demonstrate how barking all the fares are.

Speaking of Barking, Jeremy Corbyn wanted electrification of part of the line from that part of London to Gospel Oak. It was a matter, he claimed 'of national importance', which translates as 'of national importance in my constituency'. The junior minister, Theresa Villiers, told him politely to get lost. He asked her to meet the 'secret group of Barking to Gospel Oak line MPs' to discuss the matter.

A secret group? It sounds like Enid Blyton. 'Look in the hollow tree to find the next meeting of the secret group! We will have lemonade and sticky buns, and will discuss upgrading the Barking to Gospel Oak line!'

As I said, one bacon buttie short of an on-board buffet.

Our rage against Fifa, the governing body of world football that had denied us the 2018 World Cup and which awarded the 2022 event to Qatar, began to grow at this stage. The relevant parliamentary committee had a hearing.

Qatar is an absolute monarchy, most famous for its 'indented servitude', or, as we used to call it, 'slavery'. Its native populations number just 300,000. It has no tradition of professional football. Much of the country consists of barren plains covered in sand. The daytime summer temperature can reach 50°C, nearly 120°F.

So it sounds like the perfect setting for a football World Cup, right? And yes, it is the venue for the 2022 tournament! (The fact that sharia law obtains throughout makes you wonder what the penalty for hand ball might be.)

Yesterday the Commons culture committee examined the bidding process. Its first witness was Mr Mike Lee, who is credited with the strategy that won the Olympics for London, and for snaffling the World Cup for Qatar.

He thought the tiny kingdom was a spiffy place for a World Cup. We already had the technology to make new stadia cool, even in the broiling midsummer. And it would be green! The power of the sun would be harnessed to cool the heat of the sun. MPs' eyebrows shot up and down like caterpillars on a trampoline.

But the committee members were more interested in the allegations of corruption. The *Sunday Times* had told them that two members of the Fifa committee had been paid $1.5 million to vote for Qatar – which they had duly done.

Mr Lee was shocked, shocked! 'I have no reason to believe it happened. I have seen no evidence of that.' The chairman, John Whittingdale, said that a former member of Fifa had told them that committee members had been offered $1.2 million.

'I never witnessed that, I have never been involved, I have absolutely no reason to believe those allegations are correct!' said Mr Lee.

Surely he must have known something was going on? Apparently not. 'You are asking me questions about something I know nothing about.' How was that possible, given his role?

'I have never seen behaviour I believe is unethical!'

The committee realised it was getting nowhere, slowly, and changed the subject, leaving behind the topic of why, apart perhaps from the Faroe Islands in winter, Fifa had chosen the worst possible venue for a World Cup. (And at least they play football in the Faroe Islands.)

Later Lord Triesman appeared and produced a list of Fifa committee members who, he said, had demanded special favours. He told MPs that Jack Warner had wanted £2.5 million to build an education centre in Trinidad. The Thai member had wanted the TV rights to a friendly match played by England. Most bizarrely, Paraguay's Nicolás Leoz had asked for knighthood. Imagine that one being granted! The Queen would have taken one long look, declared that she had finally lost the will to live, then run herself through with her own sword.

Prime minister's questions became increasingly pointless, though entertaining for the troops. It does have some residual importance, though: a good performance by a leader can raise morale among back-benchers. A poor performance sends them off crossly to lunch.

The session began with a poser. The Tory Philip Hollobone raised the question of votes for prisoners, against which the house has already voted by a majority of 10 to one. 'Will the government bend the knee to the European court, or will they stand up and insist that on this issue Britain will not budge?'

The prime minister said that Britain was 'leading the charge' to make the court pay more attention to national parliaments. And he would 'consider our response to this issue' in the hopes of bringing it 'as close as possible to the will of the House of Commons'.

Pick the bones out of that, and it would collapse like an old Marigold glove.

'Sire, the barbarians are at the city gates!'

'Aye, and so they are, and we will lead the charge to get them to reconsider, in the fullness of time, their decision to lay siege with 10,000 men. And we will look at ways in which they may be persuaded to move closer to our judgment, which is that they don't invade at all.'

Hardly convincing, but he got away with it because Ed Miliband was up next. There followed an obtuse debate about the NHS, which I can summarise like this:

Miliband: Waiting times are up.

Cameron: No, they're not.

Socratic dialogue it wasn't.

After close study I have decided that Nick Clegg always looks sad. It's his default expression. I bet he looked sad on his wedding day. And night. If someone phoned and said, 'I think we've found your children's missing puppy,' he would look even sadder.

Yesterday we had the chance to view him at close range. He and David Cameron were, so to speak, renewing their vows after their wedding in the Downing Street garden just one year ago. They had travelled out together to the Olympic Park and the impressive handball arena. The chairs in this 7,000 seat venue (for handball!) are painted in random primary colours, so that even if it is half empty, the place will look as if every seat is taken – admittedly by people who like to dress only in primary colours. After the Olympics, it will be used for other sports, such as, I hope, pro-celebrity cage wrestling – Katie Price versus Wolverine, perhaps.

The two men walked in, Cameron smiling, Clegg's face apparently thrashed into what his personal face-trainer has assured him is a smile. They were launching yet another campaign to get young people back into work. Around 40 young persons were ranged behind them.

They sat down. At this point Clegg's visage returned to its normal mode. His mouth turned down, and his eyes spoke of an immemorial sorrow, as one who has just learned that Sainsbury's are out of Crunchy Nut Flakes, that the dry cleaners have ruined his novelty tie, or that his party has just been humiliated in the local elections.

Cameron said that youth unemployment was a big problem, even with the economy improving. We reflected that it would be an even bigger problem if the economy didn't improve, as many experts believe that it won't yet. Meanwhile, his deputy looked as if he had just asked the prettiest girl in class to the school dance and she had laughed so much that she sprayed crisp particles into his face.

'We want to help the people who fall between the cracks, who are forgotten and ignored,' Clegg said, and it sounded as if he was talking about the Lib Dems.

They answered questions about David Laws, the chief secretary obliged to resign a year ago for apparently being over-generous to himself with his expenses.

Clegg said that, Laws being a closet gay, he had fiddled the figures only to protect his own privacy. I wondered if a masked mugger could make the same plea. His face snapped back into 'I'm sure I had the winning numbers, but the ticket was in my trouser pocket and got lost in the washing machine' mode.

Old Tommy Cooper joke: 'Horse walks into a pub. Barman asks, "Why the long face?" Horse: "I've just been chatting to Nick Clegg."' Like Mona Lott in *ITMA*, it's being so cheerful that keeps him going.

And the following week, poor Nick Clegg had to announce his plans for House of Lords' reform. They gave the impression of having been worked out by a lonely schoolboy sitting in his bedroom. The scheme was met by almost universal scorn, from every direction. Tory backbenchers, I thought at the time, obliged to take it all seriously, sat and looked like Easter Island statues that had been put in suits and ties as a prank.

The question of David Laws' fiddles finally came up to the house. MPs, usually quite eager to excuse each other, were less generous to Mr Laws, who used to be a member of the Coalition Cabinet, thus hated by all Labour MPs (and, covertly, quite a few Tories).

For 10 years he had been submitting demands for rent to be paid to his partner – in several different properties over the period. He had paid his partner, from public funds, more than the market rate. He had received money for building work that should have been covered by the rent. He had claimed the house he shared in London as his second home, though he spent far more time there than in his constituency.

Kevin Barron, the chairman of the standards committee, was – like many MPs – almost as enraged at the behavior of the press as he was at Mr Laws. The judgment was theirs to make, and 'not for the media'. Perhaps so, except that it was taxpayers' money that Mr Laws had been raking in.

Yet Mr Brennan managed to contain his rage at the papers long enough to add another charge: Mr Laws had chipped in £99,000 towards one property. He was asking the public to recompense him for rent he was paying to himself.

After a short debate, the house decided, without a vote, to punish these crimes with seven days' suspension. Since it took a year to investigate the case, Mr Laws was thus in the position of a burglar who, having been tried over five days, is sent to jail for one hour. Or as a judge might say, 'You have been convicted of a heinous crime. You deserve a condign and exemplary punishment. I hereby sentence you to bunk off work for a week, and let that be a lesson to you.'

24 May 2011

At this time there was a great deal of fuss about injunctions and super-injunctions, whereby people in the public eye – TV stars, actors, footballers etc – were able to protect their privacy by preventing the media from revealing details of their love life. These injunctions (the rarer super-injunction prevents the media from even reporting that the injunction exists in the first place) cost tens of thousands of pounds, and rarely work as they are intended to do, since the names leak quickly and are bandied about everywhere. One popular formula was to put it in the form of a joke: '[name of footballer], [name of actor], and [name of TV star] go into a pub. And I'm afraid I'm not allowed to tell you any more.'

An MP yesterday named Ryan Giggs as the prominent footballer who had obtained an injunction to prevent the media from reporting his affair with a former *Big Brother* contestant. The MP cannot be identified, by me at least, since he is, *prima facie*, guilty of a breach of parliamentary convention, if not the law. (Also he is so hungry for publicity that he would willingly have gone to court to demand that the media did report his affairs.)

So my ruling is that it would not be in the public interest, or his family's interest, for me to name him.

The MP stood up during a brief session devoted to injunctions and privacy law. The attorney general, Dominic Grieve, had already announced that there would be a committee of both houses devoted to the matter. This is the government's way of saying, 'Shut up, will you, while we try to work something out.' John Prescott – now M'lord Prescott – sat in the public gallery, alternately laughing and scowling.

John Whittingdale, who chairs the culture committee, said you would need to be living in an igloo not to know the name of the footballer. There was a danger of making the law an ass. (A bit late to worry about that, I thought.)

Mr Grieve made it clear that nothing would affect parliamentary privilege. But he didn't promise that the media could necessarily report what was being said in parliament. This would truly be a politician's worst nightmare – they could beaver away to expose wrongdoing but nobody could know about their zealous work. Unless they used Twitter.

Then came the moment. I was slightly surprised that the Speaker called the MP, who I can reveal sits for a Midlands constituency and isn't exactly the hunkiest he-man in the house, not that that narrows the field much, frankly. The MP has form, and has tried to break injunctions before. But if he had not been called, he would have barged in on a point of order later, so perhaps Mr Bercow had no choice.

The MP rose to say that about 75,000 people had named Ryan Giggs on Twitter. 'It is obviously impractical to imprison them all, and with reports that Giles Coren faces imprisonment…'

The Speaker leapt up. The thought of *Giles Coren's Prison Feasts*, a 13-part series on BBC 1, was too much. He slapped the MP down, saying that these occasions were for discussing principles, 'not seeking to flout, for whatever purpose.' We were in a state of shock. Mr Bercow had used a transitive verb without an object. Can parliament sink any lower?

We were left to ponder the meaning of these events. Rich footballer has an affair: two days' wonder in the tabloids. Rich footballer tries to hush up affair: this one will run for months if not years.

The MP in question was John Hemming, a Liberal Democrat.

In late May, Barack Obama visited Britain. Some of the gloss might have worn off his image back home, but not here. He gave a speech to both houses of parliament.

After his speech, the president could barely get out of Westminster Hall. He strolled down the central aisle, being accosted by anyone within a few seats of the route. Everyone he met – Glenda Jackson MP, (Lord) David Puttnam, various unknown MPs – all reached out, all wanting to grasp some stardust and sprinkle it on themselves. I was only surprised that nobody was pushing the halt and the lame towards him to be cured.

As he moved up, spontaneous applause would break out. He was being clapped just for being here, for simply existing! Everyone he encountered had that rictus smile, like a very happy corpse, common to people meeting a superstar.

He must think that almost everyone in the world has that emoticon face. For his part, he was wearing the amiable, hesitant smile of someone at a party, introduced to someone else they did not know and will never meet again.

Mind you, the crowd – mostly MPs and peers – were well up for it. The long wait had created a strange, faintly manic feeling in the hall. Gordon Brown and Tony Blair were seated next to each other and did not have a fight. That's how thrilled they were to be there!

Even the arrival of the state trumpeters, who took up their positions under the stained glass at the south end, like the world's poshest window cleaners, raised a laugh. There was so much glee I half expected empty lager cans to be heaved over.

Simon Hoggart

When Obama finally arrived, he did seem pleased to be there. The man loves a crowd and sucks up its energy. Don't forget that he first decided he was in with a chance when he spoke to a handful of people somewhere in the sticks and a little old lady yelled, 'Fired up! Ready to go!' This lot were fired up, ready to stay.

The speech was, perhaps, less moving than we might have expected. It was more of a hand-stitched tapestry than a speech, unrolled at length before our eyes. The start was breezy: he had been told that the others who'd preceded him there were 'the Pope, Her Majesty the Queen, and Nelson Mandela, which is either a very high bar, or the beginning of a very funny joke.'

The gist seemed to be that for centuries Britain and America had led the world in promoting democracy and the freedom of the individual. He implied, though didn't actually say, that the west was pretty much washed out now, following the success of China and India, and all those other places that make cars, televisions and novelty key rings cheaper than us. But we would be the head prefects of the world, bringing our values to those who yearned for them.

It was like Peter Cook's sketch in which Macmillan, meeting Kennedy, offers Britain as an honest broker. They agree that no nation could be more honest. 'And I said that no nation could be broker.' Except that Obama knows we are both broke!

It was a largely cheer-free speech. But when he said that the grandson of a Kenyan cook in the British army stood before us as president of the United States, the applause crashed around him in waves.

I may have said this before, but the prime minister is more and more like the slapdash operator of a bungee-jumping outfit. He sends someone off the bridge, then goes for a cup of tea. The customers – like Cameron's ministers – are left dangling, bouncing up and down, wondering if they will ever be pulled up and fearing that some passing ill-wisher might cut the elastic.

His latest victim is Ken Clarke, the justice secretary, whose plans to halve sentences for people who plead guilty was binned by the PM through leaks this week. Clarke is seen by some of his more rightwing colleagues as a politically correct, sandal-wearing, *Guardian*-reading, bleeding heart liberal. Yesterday a Tory, Philip Hollobone, asked why it was that magistrates had to retire at 70, whereas Clarke, the man who appoints them, is still in office. He turns 71 next month.

The question sounded hostile, but it gave the prime minister the chance to say that Clarke was 'doing a superb job … there is plenty more fuel in his tank,' which sounded on the one hand slightly obscene, and on the other damning with high praise, like 'the board has every confidence in the manager'.

Given that Cameron has executed more screaming U-turns – on sentencing, NHS reforms and the privatisation of trees – than a getaway driver without satnav, it is surprising that Ed Miliband didn't really dent him. In fact, after much inconsequential argy-bargy, the two men began to trade personal abuse, with Miliband calling Cameron 'shameless' and Cameron accusing the Labour leader of 'an interesting use of the facts,' which I took to mean 'he's a liar'. I noticed that the bald patch had moved a short distance in a south-westerly direction, and may start to interfere with electronic communications on earth, any day now.

David Cameron likes to make policy announcements in an appropriate setting: a school for education, a hospital for health. Maybe he'll tell us about new food hygiene regulations in an abattoir.

What a superb PR man David Cameron is! All those years of training in the arts of spin and persuasion – none were wasted. He arrived at the top of Guy's Hospital in London to announce the concessions he's made to the Lib Dems in order to push through his reorganisation of the NHS.

Later it all went horribly wrong. But for the moment, everything was calm He was flanked by the health secretary *pro tem*, Andrew Lansley, who looked grim, and Nick Clegg, apparently as dejected as ever. Still no news of that missing puppy!

Behind him was a selection of Guy's staff, including nurses and doctors. It may be my imagination, but it seemed as if they had selected some of the most attractive nurses to sit there. Cameron is a lover of demotic language, and perhaps they are preparing a new slogan, 'Fit people to make you fit!'

Unlike his two colleagues, the prime minister seemed as full of beans as an overstuffed beanbag. Considering that he had suffered the humiliation of having a bill yanked halfway through its passage through parliament because everyone thought it was rubbish, he was on top of the world.

My mind strayed to the press conference the Grand Old Duke of York would have held. 'Yes, I marched 10,000 men to the top of the hill. And yes, I won't hide it from you, there was a spot of grumbling in the ranks. Some of the chaps didn't appreciate all we were trying to do. So I paused, I listened and I reflected. Then I marched them down again. That is leadership!'

He told us that he wanted a more 'bottom-up process'. I recalled the old joke about the patient whose GP prescribes suppositories. When the doctor asks if they worked, he replies, 'For all the good those pills did me, doc, I might as well have shoved them up my backside.'

Next the prime minister and his posse went on a tour of the hospital, where he and the camera crew that was following him encountered an enraged, bow-tied surgeon, who thought they were not dressed according to regulations. 'I'm not having it! Out!' he bellowed.

Quite right too. Some of these cameramen work in foreign countries where they have bacteria the size of pigeons.

Mr Cameron marched out swiftly, because he knows how vital good public relations are. Especially when a furious surgeon is barking at you, on TV.

I thought at the time that the phraseology used by the surgeon, Mr David Nunn, would have been perfect for David Miliband to use against the prime minister; something on the lines of 'The British people are not having it! Out!' But Miliband does not do jokes, and his grey cells remain resolutely grey.

The Commons can flip in a moment from matters trivial to matters horribly urgent. So yesterday they discussed the government's latest U-turn – no longer are weekly bin collections going to be mandatory for local councils; instead ministers are pondering 'incentives'.

Of course, if the incentives don't work, the smell of a dozen unfinished tikka masalas will hang over every street, reminding us all of the government's ongoing difficulty in distinguishing the desirable from the possible.

Then suddenly we were in Athens with the Greek crisis. This is no longer, to use the old cliché, the elephant in the room, but the whale in the birdbath. A Greek default, followed by financial apocalypse in the other debtor countries, could lead to a crash as bad as the one we had in 2008-9, with the world economy already beached, gasping for air.

So the matter was put in the hands of Mark Hoban, an Osborne understrapper and financial secretary to the Treasury.

Oh dear. Mr Hoban does not inspire confidence. Of some men it is said that you would follow them into the jungle. If Mr Hoban were about to hack his way in, he'd study the map carefully, look at it again upside down, discover that he'd left his sandwiches at home, then say it was a great mistake to worry about speculation that we might get lost. And he would add that he was totally opposed to us being eaten by ferocious beasts.

He had been asked what plans the Treasury had for a Greek default. Well, if they have any plans, Mr Hoban wasn't letting on. He muttered about French and German banks being more exposed to Greek debt than ours. (Yes, but as he didn't mention, our banks are exposed to the very French and German banks who are exposed to the Greek banks. If you catch my drift.)

Labour MPs were furious. Jack Straw said we were in a much worse position than Mr Hoban had admitted, and we should face the fact that the eurozone was not going to survive. He accused Mr Hoban of 'complacent words and weasel language'. Mr Hoban replied in the manner of a supply teacher working his last Friday afternoon. He gabbled, prat-tling platitudes, just desperate to get out of there.

Later he might have thought he was safe. But then arose Sir Peter Tapsell. As alarms clanged in the Hansard office, a squadron of light aircraft was scrambled to fly over England towing banners with Sir Peter's words upon them.

I have no space to quote all of his majestic contribution, save to say that we would indeed be liable to cough up for the disaster, if only through our funding of the IMF, 'to bail out the European Union from its folly with the single currency!' He hit the word 'folly' like a punchbag.

Watch for the whole speech, flying soon over a town near you!

The government finally admitted – under pressure from the opposition and the tabloid press – that it was backing down on the plan to halve prison sentences for defendants who plead guilty.

'Well, I've done many U-turns in my time, and they have to be done with a certain purpose and panache, if you have to do them at all,' said Ken Clarke, or the Lord High Chancellor of England, as he is known to friends and family.

This was said with a certain world-weary insouciance. He is, of course, an old lag in parliament – institutionalised, you might say. If you let him out with a £20 note and the address of the nearest Job Centre, he would probably re-offend just to get back to the familiar old routine.

His attitude was startlingly different from that of his boss, who was three years old when Clarke was first elected. Cameron was already doing U-turns, but on a Tonka truck in the back garden.

To Clarke, U-turns are just another fact of political life: win some, lose some, been there, done that, was his message.

To Cameron they are quite different. They are a sign of strength, as he said many times during his press conference at Number 10 yesterday. Popeye had spinach; he chugs indecision.

'Being strong means recognising that you didn't get everything right in the first place. It's not strength or leadership to be living in fear of being criticised for changing your mind.

'I don't make any apology for listening to people and wanting to change things!' he told us. 'The weak thing is to plough on and say, "I can't possibly change, I might have to face a difficult question at a press conference!"'

This was mucho macho stuff. Older readers may recall Charles Atlas. Ads in comic books showed how a 97-pound (7 stone) weakling had sand kicked in his face by a bully, until he sent off for the Charles Atlas books, turned himself into a muscular body-builder, and won back the girl who left him when he had the sand kicked in his face, the minxy hoyden.

Cameron has the same effect with U-turns. Every time he changes his mind, on the NHS, sentencing, waste collection, or anything – he gets even stronger. In his own mind, at least.

Thugs and hoods run from the beach as he saunters along, a gorgeous girl on each arm. 'There goes a geezer what's not afraid to change 'is mind,' they say in terror. 'We'd better scram!'

As well as being strong, the prime minister was tough. He demanded tough punishment, 'punishment with a purpose!' There would be 'tough' changes in the criminal justice system. 'When people cross the line and break the law, I want an incredibly tough response!'

Back in the Commons, Ken Clarke announced that 'talking tough is easy, and most politicians do it. Delivering tough is rather difficult.'

I could only assume that he was kicking sand in the prime minister's face.

The Chinese premier, Wen Jiabao, came to Britain as part of his European tour.

I love it when the British and Chinese leaders get together. You always have two entirely different cultures pretending to be much the same. It's all a little baffling and rather amusing. The two leaders strode out to their lecterns under the Union Jack and the Chinese flag. David Cameron talked about dialogue. Apparently the big thing is going to be person-to-person dialogue, and he didn't mean 'Pearl of the East oriental banquet for two, please'. We are to get together on a personal level in order to learn about our new friends. Especially young people, because they are the future. The Chinese young people will be very polite and talk about calligraphy, or gymnastics. Our young people will drink *mai tai* until they are out of their skulls.

But that is for later. In the meantime, Mr Wen had good news for his 'dear friends in the press'. He was giving two giant pandas to Edinburgh Zoo. Not more bloody pandas, I thought. Edinburgh Zoo might not be too thrilled either, because pandas cost a fortune to keep in that they only eat two types of bamboo, which are very rare, being Szechuan's answer to foie gras and Beluga.

And these particular pandas had been announced before. They are like Gordon Brown's spending on the NHS – the more often you announce the same thing, the more it seems to be more. If you see what I mean.

Then came questions. We held our breath. Adam Boulton of Sky News asked when China was going to make progress on human rights. Mr Cameron flannelled, rather well, talking about 'different stages of development', which is fair enough, since 400 years ago, political opponents in England had their heads chopped off.

But Mr Wen looked thunderous. Goodness knows what he had heard, because the translation of Mr Boulton's remarks was far longer than the question itself. Mr Wen replied by speaking at him, like a headmaster, very slowly, but in Mandarin. I guessed he was saying something along the lines of, 'You have let me down, you have let yourself down, but worst of all, you have let the Chinese people down.' We half-expected him to say that Boulton had been condemned to death in his absence, and that if he ever returned to China he would be shot and the bill for the bullet sent to Rupert Murdoch. (Mr Boulton later told us, with some pride, that he had been refused a visa for a holiday in China.)

Mr Wen's answer seemed interminable. Prime minister's questions in the Chinese parliament must be awfully monotonous. They can never get past number one.

When we finally got the translation it was indeed very cross. Mr Boulton should spend much more time in China (difficult if you're not allowed in). He should travel by bus and by metro (as senior Communist officials do all the time, no doubt). He, Mr Wen, had visited many of China's 2,800 counties. Unlike the wretched Boulton.

The Chinese people had a history going back 5,000 years. They had undergone 'untold sufferings', and this had taught them never to address other countries 'in a lecturing way'.

I took this to mean, 'You bastards gave us the opium wars, and now you hector us about human rights! Just shut it, will you?'

Mr Wen, who went to Stratford-upon-Avon on Sunday, told us that as a boy he had loved William Shakespeare and had read *Twelfth Night*, *King Lear* and *Othello*.

Proof, if it were needed, that youth culture is entirely different in the two countries, and may never be bound together by any number of person-to-person dialogues.

Index

(years and months in subentries when the sketches appeared)

333